TWEED

Textiles that Changed the World

Series Editor: Linda Welters, University of Rhode Island, USA

ISSN: 1477-6294

Textiles have had a profound impact on the world in a multitude of ways—from the global economy to the practical and aesthetic properties that subtly shape our everyday lives. This exciting new series chronicles the cultural life of individual textiles through sustained, book-length examinations. Pioneering in approach, the series will focus on historical, social and cultural issues and the myriad ways in which textiles ramify meaning. Each book will be devoted to an individual textile or to the dye, such as indigo or madder, that characterizes a particular type of cloth. Books will be handsomely illustrated with color as well as black-and-white photographs.

Previously published in the Series

Tartan
Jonathan Faiers

Felt
Willow Mullins

Cotton
Beverly Lemire

Digital Textile Printing
Susan Carden

TWEED

FIONA ANDERSON

Bloomsbury Academic
An imprint of Bloomsbury Publishing Plc

B L O O M S B U R Y
LONDON · OXFORD · NEW YORK · NEW DELHI · SYDNEY

Bloomsbury Academic

An imprint of Bloomsbury Publishing Plc

50 Bedford Square   1385 Broadway
London   New York
WC1B 3DP   NY 10018
UK   USA

www.bloomsbury.com

BLOOMSBURY and the Diana logo are trademarks of Bloomsbury Publishing Plc

First published 2017

© Fiona Anderson, 2017

British Library Cataloguing-in-Publication Data
A catalogue record for this book is available from the British Library.

ISBN: HB: 978-1-8452-0696-3
PB: 978-1-8452-0697-0
ePDF: 978-1-4742-6320-7
ePub: 978-1-4742-6321-4

Library of Congress Cataloging-in-Publication Data
A catalogue record for this book is available from the Library of Congress.

Series: Textiles that Changed the World, 14776294

Cover image © Luca Sage/Getty Images

Typeset by Fakenham Prepress Solutions, Fakenham, Norfolk NR21 8NN

CONTENTS

LIST OF ILLUSTRATIONS

COLOR PLATES

FIGURES

ACKNOWLEDGMENTS

Research for this publication evolved over a period of years, during which time I benefited greatly from the support and advice of many people. Dialogue with individuals working in industry, academia, museums and archives has influenced the book's development and greatly enriched the final work.

First, I would like to thank Jane Carmichael, Director of Collections at National Museums Scotland, who generously supported the research and writing of this publication, during my time as Senior Curator of Fashion and Textiles at that institution. I would also like to thank my former colleagues at NMS for their support, including George Dalgleish, Godfrey Evans, Georgina Ripley and Emily Taylor. This study helped to prompt the acquisition of the Bernat Klein and Otterburn Mill Collections by NMS and my subsequent research on these firms has had an important impact on the final book. I would also like to extend warm thanks to Shelley Klein for helping to facilitate illuminating conversations with her now late father Bernat Klein about his work.

During this project I traveled to various rural and urban locations, including the Outer Hebrides, Cumbria, the West of England, County Donegal, London and Paris. Research in museum and archival collections in Britain and France yielded invaluable insights. Helen Taylor, Archivist at the School of Textiles, Heriot-Watt University, generously provided access to their important holdings relating to the Scottish tweed industry. Studying extremely rare pattern books of the 1830s in that collection was of great importance in ensuring that text-based research about early tweeds was interwoven with an awareness of the materiality of these textiles. I would also like to thank Joanna Marschner at Historic Royal Palaces, Claire Wilcox at the Victoria and Albert Museum, and Isabel MacLachlan at Museum nan Eilean, Lewis, for kindly arranging access to collections.

I also owe a great debt to the Curators and Archivists who helped to make my trips to Paris enlightening and fruitful. At the Palais Galliera, I would like to thank Pascale Gorguet-Ballesteros, Marie-Laure Gutton and Alexandra Bosc for stimulating conversations about sportswear and for showing me objects in their collections. Véronique Belloir, then at the Musée des Arts Décoratifs, was also very generous in sharing her time and knowledge about French woolen manufacturing. Access to private archives in Paris also had a pivotal influence on the research. I am immensely grateful for access to important tweed artefacts and related information provided by Odile Premel of Chanel, Soizic Pfaff of Christian Dior and Gael Mamine of Balenciaga, all of whom were extremely helpful.

The prime focus of this book is on the cultural history of tweeds and the design, manufacture and sale of these textiles. I therefore owe a great many debts to individuals connected to industry. In 2013, I interviewed Alan Cumming and Stephen Rendle of the Lovat Mill; Leslie Walker and Keith Walker of Linton Tweeds; Ian Angus Mackenzie, Margaret MacLeod and Ken Kennedy of Harris Tweed Hebrides; Kathy Macaskill of the Carloway Mill; and Lorna Macaulay, Chief Executive of the Harris Tweed Authority. I would like to thank these individuals for their remarkable patience and generosity in answering my copious questions and also for making helpful comments about chapters. Their substantial expertise about the last thirty years or more of designing, making and selling tweeds internationally had a significant impact on this book.

The volume was also informed by research trips to the Outer Hebrides in 2010 and 2011 and I am immensely grateful to Terry Bloomfield, Joan Cumming, Lorna Macaulay, Donald John Mackay, Ian Angus Mackenzie and Ronnie Mackenzie who shared their great, collective knowledge about Harris Tweed with me. I would also like to thank John Gillespie for showing me the Johnstons of Elgin archive and for an illuminating conversation about tweeds at an early stage of the research. Although this volume primarily focuses on the history of British tweeds within international contexts, the development of the research was also informed by a trip to County Donegal in 2012. I offer sincere thanks to Peter McNutt of Baird McNutt; Gill Mudie of Magee; Shaun and Kieran Molloy of Molloy & Sons Weaving Ltd; Chris Weiniger of Donegal Yarns; and Tristan Donaghy of Studio Donegal for answering my numerous questions. In addition, Royston Berrett who worked in the West of England woolen industry between 1945 and 2000 shared his extensive, first-hand knowledge with me for which I am grateful. Dialogue with people connected to the tweed industry revealed the important relationships between the history of tweeds and the international design and marketing of these textiles today. I hope that this book conveys some of the enterprise and passion that has helped to sustain the manufacturing of tweeds in the UK as a small but globally relevant, niche industry.

I am immensely grateful to Lou Taylor for her encouragement, insightful comments and suggestions. Her marvelous generosity extended to undertaking the huge task of reading the entire draft manuscript of this book. I also wish to thank Christopher Breward and Lesley Miller for kindly devoting some of their valuable time to reading and commenting on chapters. The award of a Fellowship by the Arts and Humanities Research Council contributed to the development of this book and I am grateful for their support. That AHRC project, Tweed: History, Culture and Design also involved working collaboratively with the partner, Scottish Borders Council Museum Service on an exhibition and education events. I would like to thank Fiona Colton and Shona Sinclair of SBCMS for helping to make that collaboration a positive one.

Huge thanks are due Geraldine Billingham, Hannah Crump and Ariadne Godwin at Bloomsbury Academic for their patient and generous support and to Series Editor, Linda Welters for her insightful comments. When they are older, Sandy and Ellie Jackson may read this book and discover why they spent so many family holidays in places such as the Outer Hebrides. Last but not least, I thank Stephen Jackson whose unstinting support has been more important than I can say. I dedicate this book to my mother, Eleanor Anderson, a regular wearer of tweed skirts in her younger days.

1
INTRODUCTION

Contemporary perceptions about the cultural history of tweeds have largely centered on the idea that these textiles were exclusively worn in the past by the British upper classes in rural contexts.[1] *Tweed* challenges these mythologized and overly simplistic notions by pursuing an in-depth historical and cultural analysis of these textiles from their emergence in Scotland of the 1820s to the present. This investigation of the history of the group of cloths known as tweeds includes examining their origins, technical characteristics, manufacture, design and consumption within UK and international contexts. The book follows the development of these cloths from the raw fiber to the finished garment, worn on both male and female bodies. It begins in the 1820s, when the long-established Scottish woolen products of shepherd's checks were first adopted by fashionable, urban male consumers. From that decade, these coarse woolens began to evolve into the "family" of modern, fashionable commodities, which by the 1830s had acquired the collective name of tweed, as discussed in Chapters 2 and 3.

This volume incorporates significant new research about all types of tweeds, from Harris Tweed to the type of novelty, or *fantaisie* tweeds that have famously been used by Chanel. The study begins at a much earlier stage in the fashion cycle than is usually pursued within studies of dress, which has facilitated the development of new, broader perspectives about the processes of fashion change and innovation. *Tweed* adds to research by a limited number of authors, which has also considered fashion textiles and garments in a holistic way.[2] Through the example of tweed, this approach has also yielded new insights into how the cultural and social connotations of fashion objects evolve, because textiles have a "life" and acquire meanings long before they become part of a garment. Tracing the diverse and shifting factors that have shaped the history of tweeds has involved the use of interdisciplinary approaches. Material culture methods have also been at the core of this study and researching objects such as textile samples and garments has yielded invaluable insights only available from those sources.

International perspectives are embraced in this publication by focusing primarily on the study of British-made cloths and their worldwide export. Donegal tweeds are included in Chapter 2, because although these woolens originally derived from that Irish county, the name is now widely used as a generic term. In addition, research about the export of British tweeds in the archives of Chanel, Dior and Balenciaga, as well as Paris museum collections has involved comparative examples of French woolens. These investigations have informed the arguments presented about the existence of a design dialogue between Scottish and French woolen textiles, which influenced the development of novelty, or *fantaisie* tweeds for womenswear, as discussed in Chapters 5, 7 and 8.

The scant amount of academic publications about the history of tweeds means that preparing this volume has principally involved original research. Clifford Gulvin's *The Tweedmakers: A History of the Scottish Fancy Woollen Industry 1600–1914* was the last major academic book on that subject. His important study of 1973 follows a typical methodology of an economic historian of the period in that few connections are made between the production of the cloth and the consumers who wore the cloth made up into garments. Furthermore, Gulvin's research focuses almost exclusively on the mill-based tweed industry in the Scottish Borders.[3] Since 1973, there have been a small number of publications related to the history of tweed that have focused either on specific types of tweed, or on a limited time period.[4] This includes *The Islanders and the Orb: the History of the Harris Tweed Industry 1835–1995* by Janet Hunter, which embraces a major focus on the legal aspects of that textile's history. It also involves Janice Helland's research about the important role of female philanthropists in encouraging the manufacture and sale of domestically produced handwoven tweeds between 1880 and 1914.[5] The specific focus of these two publications on cloths woven in the home, means that they do not address the fact that most British tweeds have been mill-woven since the mid-nineteenth century. The history of the vast majority of tweeds produced in the UK in the twentieth and twenty-first centuries has therefore never been researched. In this book, the interconnections between the histories of cloths woven in domestic and industrial contexts are thus examined in depth for the first time.

The vast majority of publications on the British wool textiles industry take economic history approaches to the English trade in the period up until 1830. However, Beverly Lemire and Miles Lambert have argued that in addition to their economic importance between 1660 and 1820, English woolens also had social and cultural significance and they symbolized masculinity, tradition, Englishness and Britishness.[6] *Tweed* extends that research by locating itself within the broad context of developing new interdisciplinary approaches to the study of Scottish, as well as English wool textiles after 1830.

TWEED: INVESTIGATING MYTHS AND MEANINGS

Exploring contemporary fashion imagery shows that the mythical or stereotypical connotations of tweeds form a useful starting point for a deeper investigation into their history. For example, an advertisement in *Vogue* for Ralph Lauren's autumn/winter 2012 womenswear collection featured outfits that were strongly influenced by British country clothing and 1920s fashion, including fitted jackets and jodhpurs in tweed, worn with "mannish" shirts, ties and Fair Isle style knitwear. These garments were designed and styled in a way that was deeply historicized, but the fact that a herringbone tweed overcoat inspired by 1930s menswear was worn with a 1920s-style cloche hat and a fake fur leopard skin scarf reveals that this was a mythical, re-interpretation of period, country house style. The strong influence of film and television on Lauren's re-imagining of British upper-class style is shown by the fact that this campaign was shot at Highclere Castle, the English location for the internationally popular ITV series Downton Abbey. This advertisement reveals that tweeds have retained associations of traditional elite British lifestyles, which are resonant enough with a contemporary consuming public that they remain part of the brand identity of a globally successful fashion business such as Ralph Lauren. It also helps to show that film and television have played an important role in keeping these largely mythical, but partly historically accurate, connotations of tweeds present in the contemporary cultural imagination.[7]

Chapter 2 of this volume addresses the origins of the term tweed and the principal characteristics of the group of cloths that have been known by that name since the 1830s. That text is followed by a series of chronological chapters, which explore new evidence about the historical relationships of tweeds with notions of class, gender, tradition, innovation, authenticity and urban and rural contexts. This book also investigates the interconnections of tweeds with shifting ideas about Scottish, English and British identities. The volume thus presents a historically nuanced picture which contests the stereotypical connotations of these textiles while simultaneously revealing their roots of development. In Chapter 3, for example, the book shows that from the 1840s tweeds were worn in urban contexts by men at social levels ranging from Royalty to the lower middle classes. Furthermore, up until the 1870s tweeds were primarily worn for rural sports by elite men and this meant that they acquired strong connotations of land ownership, wealth and leisure, as discussed in Chapters 3 and 4.

Tweed also investigates the fact that these textiles have had important relationships with changing social conventions and sartorial practices relating to gender from the early nineteenth century to the present day. The majority of publications on dress deal with the self-fashioning of either men or women. This book provides innovative perspectives about gender identities, fashion textiles and fashionable dress by considering the design and manufacture of tweeds and their consumption by both sexes. Since the 1990s, important advances have been made in the study of men's fashion by authors including Christopher Breward, Paul Jobling, Frank Mort, and Laura Ugolini.[8] These publications have primarily focused on the consumption of masculine clothing and related representations. Published research about the history of textiles used in men's dress after 1830 has been extremely limited.[9] *Tweed* has begun to bridge the large gap between the scant research on fashion textiles for menswear and the excellent studies about men's fashion consumption. It also builds on previous research by Lou Taylor, Janice Helland and the author, by exploring new, primary evidence about shifting gender relationships and the increasing adoption of tweeds by women from the late nineteenth century onwards.[10]

A further aim of this book is to challenge the notion that tweeds may simply be related to nostalgic visions of past, traditional, country lifestyles. That view is contested with reference to work by the cultural geographer David Matless and literary historian John Glendening, which suggests that nostalgia, authenticity and tradition are far from simple concepts and that they often have an intrinsic and complex rather than simple and oppositional relationship to modernity.[11] Tweeds emerged in the Romantic era and they eloquently expressed the tensions and contradictions of a time in which industrialization and urbanization were having a transformative effect on British society. As Glendening states: "Although the romantic sensibility asserts itself in opposition to the modern world, it is the direct outgrowth of that world."[12] Chapter 3 of this book posits that the emergent fashion for tweeds of the early nineteenth century was strongly connected to the romantic search for authenticity and idealization of nature. It also argues that through their consumption by fashionable, metropolitan consumers from the 1820s, the coarse, Scottish woolens that were soon to be called tweeds were transformed into modern fashion textiles.

Tweed further pursues this enquiry by investigating the physical and conceptual relationships of these textiles with country and city landscapes between the 1820s and the present day. It argues that from the beginning of the tweed trade onwards, rural and urban influences and contexts have been deeply intertwined in the making, designing, selling and wearing of tweed cloths. Previous research about menswear tweeds in the late nineteenth century has problematized what has been the dominant paradigm within fashion history over the last thirty years, that is the pivotal relationships between fashion and the urban within the era of modernity.[13] In *Tweed*, that investigation into the relationships between fashion in modernity and rural and urban landscapes has been extended by exploring the history of tweeds in men's and women's dress since the 1820s. I do not wish to contest the view that modern fashion is principally an urban phenomenon. Instead, this book is informed by the ideas of Matless, which suggest that because of the intrinsic relationships between modernity, industrialization and urbanization, notions of the rural are often understood in opposition to this, in other words as being traditional and anti-modern.[14] These views have undoubtedly influenced the fact that tweeds have often been perceived as being "classic", traditional, or heritage fabrics. In contrast, *Tweed* focuses on approaches to landscape and modernity, which conceive of *both* urban and rural landscapes as subject to change and as dynamic processes that are pivotal to the development of modern sartorial identities.[15] In this book, Chapters 3 to 9 reveal that people's imagining of their identity and the phenomenon of fashion within modernity has not been strictly ordered into the exclusively defined categories of the country and the city.

In 2011, the journalist A. A. Gill described tweeds as a "stereotype of Britishness."[16] This quote confirms that within recent media these textiles still have strong associations with enduring ideas about a fixed and unchanging sense of British identity. In contrast, researching the history of tweeds reveals the historical complexities and mythologies linked to Scottish, English and British identities in an era of massive change within Britain and its global contexts. For example, the history of these textiles is integrally related to radical changes in landownership and usage in the Scottish Highlands, which developed from the late eighteenth century onwards. By the mid-nineteenth century much land in northern Scotland had been cleared of small tenants to make way for a huge expansion in sheep farming and the development of deer forests. From the 1830s onwards, the growing fashionability of Scottish field sports, such as deer stalking and grouse shooting led to the emergence of a sporting economy in the Highlands. The desirability of travel to northern Scotland to engage in these pursuits was also encouraged by mythical notions about that locale as an area of Britain that was an unchanging wilderness, untouched by the impact of modernity.[17] These ideas and developments had a pivotal influence on the design and consumption of the early tweeds, as discussed in Chapters 3 and 4.

INNOVATION AND TRADITION: DESIGNING AND MAKING TWEEDS

The considerable international impact and design influence of British tweeds since the mid-nineteenth century are also explored in this volume. In Chapter 9, it is argued that these textiles retain their cultural significance as a key element of Britain's fashion identity, despite the continued tendency toward dramatic decline in tweed production in the UK from the 1980s onwards. Furthermore, British firms continue to be successful in selling tweeds in fiercely competitive, international luxury markets, including to brands such as Chanel, Ralph Lauren and Dries van Noten. The exploration in Chapter 9 of contemporary practices within British firms that globally export tweeds, confirms the textile trend consultant, Beryl Gibson's view that, "It is the mix of tradition and innovation that means that UK textiles continue to be relevant in the modern design climate."[18] The volume also investigates the fact that the British export trade in tweeds has involved significant, but hidden, design interactions between fashion houses from leading, international centers and textile producers from locations considered to be peripheral to the world of fashion. Through the consideration of these business relationships in Chapters 7, 8 and 9, *Tweed* contributes to a re-assessment of the geographical mapping of the creative processes connected to global fashion.

This volume shows that the development of tweed manufacturing was a significant factor in the changing economic and social structures of specific locales in Britain, most notably the Outer Hebrides and the Scottish Borders.[19] For example, Hunter commented on the period from the 1880s onwards in the Outer Hebrides, as follows: "production of Harris tweed was a vital and integral part of Island life for over a century. Families and communities prospered in the good years and equally, they suffered during the lean years."[20] Many people on hearing that I am writing a book about tweed have assumed that it will only address the history of Harris Tweed. In fact, the volume investigates all types of tweeds and where Harris Tweed is specifically referred to that is clearly indicated in the text.

Tweed demonstrates the eloquence of these textiles in resolving in symbolic form the powerful tensions and contradictions that are inherent within fashion in modernity. That dynamic has remained a remarkably constant factor in the cultural history of tweeds since their emergence in the Romantic era. Since that time, these widely worn textiles have continued to shape our material and symbolic worlds. Irresolvable tensions between the past and present still have a powerful impact on fashion and culture today. For example, Lisa Armstrong in her report on the Chanel autumn/winter 2013 couture show, stated: "Established fashion houses are obsessed with being perceived as modern, just as new fashion houses are consumed with trying to invent a heritage for themselves. What they all want is to be both traditional and modern."[21] This study of tweeds shows that the adaptability of these textiles in expressing contradictory notions of "timelessness," historicism and contemporaneity is pivotal to their continued resonance within men's and women's global fashion.

2

TWEED: TERMS, DESCRIPTIONS, AND CHARACTERISTICS

The origins of the word tweed are of historical and commercial significance today because of the importance of authenticity and place to the past and present identities of these textiles.[1] Published texts relating to the history of these cloths have shown a marked tendency to present, or repeat, mythologized accounts of how the term was adopted. This chapter questions these myths and it begins with a detailed, critical account of the development and early use of the word tweed to describe a particular group of Scottish, woolen textiles. A key aim of this book is to undertake an extended examination of the shifting meanings and associations of that term since the 1830s. The existing literature has not yet adequately defined or described tweeds, other than Harris Tweed.[2] In this chapter, key characteristics of the wide range of woolen cloths that have been grouped together within the "family" of tweed since the early nineteenth century are examined. The technical and aesthetic properties, and geographical associations of different types of named tweeds are also explored, including Saxonies, Cheviots, homespuns, Harris, Donegal, Shetland, West of England, Welsh, estate and Yorkshire cloths. Through these examples, the chapter introduces the concept that many tweeds have strong connections with specific places or landscapes, and with notions of Scottish, English, Irish and British identities.

ORIGINS OF THE TERM TWEED

The word tweed began to be used to denote woolen cloths from Scotland in the twill weave from the 1830s.[3] Before that decade, its only form was the proper noun, Tweed, which is the name of a river that flows through the Scottish Borders region. That river became well known throughout Britain and to an extent, Europe, in the early nineteenth century because of its close associations with the famous writer, Sir Walter Scott, who lived near it.[4] The cloths that later became known as tweeds, were initially sourced by merchants from the Scottish Borders region in the late 1820s and it might be assumed that their name was directly inspired by that local river. However, the most frequently quoted account of how the term tweed developed is that it derives from the Scottish word *tweel*. In the early nineteenth century that term was used to denote any cloth in the twill weave, but it was most often applied to woolen fabrics of that construction.[5] Since before the eighteenth century, Scottish wool textiles had predominantly featured the twill structure. The textile historian Kenneth Ponting notes that this contrasted with the English woolen industry, which at that time largely specialized in fine broadcloths made in the plain weave.[6] In its most common form, the 2/2 twill, this weave involves each warp yarn floating over two and then under two of the weft yarns and at the same time progressively moving forwards to either the right or left. This results in the characteristic diagonal lines or "wales" that are evident on the surface of twilled cloths, as can be seen in the Scottish woolen samples of the 1830s in Plate 1.[7]

James Locke, a Scottish cloth merchant, features in the most frequently quoted story about the origins of the word tweed. By 1830, Locke was based in Regent Street, London and around that time he began to introduce the Scottish woolens that were to become known as tweeds to his fashionable, urban clientele. The most popular version of the story states that the term derives from a clerk working for Locke who misread the Scottish word *tweel* for tweed. The basic elements of this account have been repeated by all the published authors on the subject, with some debate about the details, such as the names of the woolen manufacturers involved. For example, most writers state that William Watson & Sons of Hawick had sent the invoice which was wrongly interpreted, whereas Ponting and Gulvin merely mention a company from Hawick. It is also disputed whether it was a clerk, or Locke himself, who misread the word *tweel* as tweed.[8] The popular story about the origins of the term tweed appears to derive from David Bremner's text of 1869, in which he states:

> Messrs William Watson & Son, of Hawick, sent a quantity of "tweels" to one of their customers in London – the late Mr James Locke, who was one of the earliest merchants of that kind of goods in the metropolis. In the invoice the word "tweels" was written indistinctly, and was read "tweeds" by Mr Locke, who, in ordering a further supply, adopted what he conceived to be a new and happy designation.[9]

This account ignores the fact that Locke and his staff would have been so familiar with the term *tweel*, they would have been highly unlikely to misread it, which suggests that a detailed re-examination of the origins of the word tweed is necessary.

The entry for tweed in the *Dictionary of the Scots Language* cites the popular story involving Locke and then states that this "theory ignores the important fact that forms of the word *tweel(ing)* with -d- were current in Scotland from the 16th c. … *Tweed* is therefore more likely to have arisen from an abbreviated form of *tweeled* or *tweedle*."[10] The noun forms of *tweedle,* such as *twidlen,* were most usually used in Scotland to describe coarse linens rather than woolen cloths, and along with Locke's own writings this suggests that *tweeled* is the more likely source for tweed.[11]

Locke himself gives a different account to Bremner in a letter that was published in the local newspaper *The Border Advertiser* in 1863.[12] Notably, Locke's writings are not cited in any of the more recent publications on the history of tweed.[13] His published letter includes a description of the adoption of the shepherd's check design for men's trousers, from about 1827 or 1828. Along with cloaks, these were the first garments made from the Scottish woolens that were to become known as tweed, which were sold to fashionable London consumers.[14] Locke states that after the initial popularity of the shepherd's checks and prior to 1830 or 1832, discussion with his clients proceeded as follows: "It was then suggested ... by some of these gentlemen that other colours and other substances should be introduced for coats, &c. Partridge brown was among the first. These not being made in checks, but in plain colours, they were called 'twells' and spelt in their invoices tweeds – hence the name of tweeds became a household or trade word."[15]

A further account about the origins of the term features in Locke's book of 1860, *Tweed and Don; or, Recollections and Reflections of an Angler for the Last Fifty Years*. He states that "Brown-and-drab tweels, often written in the invoices to the Londoners, Tweed, which was meant to be Tweelds; the word Tweed came to be the common name of all this class of goods."[16] "Tweelds" is an abbreviated form of *tweeleds*, a noun with the same meaning as *tweel(l)s*, namely cloths in the twill weave. In his two texts, Locke confirms that tweed derives from either *tweels* or *tweelds* and the presence of the letter "d" in the latter suggests that this is probably the more likely origin of the word. The accounts of Locke differ from the popular story in that he does not claim any personal involvement in the adoption of the term tweed. Furthermore, his letter makes clear that the goods referred to came from the Scottish Borders, but he does not mention any particular town or woolen manufacturer.[17]

There is yet another account of the origins of the term tweed, which has somehow become fused with the myths about Locke's direct involvement to form the most frequently repeated version of the story. The original source of the much-quoted Watsons link is a letter in the *Hawick Advertiser* of 1855, from a Mr Irvine, who recounts the story that Thomas Watson, of William Watson & Sons had invoiced a parcel of trousering to the London cloth merchant Ebeneezer Harvey & Co. and it was this invoice that Mr Harvey, not James Locke, misread as tweeds.[18]

Based on the surviving evidence it is impossible to say for certain which firms or individuals first used the word tweed to describe a woolen cloth. The derivation of the term from either *tweels* or *tweelds,* as described by Locke and the *Dictionary of the Scots Language,* appears to be the most credible theory available. Locke does not comment on whether those working in the trade saw a marketing opportunity in the adoption of the word tweed because of the great fame of Sir Walter Scott and his associations with the river of that name. However, the commercial potential of the term means that it is entirely possible that, as Bremner argues, the use of "tweed" was encouraged by Locke, or by others in the industry.[19]

Whoever first employed the term tweed, what remains historically significant is that by the early 1840s the word had become widely adopted within the textile and tailoring trades. Gulvin posits that the name does not appear in any business data he surveyed before the early 1840s, but research for this book indicates that it began to be used at a slightly earlier date. For example, Locke suggests that "tweed" was being used in trade invoices by 1832.[20] Furthermore, an advertisement for his London establishment in an 1838 edition of *The Satirist,* lists "a new thick Tweed for Trousers." That source is also useful in confirming Locke's pivotal, but not singular, role in promoting and selling tweeds to the higher echelons of the London market in the 1830s.[21] Other early examples of the use of the term can be found in *Punch,* including three articles in 1844, which refer to "Tweed trousers," meaning shepherd's check trousers, and two editions of the following year that feature the expression "Tweed wrapper," which is used to denote large plaids that were used by men as garments and traveling wraps.[22] These examples clearly indicate that the name tweed was in wide circulation in Britain by 1844, most prominently with reference to trousers and large plaids.

Further insights into the early use of the term are provided by the letters of the renowned writer Thomas Carlyle (1795–1881). On July 4, 1843, he wrote to Charles Redwood that "Today is wet; but in old trowsers and a water-proof blanket coat (Tweed I think they call it) and other uninjurable apparatus, I mean to perambulate Bristol nevertheless."[23] Carlyle also wrote to his brother John two weeks later, that, "I go always in the Tweed – one of the best of coats!"[24] These letters are useful, in revealing that at this early date, tweed was being used to make overcoats, as well as traveling wraps and trousers. The way that Carlyle uses "Tweed" in his letter of July 4, 1843, also confirms that it is a relatively new term at the time.

WHAT IS TWEED?

Since its emergence in the 1830s, the name tweed has been used to describe an increasingly wide range of woolen cloths. The fact that this term denotes a "family" of textiles, rather than one fabric of set characteristics, means that tweeds are much harder to define or describe than many other cloths. An important exception to this is Harris Tweed, which has been protected by trademark certification from 1910 and by an Act of Parliament since 1993. These measures mean that there are precise legal definitions of what can be stamped with the official Orb mark, which denotes that a textile is Harris Tweed, as discussed in detail later in this chapter.[25] A working description of other types of tweed, which relates to the range of cloths that have been linked to that generic name since the 1830s, will now be established.

It is pertinent to start with an exploration of some descriptions of early tweeds from key, nineteenth-century publications. Studying published letters by the merchants James Locke and Alexander Craig, and *The New Statistical Account of Scotland,* reveals that tweeds evolved from the established Scottish woolen products of shepherd's plaids, Highland "home stuffs" and *tweels,* as discussed in depth in Chapter 3. These cloths were usually of medium weight and made from coarse wool in the twill weave (see Plate 1).[26] A wide range of sources confirm that tweeds have predominantly been made from wool, from the 1830s to the present.[27] Key developments in the types of wool used to make mill-woven tweeds in Scotland are indicated in a promotional booklet produced by Peter Anderson, Ltd of Galashiels in about 1900. It states:

> Scotch Tweeds are made from pure new wools. In the early days of the industry home-grown wools, such as Cheviot, were principally used, but as the industry developed, imported wools from New Zealand, Australia and South Africa were introduced, and at the present time practically all types of wool produced at home and abroad find a place in the manufacture of the wide range of ... cloths produced in the Scottish woollen industry.[28]

Christie correctly identifies that the early tweeds of around 1830 were made from local, Scottish Cheviot wool. The imported merino qualities, which he discusses, have also been used since the 1830s to make a type of tweed known as Saxony. The two key categories of Cheviots and Saxonies have retained an important place in tweed manufacture between the 1830s and the present day, which has largely determined the wools used to make those textiles.[29] Christie also emphasizes the important point that because the term tweed relates to a broad "family" of textiles and a huge range of varieties and qualities of wool exists, fibers from many other types of sheep, as well as Cheviots and merinos have historically been used to manufacture tweeds. Luxury fibers, such as cashmere, silk and mohair, have also been used since the late nineteenth century to extend the visual appeal and handle of some mill-woven tweeds.[30]

Ponting notes that from the mid-twentieth century, new synthetic fibers such as nylon began to be incorporated along with wool, which produced more hard-wearing tweeds. However, pure new wool remains the essential ingredient for a high quality tweed, as recognized by the Textile Institute's statement that "Descriptions of tweed not made substantially of wool need qualification."[31] There are exceptions to this, however, because from the 1950s good quality tweeds made from wool and synthetic fibers, often combined with mohair, were being produced for the women's designer level fashion market, notably by the British firm of Ascher.[32] A further example features in an Escada outfit of 2005, in the collections of National Museums Scotland. It is made from a *fantaisie* tweed by Neill Johnstone of Langholm, Scotland, which is composed of viscose (30 percent), nylon (24 percent), cotton (18 percent), wool (16 percent) and polyester (12 percent).[33]

Another key characteristic of tweed is that it has always been a woolen cloth, as distinct from a worsted. This means that these textiles are exclusively, or predominantly, made from yarns spun

Figure 2.1 Womenswear tweed sample from bunch in red, white, and dark brown herringbone pattern, 1934, 113/3, Otterburn Mill Collection. © National Museums Scotland, Edinburgh.

on the woolen system, which involves carding but not combing. Significantly, yarns made using that system may contain fibers other than wool. Carding is a manufacturing process that involves disentangling fibers so that they lie in a straighter position before spinning. The fine, long wool fibers that are used to make worsted yarns undergo a further process called combing, which helps to create a smoother, more even surface than is characteristic of the appearance of a typically "hairy" woolen yarn.[34]

Twill weave has been by far the most popular one for tweeds since the 1830s, primarily because of its huge potential for variety in color and design. For example, a womenswear tweed sample produced by the Otterburn Mill in 1934 in a herringbone pattern is based on an undulating twill structure, rather than the more common regular twill structure, which results in the v-shaped lines being curved (Fig. 2.1). Other methods of construction have also been used: in particular, the plain weave has played a notable secondary role in the design of tweeds, although it offers less scope than the twill for creating color and weave effects. Donegal tweeds have often featured the plain weave and this structure also forms the foundation of thornproof tweeds.[35] The fact that simple methods of construction have dominated in the manufacture of tweeds was emphasized by Ponting, who characterized "Scottish designing skill" as fundamentally based "on colour sense rather than pure design (that is, the making of complicated weaves)."[36]

The difficulties of arriving at a precise definition for tweeds, other than Harris Tweed, were acknowledged within the industry itself in the mid-twentieth century. The National Association of Scottish Woollen Manufacturers published a series of pamphlets between 1931 and 1956 on various aspects of their trade. That organization represented most Scottish producers of tweed, but not the Harris Tweed industry, because it was structurally distinct. The pamphlets were mostly written by Edward. S. Harrison (1878–1977), who was then Chairman and Managing Director of Johnstons of Elgin.[37] Harrison's expertise on tweeds was considerable, but even he found defining these textiles challenging. For example, in a pamphlet of February 1944 titled "WHAT IS TWEED ?" he concluded:

> Tweed could perhaps be described rather than defined as a cloth of medium weight, best adapted for suits for men and women. Not very smooth in texture. Tending, but only tending, towards Cheviot qualities. Tending, but by no means limited to broken effects of colour, attained either by pattern or by blends of colour; quite definitely limited to wool spun on the Scotch system—that is, woollen, not worsted yarn. It should show that slightly rough surface and that kind of broken or varied colour that is more suited to informal use than to ceremonial occasions.[38]

Harrison's description is necessarily vague at points, but it captures the visual and textural characteristics of tweeds more successfully than any other published text. Some further important characteristics of these cloths are described in *Textiles for Tailors,* which was published by the trade journal, *The Tailor and Cutter,* around 1950. It states: "The name 'tweed' includes a very large range of fabrics, made in various weaves, varying weights and qualities. Tweed textures are open and elastic in nature, and all grades are met with from the coarse homespun to the finest Saxony cloths."[39] Another useful description of tweeds features in a *British Wool Cloth Sample Book,* which was published by the International Wool Secretariat in the mid-1960s. It states:

> Tweed is a very popular woollen cloth used for men's and women's suits and overcoatings, especially for informal and sports wear. According to the weight, finish and type of cloth

Figure 2.2 Chanel suit in black-and-white *fantaisie* tweed, haute couture collection, spring/summer, 2013. Photograph by Dominique Charriau/WireImage. Getty Images.

required, many grades of wool are employed in the manufacture of tweeds. The term 'tweed', therefore refers to the colour and design of the cloth rather than to the material and weight.[40]

This description reinforces Harrison's arguments that tweeds are woolen cloths in which design, color, and surface texture are key elements, which meant that they were particularly, but not exclusively, associated with informal wear up until the 1960s. Significantly, there is evidence of a shift within the group of textiles that have been known as tweeds by the inter-war period.[41] This relates to the development of the type of fabrics that have characterized many of the women's suits by Chanel since the 1950s and which are widely described in fashion media as tweeds (see Fig. 2.2).[42] In the British textile industry these are called novelty tweeds and in France the term *les tweeds fantaisie* is used.[43] These fabrics have only been used for womenswear and they are characterized by the use of novelty, or *fantaisie* yarns, such as bouclé, slub, knop, gimp or loop. In addition, they commonly feature a simple weave and they rely on these fancy, often colorful, yarns in order to create appealing visual and textural effects. Novelty tweeds became prominent from the 1930s when British tweed manufacturers placed more emphasis on modifying their cloths for the womenswear market, principally by introducing more highly textured yarns.[44] The historical evolution of these tweeds, including their links with earlier menswear cloths and French womenswear fabrics, is discussed in detail from Chapter 5 onwards.

Bernat Klein (1922–2014) was an important designer of these novelty fabrics for womenswear and one of his houndstooth mohair tweeds of 1964, appears in Plate 2. It is made from section-dyed brushed mohair and wool, which creates a highly textured fabric featuring many different colors. This textile matches well with Harrison's earlier description of tweed in that it is "Not very smooth in texture" and features "broken or varied colour." It differs from Harrison's description in that these color effects are not achieved "by pattern or by blends of colour" but by Klein's development, prior to 1962, of the technique of section dyeing. This new method involved dipping sections of the yarn in different dyes to yield a yarn of varying colors along its length.[45] These variegated color effects are, however, very much in the spirit of earlier tweeds and Harrison's description. In addition, studying a Chanel couture suit of 1964 in the collections of the Victoria and Albert Museum, which is made from an Ascher tweed that has a similar visual effect to a heather mixture, reveals that this appearance has been achieved by twisting together a range of yarns of different shades of purple, rather than featuring blended yarns.[46] Examining these examples of *fantaisie* tweeds reveals that Harrison's description could be updated, so that as well as stating that the appearance of tweeds involved "Tending, but by no means limited to broken effects of color, attained either by pattern, or by blends of color," it also stated "or by incorporating section-dyed yarns, or different-coloured yarns."[47]

Crucially, however, it is also possible for tweeds to be predominantly of one color. The cloth merchant Alexander Craig writing in 1874 refers to "Black Tweeds," for example, although close examination of tweed garments in the Victoria and Albert Museum's collection reveals that a man's "black" coat of about 1914, includes coarse, white, kemp fibers in the yarn. Furthermore, the "black" surface of a riding habit jacket and skirt of 1890 is broken by grayish white fibers.[48] In the vast majority of tweeds, therefore, the interplay between two or more colors is fundamentally important to their belonging to that group of cloths.

NAMED VARIETIES OF TWEED

The term tweed incorporates cloths that have more strictly defined characteristics, or associations with place, than is inferred simply by a generic nomenclature, as Taylor and Ostick confirm.[49] It is therefore now necessary to explore the technical and aesthetic properties and geographical associations of different types of named tweeds, including Saxonies, Cheviots, homespuns, Harris, Donegal, Shetland, West of England, Yorkshire, Welsh and estate tweeds. Investigating these named cloths is essential to developing an understanding of the history of tweed because, for example, the terms Cheviot, Saxony or homespun are frequently used in primary sources instead of the word tweed.[50] That fact is illustrated by the following quote from the company history of Henry Ballantyne & Sons Ltd of 1929, which states: "Though made in infinite variety, the Scotch Tweeds of to-day may be divided broadly into the two great categories of Saxonies and Cheviots and the smaller class of Homespuns."[51] The characteristics of these three types of tweed and how they relate to cloths whose name is linked to their place of origin, or manufacture, will now be explained.

Saxonies

Locke and Craig argue that merino wools from Saxony and Silesia began to be imported into Scotland to be made into tweeds, from as early as 1834. These superfine fibers were soon replaced by cheaper versions from Australia. The name Saxony was, however, retained and it is still used today to denote fine tweeds made from merino-grade wool.[52] Saxonies are fine and densely woven and they have a soft, smooth handle. The finest versions are hard to distinguish from worsted cloths.[53] By the 1860s, Saxonies were primarily being used to make men's tweed suits for informal, summer wear and since that time they have continued to mainly be employed as suiting cloths. Today, these textiles continue to form part of the ranges of leading British manufacturers of mill-woven tweeds, such as the Lovat Mill.[54]

Cheviots

The name of these woolens derives from the Cheviot breed of sheep, which by 1791 was being widely introduced into the Scottish Borders.[55] By the 1880s, it had become well established that the character of a Cheviot tweed might also be achieved by using a range of other wools, or blends with them, including, in particular, Colonial Cross-breds.[56] In their definition of 2002, the Textile Institute state that the term relates to "A tweed made from Cheviot wool or wools of similar quality."[57] The word "quality" has a specific meaning in relation to wool, it refers to the diameter of the fiber, which has a significant impact on the characteristics of yarn and cloth made from it.[58] Cheviot tweeds have a crisp, springy handle, a rougher appearance and a more open texture than Saxonies.[59] These characteristics and their aesthetic appeal largely derive from the broader qualities of wool that Cheviots are made from, as Harrison stated in 1944:

> Being of a thicker fibre it is usually stouter in the yarn and bolder in the twill or more open in the weave. It therefore presents to the eye a bigger pattern or effect. Saxony lends itself more to quiet colourings and restrained designs, while Cheviot offers unlimited scope to the designer for bold patterns and gay colourings.[60]

Cheviots were popular as men's suitings during the late nineteenth and twentieth centuries. These cloths are still woven by UK-based mills today, including Alexanders of Scotland.[61]

Homespuns

These tweeds have a rough, textured appearance and many of them include white, brittle kemp fibers, parts of the sheep's fleece that are usually discarded before making other woolens. Kemp fibers are resistant to dyeing and therefore they appear as a pale, textural feature on the surface of the cloth.[62] Between the late nineteenth century and the mid-twentieth century, all types of homespun tweeds were principally worn by men and women for sporting or leisure wear, as clarified in Chapters 4 to 7. The popularity of the early tweeds of the 1830s and 1840s, which were mostly made in mills in the Scottish Borders, prompted the subsequent development of domestically based tweed industries in the Highlands and Islands of Scotland and Ireland.[63] From the 1880s, these industries became fully established as selling tweeds that were handwoven using handspun yarn, processes that were carried out in the home, hence the adoption of the name "homespuns" for these cloths. Harris Tweed was the most famous product related to these developments and Hunter argues that the commercial success of these particular homespuns had, by 1906, led to extensive copying of them by manufacturers using mill-spun yarn and power looms. The term homespun therefore also became widely used to denote coarse, or coarse-looking tweeds made in mills by mechanized methods.[64]

From 1934, the Harris Tweed Trade Mark was amended to allow the use of mill-spun yarn, although because these cloths continued to be handwoven at home they were still known, however illogically, as "homespuns."[65] *Textiles for Tailors*, published in about 1950 reveals that the name, carefully qualified by the word "Imitation" to avoid litigation, was still being widely applied to "coarse fabrics of a tweed character" that were machine-spun and power-woven.[66] It is difficult to determine exactly when the term "homespun" fell out of widespread use in the textile and tailoring trades, however, it is notable that the 7th edition of *Textile Terms and Definitions* of 1975 does not include it.[67] Although this nomenclature is no longer used, tweeds of this character such as Harris Tweed and the coarser types of Donegal tweed are still woven today.

Harris Tweed

This tweed is intrinsically related to a specific location, namely the remote islands of the Outer Hebrides, which lie far off the northwest coast of Scotland. Because Harris Tweed is handwoven and sold in some volume, it holds a distinctive position within contemporary global markets. The concise definition in the Act of Parliament of 1993 reads as follows: "Harris Tweed means a tweed which has been handwoven by the islanders at their homes in the Outer Hebrides, finished in the Outer Hebrides and made from pure virgin wool dyed and spun in the Outer Hebrides." This Act also sets out that detailed specifications and standards must be met in order for the cloth to be stamped with the Orb mark by the Harris Tweed Authority Inspectors.[68]

Today, Harris Tweed is mainly woven from Cheviot wool in twill, or broken twill constructions. These cloths are produced in a wide range of patterns and they usually feature mixture yarns that give attractive, variegated color effects. Another characteristic feature is the presence of kemp fibers in the yarn, which help to create visual and textural, surface interest. Although these textiles are often perceived as solely being heavy cloths, today they come in a wide range of weights from 390g to 550g per square meter, with the heaviest versions now mostly being used for interiors.[69] In 2014, the dyeing, spinning and finishing processes were carried out in three mills on Lewis, namely Harris Tweed Hebrides, The Carloway Mill and Harris Tweed Scotland. All of the weavers in the industry are self-employed and the majority of them work solely with the mills, although a few work independently as small producers.[70] An example of a Harris Tweed in a heather mixture woven by the independent producer Donald John Mackay in 2010 for use in Nike trainers features in Plate 3.

Donegal Tweeds

A handwoven tweed industry developed in County Donegal from the 1880s and these textiles became the best-known type of Irish tweed. The historian, David Jenkins states that the cloths produced were "made from coarse local wool in a plain weave with contrasting colours in warp and

Figure 2.3 Model (right) in trousers made from Donegal tweed, which show the classic "pepper-and-salt effect," 1947. Photograph by J. A. Hampton/Topical Press Agency/Getty Images.

weft and little bits of uncarded wool spun into the yarn to give distinctive effects. This tweed … tended to be copied in cheaper imitations by Yorkshire manufacturers."[71] The small flecks of dyed, felted and carbonized wool, which are intrinsic to the appearance of a "classic" Donegal tweed, are known in Britain as knops, whereas the terms nepps, or burrs, are used in Ireland (see Fig. 2.3). Studying archival range books related to the mills, Convoy and Magee of Donegal revealed that the design of tweeds by local firms since the 1960s has extended well beyond solely producing the type of cloths described by Jenkins. For example, although the plain weave has been a typical characteristic of Donegal tweeds, twill and broken twill constructions have also featured in these woolens.[72] Significantly, tweeds woven in Donegal have not enjoyed the legal and trademark protections that have been of vital support to the Harris Tweed industry. Furthermore, by the mid-1970s, all of the County Donegal-based tweed manufacturers were using power looms for some, or all, of their cloths.[73] Today, Donegal tweed is widely used as a generic term to describe fabrics woven in the plain weave from contrasting colors of flecked yarn, at a range of quality levels around the world.[74] Despite that global competition, a research trip of 2012 revealed that a few firms including Magee of Donegal, Studio Donegal and Molloy & Sons Weaving Ltd continue to make high quality, machine and handwoven tweeds in County Donegal, many of them for international export.[75]

Shetland Tweeds

Wool from the native sheep of the Shetland Islands (which lie far off the north coast of Scotland) was originally used to make tweeds of that name. The very limited supply of this wool, and its desirable, soft handle, prompted a Scottish Borders tweed manufacturer to state in 1929 that, "a real Shetland suit or costume is distinctly a luxury."[76] These homespun tweeds were generally made in the plain weave from un-dyed wool, with the natural colors of the fleece being sorted to create the required design. The majority of cloths described as "Shetlands" have, however, not been made from pure wool from those remote islands.[77] Harrison quotes an individual involved with the textile industry as stating in 1935, that "Most of the so-called Shetland is woollen or shoddy mixture, and has no relationship to actual Shetland wool."[78] Safeguarding that local, raw material proved elusive until 2011, when EU, Protected Designation of Origin status was secured for organic "Native Shetland Wool," which comes from pure-bred, sheep reared on the Islands. Today, Shetland tweeds continue to form part of the ranges of leading British woolen manufacturers, such as Abraham Moon & Sons. They are also made on the Islands themselves by Jamieson's of Shetland.[79]

West of England Tweeds

The majority of tweeds woven in the West of England region were Saxonies, made from merino wool.[80] Between 1835 and 1914, the formerly pre-eminent woolen industry in that area experienced significant decline. By the 1840s, its famous broadcloth trade was already close to its end and by the late nineteenth century manufacturers were producing a wide range of woolen cloths, including cavalry twills, venetians and tweeds.[81] Jenkins and Ponting make a comparison between tweeds produced in Scotland and by West of England mills between 1870 and 1914 and they conclude in relation to the latter that the "only successful attempt to compete in this new, high quality tweed trade came from one firm, William Bliss of Chipping Norton."[82] Ponting, who previously worked as a designer in the West of England woolen industry between 1945 and 1965, also described tweeds from that region as being "somehow between the best Scottish tweeds and run-of-the mill Yorkshire."[83] In 2014, the only manufacturer of woolen apparel cloths left in that locale was Fox Brothers & Co. Ltd, who are based in Wellington, Somerset. This mill is most famous for its flannels, but they also create other luxury wool cloths, including tweeds, which they sell to Savile Row tailors and other high end, international customers.[84]

Yorkshire Tweeds

Following on from the growing popularity of Scottish tweeds from the early 1830s, Yorkshire woolen manufacturers began to make these textiles. Gulvin argues that by the late nineteenth century they had achieved great success in selling them at the middle and lower levels of the British market.[85] An article of 1878 in *The Textile Manufacturer* discussed the importance of "cheap tweeds" to the Huddersfield trade, thus indicating that Scottish designs were widely imitated by Yorkshire woolen manufacturers at mass market quality standards.[86] In Scotland, tweed producers chiefly used pure new wool, whereas in Yorkshire, combinations of cotton and wool, lower grades of wool and shoddy (wool recycled from soft rags) were principally employed in the late nineteenth and early twentieth centuries. Notably, Jenkins and Ponting argue that despite the major reliance on shoddy, cloths from that region were not exclusively made from it and Yorkshire tweeds in the coarser types of new wool were also woven.[87]

A *British Wool Cloth Sample Book* produced by the International Wool Secretariat in the mid-1960s, gives specific descriptions of various types of tweeds but simply says that "A large variety of other tweeds are made in the West Riding of Yorkshire."[88] This implies that tweeds from Yorkshire did not have distinctive design characteristics related to that locale, but that manufacturers produced a wide range of different types, according to shifting consumer tastes. In 2011, Peter Ackroyd, then President of the International Wool Textile Organisation, commented on the decline and changing character of the Yorkshire worsted and woolen industry. He stated that "What we have left is a niche sector producing high quality designs and products mainly for the luxury and upper end of the market."[89] Yorkshire-based manufacturers of tweeds have also benefited from the renewed interest of high street retailers such as Marks and Spencer in British "heritage" woolens. Today, firms trading in that locale that make tweeds and other woolens include Abraham Moon, Marling & Evans, Marton Mills, and William Bliss & Son Ltd.[90]

Welsh Tweeds

In the second half of the nineteenth century, woolen mills in Wales produced mainly flannel, shirtings and blankets. However, by the 1860s, tweeds had become so popular that firms such as The Llanidloes Welsh Flannel, Tweed and Wool Stapling Company Limited, were also making them. John Geraint Jenkins posits that most of the "homespuns" produced by Welsh mills were made in the plain weave and they were similar to the local flannels.[91] From the 1920s, the woolen industry in Wales entered a period of major decline, although subsequent attempts at diversification meant that between 1949 and 1969 "light tweeds" were still being produced by a small number of Welsh mills.[92]

Estate Tweeds

Many tweed designs have evolved from the shepherd's check pattern, which was adopted for fashionable menswear from the late 1820s. In particular, E. P. Harrison argues that this simple black-and-white design has formed the basis of several patterns within the group of cloths known as estate tweeds, or district checks. These tweeds first emerged in the 1840s because of the desires of landowners to create a specific identity for their estate and their development was intrinsically connected to major social and economic changes within the Scottish Highlands. By the late nineteenth century much land there had been purchased by new owners and converted into deer forests and grouse moors, as confirmed by Devine.[93] Stillie suggests that some of the individuals

Figure 2.4 Glenurquhart check, woolen sample, 2013, Lovat Mill. Courtesy of Fiona Anderson.

who bought or rented land in the Highlands from the 1840s were influenced by the popular notion that specific tartans related to particular Scottish clan names. He argues that these romantic perceptions encouraged the development of new cloth designs, as follows:

> many of the new landowners and tenants did not have claim to a tartan but wished some distinctive garb for themselves and their estate workers. It was in this environment that the cloths which later became known as the District checks developed; the name tends to be misleading as the cloths were attached to some estate, organization or regiment rather than a district.[94]

The key publications on the development of these textiles, *Our Scottish District Checks* of 1868 by E. S. Harrison, and *Scottish Estate Tweeds* of 1995 by E. P. Harrison, contain useful, illustrated summaries of the histories of many of the existing patterns.[95] The latter text indicates that one of the earliest estate tweeds was the Glenurquhart, which is a black-and-white check that, with the addition of a blue or red over-check, has been widely known as the Prince of Wales check (Fig. 2.4). This pattern was adopted by Caroline, Countess of Seafield on her estates from the 1840s. The Glenurquhart is one of the few seminal wool textile designs that have remained popular since the late nineteenth century.[96] Its history illustrates that although estate tweed patterns were created solely for private use, many of them have constantly been re-interpreted to form commercially successful designs. New estate tweeds are still being privately commissioned from a handful of Scottish firms, including Johnstons of Elgin and the Lovat Mill.[97] The design processes linked to these cloths were described by Stephen Rendle of the latter firm, as follows: "tweed is tied to the land and the cloth's designs reflect that ... On one estate, for example, we're working from photographs that capture its many qualities in the shooting season."[98]

CONCLUSION

In this chapter, the development of the term tweed and its associated myths have been re-considered through the use of original writings by Locke, which have shown that the use of this word to denote a textile derived from either *tweels* or *tweelds*.[99] A working description of tweeds has also been developed, which will form the basis of the analysis of these textiles in the remainder of the volume. This chapter has also begun to explore the shifting and complex meanings associated with the evolving group of woolens that have been described as tweeds since the 1830s. In particular, it has shown that some British tweeds retain powerful connotations of place, heritage and authenticity today.

3

ORIGINS AND EARLY DEVELOPMENT OF TWEED TO 1850

Tweeds have specific origins that in the nineteenth century gave them a particular named identity, that of Scotch tweeds. This chapter explores the early development of these woolens and how they came to be fashion textiles woven in mills and crofts and sold to the Edinburgh and London markets. It also examines the new relationships that developed between modernity, romanticism, Scottish sporting tourism and the growing fashion for tweed from around 1830. That analysis draws on the work of the literary historian John Glendening, historian Tom Devine and the cultural theorist Elizabeth Wilson. It is also based on new research, which examines extremely rare tweed samples of the 1830s in the Heriot-Watt University Archive along with written accounts about the early tweed trade by James Locke, Adam Cochrane and Alexander Craig.[1] The limited discourse on men's fashion textiles of the Romantic era remains dominated by discussion of English broadcloths in black or other dark colors.[2] Exploring the early history of tweeds within the context of late Romanticism therefore offers important new perspectives about the design, colorings and cultural meanings of menswear woolens between the late 1820s and 1850. The chapter also challenges the historical stereotype that tweeds were exclusively worn by the British land-owning elite in rural contexts, by considering new primary evidence about the shifting interrelationships between masculinities and class between 1829 and 1850. The historical background to the development of tweed manufacturing will now briefly be discussed.

THE SCOTTISH WOOLEN INDUSTRY BEFORE THE TWEED TRADE

Gulvin argues that improvements made in the Scottish woolen industry between 1770 and the late 1820s helped to lay the foundations for the later successful development of tweed production. Prior to the 1770s, the production of woolens in Scotland was considerably less advanced than that of its neighbor England in terms of its economic success and the quality of its cloths. By the late eighteenth century, England had long been renowned for producing fine broadcloths, which at that time were principally made in the West of England and Yorkshire.[3] Ponting confirms that these woolens were woven in the plain weave to "about 100 inches wide which was then fulled to about 63 inches." They were then raised and cut to give a luxurious smooth finish.[4] In contrast, prior to the 1830s, the woolen industry in Scotland mainly produced coarse gray or blue cloths that were woven in the twill weave from home grown wool. This prominence of plain Scottish woolens has received little scholarly attention, except by Gulvin, primarily because of the extensive interest in the history of tartan.[5]

Gulvin notes that the Scottish woolen industry had by the 1820s made considerable improvements in terms of raising levels of output, improving the quality of wool and finishing and making the transition away from domestic, often-subsistence production toward factory-based manufacturing.[6] In that decade, however, this progress was set back by a temporary decline in the quality of the native Cheviot wool and increased competition from Yorkshire manufacturers. Owing to these circumstances and an overall lack of enterprise and innovation, many woolen producers in Scotland went bankrupt between 1828 and 1830. Despite these severe problems, this period was to prove a pivotal time of change and opportunity for Scottish woolen manufacturing.[7] In that era, this industry began a transformation, which is described by Gulvin as follows: "From its preoccupation with coarse inferior homespuns for local country wear … Scottish woolen manufacturing after 1830 evolved into the most aristocratic branch of the British wool-textile industry. The impetus behind this radical change of emphasis was largely fashion."[8]

THE DEVELOPMENT OF THE EARLY TWEED TRADE, 1829–1850

The shift of the Scottish woolen industry toward producing the fancy cloths that became known as tweeds was largely precipitated by the adoption as a fashion textile of the simple, checked plaids worn by shepherds in the Scottish Borders (Fig. 3.1). These lengths of cloth made in the twill weave from two contrasting shades of un-dyed Cheviot wool were known in that region as mauds, although the Highland term plaid was also used to describe them. The shepherd's check, as it became known, was worn by fashionable urban men as a trousering cloth from the late 1820s. This design is usually made in black and white, in a 2/2 twill, with the warp and weft arranged in the order of five or more light and five or more dark. The pattern is similar to that in a fragment of woolen cloth now held by National Museums Scotland, which was found at Falkirk in Scotland and that has been dated to the third century AD. Simple weaving, which creates contrasting decorative effects from light and dark natural shades of yarn was known in many early human cultures. It is not appropriate therefore to say that the shepherd's check pattern is exclusively of Scottish origin. However, in 1874 Craig suggested that this design first became used as a textile

Figure 3.1 Scottish shepherd wearing a black-and-white shepherd's plaid. Early twentieth century. © National Museums Scotland, Edinburgh.

for fashion through the masculine adoption of Scottish cloths. Although based initially on well-established products, this move toward a novelty trade was a significant departure for the Scottish woolen industry and it signaled the beginnings of strong and important connections with London-based cloth merchants.[9]

Designing and Selling the Early Tweeds

Urban contexts were central to the development of the early tweed trade, because most of the cloth merchants who acted as intermediaries between the woolen manufacturers, tailors and consumers were based in either Edinburgh or London. In 1875, Craig stated about the pivotal contribution of James Locke that "Although Mr Locke was not the first to introduce Scotch tweeds into the Metropolis (for I claim that honour), he perhaps did more work, both in getting his own designs made and the goods introduced into influential quarters than any other man of that time."[10] Craig was the employee of an Edinburgh-based merchant and he also played an important role in encouraging the sale of the new, fancy, Scottish woolens.[11] Other cloth merchants who helped to introduce "Scotch tweeds" into the London market included, Ebenezer Harvey & Co. of 9 Bow Church Yard and Binnie & Richardson, of Old Bond Street. The Edinburgh-based drapers and influential tweed designers James and Archibald Ogilvie also sold to metropolitan customers from the 1830s.[12]

Locke was initially based in Covent Garden, but around 1830 he moved to the more prestigious location of 119 Regent Street.[13] Craig describes how the success of Locke's firm helped to establish a wider trade in tweeds, as follows:

> The Messrs Locke's new shop being in one of the best thoroughfares in London, it was not long before members of the nobility and fashionable West End people found them out, so that the increasing demand sufficiently encouraged the new manufactures. Her Majesty sent for them the first time that she went to Scotland, and gave a large order for Royal Stewart and other tartan dresses and shawls. Prince Albert also selected various tweeds for suits. After tweeds got introduced into such influential channels, the middle classes were not long in following. The trade rapidly extending the Messrs Locke found it necessary to keep a large … stock of various kinds of Scotch woollen goods, which enabled them to go into the wholesale branch and to supply the leading tailors and clothiers in both London and the country.[14]

The characteristics of the cloths woven by the early manufacturers of tweed were inextricably linked to their relationships with merchants. These individuals played a role in directly designing cloths and they also acted as conduits for the ideas of tailors and consumers.[15] For example, Locke posits with regard to the early years of the fashion for shepherd's check trousers that "gentlemen of education and taste" gave his business "more ideas and designs than what we got from the makers themselves."[16]

The initial success of the fashion for trousers in that check was followed by design adaptations that took place around 1831/32, which further stimulated consumer demand for these cloths. This primarily involved dyeing the black-and-white checks and subsequently creating larger scale and broken checks. Many of these new designs were given contemporary names such as "Victoria" and "railway."[17]

In the early 1830s, at the suggestion of some of his London-based gentlemen clients, Locke ordered woolens from Galashiels that were "*tweels* in thin granite colours ... in black and white, brown and white running into lighter and darker mixtures."[18] Cloths known as "mixtures" include different shades of dyed wool that are blended together before the yarn is spun, which gives attractive variegated color effects. Although this type of yarn was not unique to Scotland, it undoubtedly came to be a characteristic feature of tweeds from that locale. Ponting emphasizes that the Scottish trade developed "mixture colours not known before, heather mixtures, for example."[19] Although it is made up of variegated shades, the heather mixture design has an overall purple appearance. Locke recalled in 1863 why these new, more colorful designs of the later 1830s developed:

> When first mixtures were enquired for which should resemble the moors and different shooting grounds, by many gentlemen of the rod and gun, we at this time had nothing of the kind, neither was there any in the market. We ... wrote to a house in Galashiels ... but as we anticipated, they replied they had never heard of such a name or article.... . we requested them just to imitate the side of Buckholm Hill which overshadowed them ... A boy was despatched to fetch home some.... . Now when a handful of this was "squashed" together it had different shades ... This proved to be the very thing we wanted and led to the introduction of a variety of colours before unknown. These first obtained the name of *heather mixtures*.[20]

Locke clearly posits that creating mixtures, whose colors were designed to blend in with the rural Scottish landscape was an entirely new idea. Furthermore, he argues that the impetus for these new designs came directly from sportsmen who wished to be camouflaged in those environments in order to better stalk their prey. Notably, the timing of the emergence of these new mixtures coincided directly with the significant growth in popularity of Scottish field sports among upper- and upper-middle-class men from the early 1830s onwards, as confirmed by Durie.[21] In addition, an advertisement of 1838 for Locke's Regent Street premises shows that he was selling "Heather and Granite Stone Mixtures for Shooting Jackets" to customers who shopped in that fashionable, upmarket locale.[22] Locke commented further about how the tastes of sporting customers and the colors and patterns of Highland "home stuffs" influenced some of the early tweed designs, by stating that his firm introduced:

> a yellow colour never seen before in town, although we remembered to have seen it on a Highland drover. This colour, so hateful in general, has become, when tastefully contrasted with others a very favourite one and we maintain that "Scotchified" patterns did not originate with the makers of Scotch tweeds. It was the Highland glens that gave many of them to the trade. Gentlemen brought the colours up from their shooting boxes, as they could not be produced there in any quantity. [23]

Locke confirms that the domestic Highland weavers of these "Scotchified" patterns only wove small quantities of the cloths that were desired by his customers. In order to meet the demand for that type of cloth for shooting attire, he therefore had designs based on these "home stuffs" made up in large quantities, principally by mills in the Scottish Borders. Locke identifies that the bright colors he used within tweeds were inspired by the yarns used in the Highlands for home-produced tartans. However, the way that vivid shades were employed in menswear tweeds from the 1830s was different to their use in tartans, in that it was influenced by rural landscapes.[24] These new ways of using bright colors, such as yellow and orange, within men's fashionable, sporting textiles can be seen in textile samples of the era.

An extremely rare pattern book of 1836–7 from the drapers and designers, J. & A. Ogilvie, fleshes out in material form and provides an important supplement to the contemporary accounts by Locke, Craig and Cochrane. James and Archibald Ogilvie ran their Edinburgh-based firm from around 1827 to 1863.[25] Craig states that they "took a lead in designing patterns, in fact they were undoubtedly the first designers of their day. Their patterns became well known, and were much sought after by the leading wholesale houses in London."[26] The majority of the samples in the Ogilvie book of 1836–7 show a strong continuity with, or signs of evolution from, well-established Scottish woolen products. This artifact contains a lot of black-and-white checked samples, including both shepherd's checks and dogtooth checks (see Plate 1). Significantly, this suggests that the famous dogtooth check may also have first entered fashionable dress through the 1830s fashion for men's trousers in Scottish woolens. Notably, some of the black-and-white checked samples have been over-dyed in dark blue, bright blue, green and brown, as described by Cochrane and Craig (see Plate 4).[27]

Although *tweels* have been much discussed as the word from which the term tweed developed, none of the scholarly sources on the history of those textiles describe their appearance.[28] The Ogilvie book of 1836–7 resolves this problem because it contains several coarse, woolen samples that are made from mixture yarns and which have an obvious diagonal twill (see Plate 1). Comparison with Locke and Craig's texts reveals that these are *tweels* and the majority of these swatches match Locke's description of the ones that he first sent to London in the early 1830s.[29] Further samples in the Ogilvie book of 1836–7 show the early development of what were to become the key characteristics of many tweeds. These features include a strong emphasis on the use of "broken effects of colour, attained either by pattern, or by blends of colour," as Harrison noted in his tweed description of 1944.[30] It also involves the use of shades linked to rural landscapes, including both subdued and vivid tones, as shown by the bright green, black and orange checked sample in Plate 4. A further group of swatches are predominantly black and white, but they feature spots of bright orange, which echoes the mottled effects of rocks, as described by Locke and Craig.[31] This use of vivid colors derived from nature in small amounts, so that they give subtle, variegated color effects rather than a stridently colored cloth overall has formed part of the distinctive appeal of many tweeds since the 1830s.[32] Notably, studying the J. & A. Ogilvie book of 1836–7 strongly endorses Locke's account, which has shown that the group of textiles known as tweed evolved from the established Scottish woolen products of shepherd's plaids, Highland "home stuffs" and *tweels*.

Early Scottish Tweed Production: Products, Location, Organization, and Power

Tweeds, ladies' shawls, and cloakings, as Locke noted in 1863, were the three main types of woolen goods manufactured in Scotland up until 1848, when the latter began to decline in popularity.[33] Cochrane explains that the fine Saxony fabrics that were known as "cloakings" were, in fact, primarily made into dresses in "clan and fancy tartans and plain checks."[34] Locke confirms that although tartans were the most popular Scottish textiles for womenswear up to 1850, females also wore fine woolen dresses in tweed patterns such as the shepherd's check.[35]

The social impact of the changes in the Scottish woolen industry was felt in Galashiels as early as 1832 when the Rev. Nathaniel Paterson commented that "the gleam of fashion, like a May sun, has given a new stir to the working bees of this town."[36] By the 1820s, the Scottish Borders had become established as the main center in Scotland for woolen and hosiery manufacture and by 1850 one third of factory workers in that industry were located there.[37] Gulvin confirms that the expansion of tweed manufacturing from the 1830s onwards was a key driver of the continued economic and social transformation of the Scottish Borders from an exclusively rural area, to one where the countryside was interspersed with several, small industrial towns.[38] Tweeds were also woven in the semi-rural, Hillfoots district, although tartans and shawls were chiefly made there between 1830 and 1850. Aberdeen and its environs was also a major woolen-producing area and Allan notes that J. and J. Crombie Ltd had great success making tweeds and overcoatings from the 1830s. Along with this major trend toward regional concentration, woolen production remained widespread throughout Scotland. This included the rural Highlands region, where Johnstons of Elgin began to play a prominent role in tweed design and manufacture from the 1840s.[39]

The tweeds produced on the Scottish mainland in the 1830s were predominantly woven by hand, but their manufacture was increasingly linked to modern industrial methods and forms of organization. In 1839, Galashiels was one of the most advanced centers of production in the Scottish woolen industry and a government report noted that "all the weaving with trivial exceptions" was performed there in factories.[40] This grouping of hand-loom weavers together in mills was primarily about more efficient organization of production, as the weaving of woolens was yet to be widely mechanized.[41]

Gulvin argues about Scottish manufacturing that: "steam-operated looms only gradually displaced the hand-loom weaver … mainly due to technical difficulties – especially the ease with which woollen weft broke under machine conditions."[42] These technical problems meant that the introduction of power weaving proceeded much more slowly in woolen production than in cotton and worsted manufacturing, throughout Britain and Europe. Furthermore, Jenkins argues that setting up looms to make fancy woolens took a significant portion of the weaver's time, so that the "advantage of the power loom was for long minimal."[43] The growing emphasis within Scotland after 1830 on producing short runs of fancy tweed cloths therefore encouraged the slow rate of adoption of powered weaving. As Gulvin states, "although the first power looms in the Borders were installed in Hawick as early as 1830 … There were only 247 in the industry by 1850."[44] The rapid expansion of the Scottish woolen industry between 1835 and 1850 meant that the number of mills doubled to around 182 by 1850, while the numbers employed almost tripled to reach 9,500.[45] The emergence of domestically-based tweed weaving in the Outer Hebrides will now be discussed.

THE ORIGINS AND HISTORICAL BACKGROUND OF THE HARRIS TWEED INDUSTRY

The beginnings of the Harris Tweed industry need to be understood within the contexts of the profound social and economic changes that took place in the Highlands and Islands of Scotland between the late eighteenth century and the mid-nineteenth century. Devine emphasizes the complex interrelationships between growing industrialization in Scotland, which prompted a huge rise in demand for food and raw materials such as wool, and the dramatic transformation of rural Scotland.[46] He also confirms that "In the first half of the nineteenth century, the Highlands suffered the trauma of widespread eviction of local communities (the Clearances), mass emigration and in the 1840s, large-scale famine."[47] The "removal" of local people by Highland landowners was principally to make way for the development of large-scale sheep farming. By the mid-nineteenth century, much land on Highland estates had also been converted to deer forests and grouse moors, which signaled the development of a profitable, sporting economy.[48]

By the 1840s, the crofting system had become firmly established by landowners and Devine argues that the most notable feature of this re-distribution of land to form smallholdings was that a croft would "provide only partial subsistence and to make ends meet … the crofter and his family had to have recourse to supplementary jobs," which turned out to be a "disastrous policy for the people of the western Highlands and Islands."[49] The social impacts of these changes, including the threat of destitution linked to the major Potato Famine of 1846 to 1851 were felt particularly severely in the Outer Hebrides. This time of social and economic crisis presented a critical impetus to develop new sources of employment that would supplement income from crofting and these contexts were pivotal to the emergence of the Harris Tweed industry.[50]

There are several conflicting accounts about the early development of Harris Tweed weaving. Firstly, Janet Hunter's detailed discussion of these debates is summarized, rather than repeated in full here. Alexander, the 6th Earl of Dunmore (1804–45) inherited the island of Harris from his father in 1836 and his wife, Catherine, Countess of Dunmore (1814–86) has been credited with a pivotal role in the early development of Harris Tweed production. However, it is not clear whether the 6th Earl started to encourage the weaving of Harris Tweed before 1845, when he died, or if his wife helped to initiate it at some time between 1839 and 1851. The most popular version of the story involves the claim that in 1844 the 6th Earl of Dunmore ordered Murray tartan to be made up in tweed for his gamekeepers and outdoor servants to wear on his estate. In consequence, the Countess of Dunmore saw weaving as a good potential source of employment for the local islanders and this effectively was how the Harris Tweed industry began.[51]

Based on the surviving evidence, it is impossible to establish precisely when the Harris Tweed industry started, or what exactly is the most accurate account of its origins. Key nineteenth-century accounts, such as that from Kenneth MacDonald the Factor for North Harris to the Napier Commission of 1884 and the essay by Mrs MacDonald in a Scottish Home Industries Association publication of 1895 confirm that the 6th Countess of Dunmore did have a pivotal early role in encouraging the production of tweeds. However, given the death of the 6th Earl in 1845 and Mrs MacDonald's claim that his wife did not visit Harris until 1851, it seems unlikely that there was much Harris Tweed produced before that date. More significantly, as Hunter argues, the desperate economic circumstances during the Potato Famine of 1846 to 1851 also suggest that little, if any, income was being received from making Harris Tweed during that time. This places the real expansion and consolidation of Harris Tweed production as taking place after 1851, as discussed in Chapter 4.[52]

ROMANTICISM AND THE EARLY FASHION FOR TWEED

By the 1820s, the literary and artistic works of the Romantics had a high public profile in Britain and Europe. Ian Duncan argues that, in particular, the novels of Sir Walter Scott had "saturated the British fiction market, outselling all other novels combined."[53] The strong links between Scottish Romanticism, Scott and the growing fashionability of tartan in the early nineteenth century have been well established. The relationships between the Romantic movement and the fashion for tweed have, however, not yet been examined in depth.[54] Elizabeth Wilson places the complex cultural developments related to the term Romanticism within their wider, historical contexts. She states that the:

> Romantic movement of the late eighteenth century and early nineteenth century was one early response to the advance of science and the "dark Satanic mills" of industrialism. It offered a counter-ideology that spoke against the machine age and yet espoused the intense individualism of the new order.... . nature began to be idealized just at the time when a new and much more wholly urban society was being created by the industrial revolution.[55]

This era produced a pivotal change in men's fashionable dress, the adoption of the English country style, which in the late eighteenth century comprised a fine broadcloth coat and close-fitting breeches that derived from riding dress. Fashionable men's daywear of the late 1820s and 1830s involved a modified version of that look, which included trousers. The embrace of woolen cloths in dark or subdued shades rather than the patterned, colorful silks that were previously fashionable for menswear was closely linked to the emphasis within Romantic sensibilities on the natural and authentic.[56] For example, Hollander states that "English country dress, besides harmonizing with the earth and its fields, forests and rocks, came to suggest the comfortable coat of horse and dog, the smooth fit and dun colour of the stag's hide."[57] In this quote, Hollander is mainly referring to men's coats, which she notes were primarily made from smooth-textured broadcloths in the plain colors of black, brown, dark green and dark blue.[58] These uniform colorings suggest that she has overstated the degree to which these cloths visually harmonized with the variegated tones of country environments. They also indicate that the emergence of sporting tweeds in the late Romantic period represented a more direct influence of "natural" rural environments on the design and colorings of menswear woolens than had previously existed.[59]

The Shepherd's Check: Romanticism, Masculinity, and Class

The origins of shepherd's check trousers are described by Craig, who discussed what he observed in Glasgow in 1829, as follows:

> a rather conspicuous object attracted my attention ... namely, a man dressed in a pair of black and white large-check trousers.... .I think it highly probable that this man's trousers were made out of either his grandfather's plaid, or his grandmother's shawl... . These trousers were the very height of ugliness, but they were the first shepherd's-check trousers I had ever seen.[60]

Craig noted that this new style was particularly striking, because at that time men's trousers were only made in plain fabrics in colors such as "drabs, greys and blacks." He also commented that later in 1829: "one of my friends in the cloth trade wrote me from London inquiring about 'a coarse woollen black and white-checked stuff, made in Scotland and expected to be wanted for trousers'... . I believe these were the first Scotch tweeds that were sent to London in bulk. They were good strong Cheviot (unfinished) checks, at a wonderfully low price." Craig's friend was James Locke and in his account he recalled that the introduction of these trousers to elite students at Oxford and Cambridge prompted an "unprecedented demand" for them.[61]

The few secondary sources that discuss the early history of tweed give Sir Walter Scott and the politician Henry Peter Brougham, first Baron Brougham and Vaux (1778–1868) important roles in encouraging the adoption of shepherd's check trousers. These texts have contributed to the mythology surrounding Scott's supposed pivotal role in promoting this fashion by wearing the garments himself from the mid-1820s.[62] Studying a pair of black-and-white checked trousers displayed at Scott's home, Abbotsford, which reputedly belonged to him, reveals that they have a woven border stripe, a style that began to be fashionable between 1835 and 1844. That detail suggests that these trousers cannot have been worn by him, because he died in 1832.[63] The only evidence found while researching this book about Scott wearing shepherd's check trousers is an eyewitness account of his visit to Malta in 1831, in Lockhart's *Memoirs of the Life of Sir Walter Scott*. This source suggests that Scott did wear that style of checked trousers, but he was not the direct originator of the fashion because it started in the late 1820s.[64] Cochrane's assertion that through the indirect, but substantial, public influence of his writing Scott encouraged consumer interest in goods made from the shepherd's check is, however, entirely credible. For example, in his famous novel *Waverley*, the ghost of Halbert Hall wears "a grey plaid, such as shepherd's wear in the south of Scotland."[65]

In contrast, Lord Brougham became so closely associated with wearing shepherd's check trousers that they were sometimes known simply as "Broughams."[66] This Scottish politician was a

THE JUDGMENT OF PARIS.

Out of regard to the delicate feelings of the Society for the suppression of vice, HB, has made free with classic truth, by enrobing the rival beauties.

Published by Thos. McLean, 26 Haymarket, Nov. 30th 1830.

Figure 3.2 "The Judgement of Paris," by John Doyle. Lithograph, published November 30, 1830. © National Portrait Gallery, London.

Figure 3.3 John Murray (1808–92). Photograph by David Octavius Hill and Robert Adamson, mid-1840s. © Special Collections, Glasgow University Library. Licensor www.scran.ac.uk

prominent Whig, who played an important role in ensuring the passage of the socially progressive Reform Bill of 1832. He is depicted in a lithograph of 1830 (Fig 3.2), which features the Prime Minister, Lord Grey (1764–1845), offering a full-bottomed wig, which symbolized the Lord Chancellorship, to the potential candidates of Brougham, Lord William Plunket (1764–1854) and Sir John Leach (1760–1843).[67] It is notable that only Brougham is wearing newly fashionable, tweed trousers, which are in stark contrast to the legal dress of formal, eighteenth-century-style breeches worn by his colleagues. A satirical letter in *Punch* of 1844, suggests that Brougham was identified as a radical figure who had brought this informal fashion into the formal, public sphere of the British Parliament. This text states that, "There is a dangerous sympathy between common garments and the common people. The Reform Bill had never been carried if Lord Brougham had not worn tweed trousers."[68] Although satirical, the letter suggests that wearing shepherd's check trousers in Parliament challenged sartorial and social conventions in an era when British power and class relationships were in a major state of flux.[69] It also shows that from this early date, tweeds were closely associated with the development of more modern and democratic forms of male attire.

Tweed trousers in the shepherd's check and other patterns, continued to be fashionable in Britain in the 1840s, as shown by the image of the well-known publisher John Murray in (Fig. 3.3). Contrary to the stereotypical image of tweeds as exclusively worn by the British upper classes in rural contexts, these garments were primarily adopted as urban wear by a wide range of social classes. Men who wore tweed trousers included Prince Albert, as noted in *The Morning Chronicle* of December 8, 1843. An article in *Punch* of 1844 suggests that these garments were also widely worn by young upper-, upper-middle and middle-class men. Significantly, this text indicates that along with a black coat these trousers were considered appropriate as formal daywear to be worn in the afternoon.[70] An advertisement for L. Hyam's Pantechnetheca of 1844, indicates that tweed trousers were also being sold to that firm's predominantly lower-middle-class customers. This company was one of the largest ready-to-wear tailoring firms in Britain and they catered to an extensive clientele. The advert includes "Woollen Tweed Trowsers," which were being sold for 4 shillings and 6 pence, which was considerably cheaper than any of the other wool trousers listed. The relative cheapness of tweed trousers is therefore likely to have helped this fashion, once established, to spread down the social scale in Britain.[71] The consumption of tweeds before 1850 was also intrinsically linked to the early development of new, modern conceptions of sport and masculine sportswear, as will now be discussed.

Romanticism, Sport, Scottish Tourism, and Tweed

By the late eighteenth century, a limited flow of English sportsmen to the Scottish Highlands in pursuit of fish and game had become established. Durie argues that it was not until the 1830s, however, that Scottish field sports became a fashionable activity pursued by considerable numbers of upper- and upper-middle-class British men. This shift involved an increasing commercialization of sport in the Highlands, as many tourists began to rent properties and shootings rather than relying on the hospitality of local landowners. The growing popularity of tourism to Scotland was made possible by the transformation in accessibility of the Highlands, wrought first by the steamships of the 1820s, improved coach services from the 1830s and the railways from the 1840s.[72] Glendening discusses the relationships between modernity, romanticism and the increased popularity of travel to Scotland, as follows:

like modern tourism, romanticism helped promote the Highlands as the real thing, a genuine, exotic, and commodifiable otherness that writing had already rendered familiar. Aided by its accessibility, Scotland became a prime destination for romantic tourism because of its ability to signify this simple, revitalizing genuineness for the English, who were facing unprecedented economic and material dislocations created by such factors as industrialisation, urban growth and a promotion of individualism.[73]

In the early nineteenth century, the Highlands increasingly represented a mythologized place in Britain that functioned as an imaginative environment where truly "natural" and "authentic" experiences such as deer stalking could be enjoyed. That image of northern Scotland as an unchanging wilderness, which was untouched by the radical, economic, political and social changes associated with modernity was far from the contemporary reality. The growth in tweed manufacturing from the 1830s onwards was integrally connected to the increasing popularity of Scottish field sports and by implication to the profound changes in land ownership and usage in the Highlands, already discussed.[74]

The growth of the sporting economy in Scotland had important social, political and economic dimensions, for those who bought and rented properties and shooting rights. Travel to the Highlands in August for grouse shooting became part of the season—the social calendar—which, from the 1820s, began to form an integral part of elite lifestyles in Britain. Leonora Davidoff clarifies that the exclusive social rituals of the season were an important means by which the British aristocracy maintained their unrivaled power, wealth and prestige.[75] In her influential work, *The Best Circles*, she gives a definition of Society and the season, as follows:

> Sociologically, Society can be seen as a system of quasi-kinship relationships which was used to "place" mobile individuals during the period of structural differentiation fostered by industrialization and urbanization. As such it can be understood as a feature of a community based on common claims to status honor which were in turn based on a certain lifestyle… .Like all status groups, the traditional aristocratic elite were obsessively concerned with the question of access to their ranks.[76]

The ritualistic set of social practices and events that constituted the season, along with the careful selection of marriage partners, played a significant role in helping to ensure that until the mid-nineteenth century, the British aristocracy was the most exclusive elite in the world.[77] For men and women, participating in the season involved negotiating formalized, but shifting, models of social and sartorial etiquette, including what was acceptable attire at certain times of day, in particular social settings, and for specific types of physical activity.[78]

The expansion in Scottish field sports from the 1830s presented the question of what was suitable masculine attire for the newly fashionable activities of deer stalking, grouse shooting or salmon fishing in Scotland. Engaging in these sports often entailed dealing with harsh weather conditions and demanding mountainous, or boggy terrain, as indicated in a sporting handbook of 1838, *The Art of Deer-stalking* by William Scrope. This text contains a rather overblown chapter on the necessary qualifications for a deer stalker, which include being able to "Run in a stooping position, at a greyhound pace, with his back parallel to the ground … for miles together. He should take singular pleasure in threading the seams of a bog, or in gliding down a burn, … accomplished he should be in skilfully squeezing his clothes after this operation."[79] As Scrope indicates, these masculine sports were carried out on foot and therefore it is not surprising that alternatives were being sought to the superfine woolen coats, and cotton, linen or fine wool trousers that characterized the male wardrobe of the early 1830s. Tweeds were much less susceptible to surface damage than fine, napped broadcloths, and for sporting purposes they also had greater elasticity in wear.[80]

Scrope strongly emphasized in his text of 1838 the links between particular masculine ideals and the desirable qualities of the "consummate deer-stalker."[81] Although his text is somewhat exaggerated, the gender characteristics Scrope describes closely mirror John Tosh's arguments about the nineteenth-century ideal of manliness. He states that it "comprised a set of core values which had characterized masculine culture long before the Victorians.... . Manly vigour included energy, virility, strength ... Next came the moral qualities which enabled men to attain their physical potential – decisiveness, courage and endurance."[82] The powerful associations between idealized masculinities, the Highland landscape and Scottish field sports that developed from the 1830s and the links of tweeds with clothing worn for these sports meant that these textiles began to acquire strong connotations of manliness.

"Highland Hospitality," Romantic Bohemians, and the Fashion for Tweed

Studying the painting "Highland Hospitality" of 1832, by John Frederick Lewis (1804–76) provides revealing insights about the contemporary associations of tweeds with romanticism, sport and gender (Plate 5). It also shows the origins of the connections between tweeds and male bohemian sartorial identities, which continued to be relevant into the inter-war period. Lewis visited the Scottish Highlands in 1830, with his friends, the artists William Evans (1798–1877)

Figure 3.4 "Coming In For A Shot." Illustration after Charles Landseer, by William Scrope from *The Art of Deer-stalking*, 1838. © National Museums Scotland, Edinburgh.

and George Cattermole (1800–68). He subsequently completed "Highland Hospitality" and exhibited it in London in 1832. This work also received significant popularity as an engraving, as Bulman confirms.[83] The painting depicts Cattermole and Evans in a Scottish Highland interior having an encounter with a local family. The presence of dogs and guns in the picture confirms that these artists have been engaging in the sport of shooting.

In Jackson's analysis of the furniture depicted, he argues that although accurate in some respects, the scene also features fanciful elements. For example, the "ornately carved mid-seventeenth century cabinet" is an improbable feature of this Highland interior.[84] The accuracy of the clothing worn by Cattermole and Evans can, however, be verified. Taking Cattermole as the first example, his hairstyle and outfit are totally in keeping with fashionable men's styles of the period, which is highly suggestive that the cloth of his jacket and waistcoat are also accurately represented.[85] These garments are made from a thick, coarse, checked woolen fabric, similar to that of Evans's plaid, in other words from tweed. This painting therefore includes a very early depiction of this type of clothing in tweeds being worn by a fashionable London artist in a Scottish sporting context.[86]

Cattermole's attire is striking in its similarity to the outfits illustrated in Scrope's *The Art of Deer-stalking* of 1838. The visual evidence in this publication also relates closely to the clothing worn by the bohemian artist, Evans, in "Highland Hospitality." These drawings depict the clothing worn for deer stalking in Scotland: for example, in "Coming In For A Shot" a sportsman is wearing narrow, checked tweed trousers, and a shooting jacket in the fashionable cut of the 1830s (Fig. 3.4). In the illustration, "Lifting the Dead Deer From A Burn," a gentleman stalker wears tweed trousers, a shooting jacket and a blue bonnet. A shepherd's plaid has also been laid

Figure 3.5 "Lifting the Dead Deer from a Burn." Illustration after Charles Landseer, by William Scrope from *The Art of Deer-stalking*, 1838. © National Museums Scotland, Edinburgh.

on the ground (Fig. 3.5). Notably, Scrope's text refers to both shooting jackets and plaids being worn by sportsmen visiting Scotland.[87]

Evans is depicted in "Highland Hospitality" wearing a shepherd's plaid in a Scottish rural location a few years before Locke discusses wearing one "in town" as a fashion accessory. These plaids also began to be used by British consumers as traveling wraps at a time when there was a marked increase in the distinctly modern pursuits of travel and tourism.[88] Evans also wears a black velveteen shooting jacket, pale-colored trousers in a fashionable cut and a blue bonnet, which was the usual headwear of the male lower orders in rural Scotland at that time.[89] Notably, Jackson states that "Like most genre artists … Lewis was … absorbed in the visual effect of 'the other.'"[90] The adoption by Evans of the shepherd's plaid and blue bonnet are clear evidence of the sartorial influence of Romanticism, which resulted in sporting tourists adopting "traditional" and "authentic" Scottish dress, albeit in a highly specific and mediated way. Notably in "Highland Hospitality" and Scrope's deer-stalking illustrations of 1838, local Highlanders, including stalkers and other outdoor servants, are depicted in tartan livery, while sporting tourists wear tweeds (Plate 5; Figs 3.4, 3.5). This suggests that sportsmen visiting the Scottish Highlands in the early nineteenth century maintained sartorial distinctions that socially distinguished them in class, ethnic and gender terms, from "the other," meaning Scottish Highlanders. Significantly, Cochrane confirmed in 1864 the growing popularity of Scottish woolens from the 1820s in Britain. At that time, he noted, male fashionable consumers tended to wear the shepherd's check and related designs, rather than the more "exotic" and feminized option of exuberantly colored tartans, which were predominantly worn by women.[91]

The sartorial choices of Cattermole and Evans were influenced by a range of social, cultural, and fashion contexts around 1830. Cattermole had a taste for Scott's writings and he produced drawings, which were published in later editions of the Waverly novels and in *Heath's Pictorial Annual for 1835: Scott and Scotland*. He also lived and socialized at the center of male fashionable London. After Cattermole moved to the metropolis in 1819, he became part of Count d'Orsay and Lady Blessington's fashionable circle, which included leading figures from the spheres of literature and art. His close friends included Edward Bulwer-Lytton, Sir Edwin Landseer, Daniel Maclise and Charles Dickens. By the late 1830s, Cattermole had moved into the Albany to a suite of private chambers that were previously occupied by Lord Byron.[92] Breward discusses men's fashion from the 1830s to the 1850s and its relationship to individuals within Cattermole's social circle, as follows:

> Romantic in inspiration … the fashionable male figure … celebrated a loudness in pattern and colour alien even to the music hall habitues of the 1890s (whose clothing and comic turns often referred back nostalgically to this lost period of 'bohemianism'). Fashion plates and portraits record a preference for light checked trousers … colourfully eccentric waist- coats and richly textured velvet jackets … . This was a look espoused by the leisured man of letters, which found its most celebrated adherents in Charles Dickens, Edward Bulwer Lytton and Benjamin Disraeli in London, and Restoration dandies including the Count D'Orsay, Balzac and Baudelaire in Paris.[93]

Cattermole clearly shared the sartorial interests of his friends, because the art historian Sperling declared in 2004 that "Few artists dressed as well as he."[94] Evans also moved in prominent artistic circles and Bulman states that he was influenced by "his bohemian friends George Cattermole, Edwin Landseer, and above all John Frederick Lewis."[95] It appears that the fascination of

Cattermole and Evans with romanticism, fashionable appearances and sporting practices, along with their travels to Scotland, coalesced to make them early adopters of the shepherd's plaid and other tweed garments.

CONCLUSION

The early development of the tweed trade involved the evolution of the traditional Scottish textiles of the shepherd's plaid, *tweels* and Highland "home stuffs", which initially functioned as symbols of "otherness," into a group of constantly changing, fashionable commodities, which became known under the collective name of tweed.[96] Raymond Williams stated about the meaning of the word "tradition" that "It is sometimes observed … that it only takes two generations to make anything traditional: naturally enough, since that is the sense of tradition as active process. But the word tends to move towards age-old."[97] In that sense, the wearing of shepherd's plaids by men of lowly, rural origins in the Scottish Borders, might be seen as traditional. However, the adoption of that pattern in the form of plaids and trousers by sporting tourists and urban consumers from the late 1820s must be seen within the contexts of modern, fashionable consumption. The modernity of the fashion for tweeds is further underlined by its connections with the pursuits of travel, tourism, and sport. In the early nineteenth century, when industrialization and urbanization were having a transformative impact on British society, the powerful associations of tweeds with the Romantic search for "natural" and "authentic" experiences only reinforced their intrinsic connections to modernity. As Glendening states: "Although the romantic sensibility asserts itself in opposition to the modern world, it is the direct outgrowth of that world." [98] These apparent contradictions were also reflected in the fact that urban and rural contexts were deeply intertwined in the processes of manufacturing, designing, selling and consuming tweed cloths. This chapter has also shown that although tweeds were primarily consumed as sporting cloths by upper- and upper-middle-class men before 1850, these textiles were also worn in urban contexts by everyone from Royalty to the lower middle classes, according to sartorial etiquette codes.[99]

4

TWEED, MALE FASHION, AND MODERN MASCULINITIES, 1851-1918

Tweeds are strongly associated with the development of the modern male wardrobe in that they were one of the most popular fabrics for making lounge jackets and suits from the mid-nineteenth century.[1] This sportswear-inspired shift toward greater informality in male attire was accompanied by the increased participation in sport by middle-class men from the 1870s onwards. By the following decade, shifts within the British and international wealth elite encouraged the further expansion in popularity of Scottish field sports. These changes meant that tweeds were worn within specific social contexts by an increasingly diverse range of male consumers including plutocratic deer-stalkers, middle-class cyclists and bohemian modernists in the late nineteenth and early twentieth centuries. Previous research about these textiles has examined the complex relationships between modernity, masculinities, landscape, imperialism and men's fashion between 1860 and 1900.[2] This chapter extends that research by exploring the range of cultural and social meanings linked to menswear tweeds between 1851 and 1918. That inter-disciplinary analysis is informed by the work of a range of authors including Christopher Breward, Peter Brooker, David Cannadine, W. J. T. Mitchell and John Tosh.[3] Changing developments within the design, selling and production of tweeds for menswear will now be examined within their British and international contexts.

DESIGNING AND SELLING SCOTTISH TWEEDS

Tweed trousers in shepherd's checks and other fancy patterns remained popular in Britain and Europe in the 1850s and 1860s.[4] The Juror's Report on Woollen Goods in the International Exhibition of 1862, which was held in London, discussed the important design influence of tweeds from Scotland. It stated: "To the Scottish manufacturers belong the credit of ... having led for a considerable period the public taste. So largely have their productions been imitated on the Continent, that many of the choicest fancy trouserings of France and other countries are easily traceable in design and colouring to their Scotch origin."[5] Locke's account of going to the *Exposition Universelle*, which was held in Paris in 1855 suggests that there was also a two-way exchange of ideas between merchants dealing in Scottish tweeds and exhibitors at international events. He stated that, "we saw a good many new ideas. On our return the ranges got quite a new impulse in a new style of check."[6]

Studying a pattern book of 1852 from the manufacturer R & A Sanderson & Co. Ltd of Galashiels reveals the huge range of tweed designs produced by that mill.[7] The majority of the samples in this book are men's trouser cloths, which have a border that in wear would have formed a side seam stripe. These swatches are made in a wide range of fancy patterns including checks, herringbones and stripes, thus demonstrating that the range of designs available for tweed trousers had greatly expanded since the 1830s. The samples are mostly made in the twill weave in shades of gray, black, white and brown. However, it is striking that many of them also have bright pink, orange, red, blue or purple yarns in them, which from a distance create subtle, variegated, visual effects, as can be seen in Plate 6. These vibrant colors have been incorporated mainly by the twisting of contrasting single yarns together, but also through the use of mixture yarns. Furthermore, contrary to the popular perception that men's nineteenth-century tweeds were all heavy in weight, almost all of the samples in this book are medium weight. For example, quite a number of the trouser cloths are 14 oz and most of them are 11oz.

This pattern book is invaluable in showing the detailed, colorful characteristics of tweeds for menswear, which are impossible to trace through contemporary black-and-white photographs. It also greatly adds to the visual and textual evidence available in fashion journals. An article in the November 1858 edition of the *Gazette of Fashion* stated that, "In 'Cheviots' and 'Heathers' there is a large assortment of mixtures, some of which are bright enough, we should think, to satisfy the *fastest* man to be found."[8] However, a survey of that journal between 1857 and 1858 reveals that only two colors were ever employed in the many fashion illustrations of tweed trousers, so the variegated effects linked to brightly colored mixture yarns cannot be seen.[9] The R & A Sanderson book shows their range of designs for 1852, but it does not clarify which patterns were actually sold. Nevertheless, studying these samples provides a much deeper understanding of the colors and characteristics of the textiles that were offered to merchants and subsequently worn by men than is available through the contemporary fashion press. Fashionable novelty and variety were clearly hugely important within the high class market for men's woolen textiles in that era, which meant that manufacturers invested considerable time and money in the production of a phenomenal range of designs each season. Gulvin argued that these practices remained central to Scottish tweed production between 1880 and 1914. He states:

> The Scotch tweed trade was largely a "one-off" trade, with few lengthy runs … Such a trade put a premium on designers and pattern-weavers, who were expensive to maintain; large numbers of trial patterns had to be produced from which merchants could choose … . Designing was therefore, an exceptionally costly part of the productive process, since most of it fell on the manufacturer himself.[10]

The skilled and inventive use of color in design and an emphasis on using pure, new wools were key characteristics of Scottish tweed cloths. That focus on quality was summed up by Mr Irvine, a Hawick manufacturer, who stated in a local newspaper of October 27, 1855, "Spare no expense of a true character on your wools – your dyestuffs … aim at excellency of fabrics … and beauty of design; repel with true pride and scorn every attempt to compromise a character so patiently earned."[11] Gulvin notes that not all Scottish manufacturers of tweeds consistently kept up these high standards and in the 1890s some producers aimed to cut costs by using Belgian yarn that incorporated about 10 percent cotton.[12] Significantly, he also argues that these tactics usually led to failure and the "more important firms in the industry … refused to lower the standards that had given their products their superlative reputation," which was largely based on design and good quality raw materials.[13]

Tweed Design and Landscape

A promotional booklet of the early twentieth century from Peter Anderson Ltd of Galashiels reveals the strong continued influence of rural landscapes on the design of tweeds. It states, "Many of the colourings in Scotch Tweeds have found their origin from blending colours of the heather bloom, brackens, grasses, mosses and rocks seen on the Scottish hills and moorlands. There are mixtures of the browns, reds and gold which remind me of the moors during the autumn months when Nature runs riot with colours."[14] This quote reveals that the use of small amounts of bright shades, so that they provided subtle visual interest, rather than a vibrantly hued cloth overall had by the early twentieth century become a long-established key characteristic of Scottish tweeds. Although this approach to color initially derived from the interplay of shades within rural environments, as discussed in Chapter 3, it subsequently influenced tweeds worn in both the town and the country. For example, a range book of winter 1907 from the Hawick-based manufacturer Blenkhorn Richardson & Co. Ltd mostly contains very dark tweed samples, which would mainly have been worn as urban suiting cloths.[15] Many of these predominantly dark-colored woolen swatches have wool or silk yarns in bright shades of red, yellow, green, purple, or orange in them, which creates subtly appealing color effects in the overall cloth. This range book of 1907 also contains tweeds designed for country wear that are lighter and more colorful than the urban suitings (Plate 7). Significantly, the windowpane checks and highly colored twist suitings illustrated reveal that men still had more varied opportunities to exercise a taste for pattern and color in cloths that were worn in informal, rural or sporting contexts.

From the 1840s, the landscapes of specific Scottish sporting estates influenced the development of estate tweed patterns, as discussed in Chapter 2. Although these designs were initially commissioned for private use, many estate tweed patterns and variations on them became an important element of the ranges of Scottish manufacturers in the late nineteenth century. In particular, Gulvin indicates that variations of the Glenurquhart check and the Coigach, or gun club check were highly popular in the North American market.[16]

Selling Tweeds: London Merchants, Agents, and Exports

From the mid-nineteenth century, London-based merchants continued to play a significant role in acting as middlemen between Scottish tweed producers and tailors. These merchanting firms still had a major influence on the ranges of designs made by manufacturers and their expert knowledge of shifting market trends was invaluable in securing sales. Gulvin argues that the focus of Scottish firms on making tweeds for the upper levels of the market meant that even by 1914 their cloths were principally used in Britain by bespoke tailors, rather than the growing ready-made clothing trade. The emphasis on that market encouraged the continuance of strong inter-connections between merchants and woolen manufacturers from Scotland. In contrast, by 1907, the expansion in production of ready-made tailored clothing meant that Yorkshire woolen manufacturers increasingly dealt directly with large clothing wholesalers, rather than merchants. A key shift that was prompted by the great demand for Scottish woolens after the Great Exhibition of 1851 was that many tweed producers engaged London-based agents for the first time. It subsequently became common practice for tweed manufacturers from Scotland to employ these urban-based representatives, to show patterns to and take orders from customers such as merchants and tailors.[17]

The early Scottish tweeds were primarily sold to the British market, but by the late nineteenth century exports accounted for a significant proportion of sales. It is difficult to ascertain precise figures for international exports, but Gulvin suggests that in the 1880s about half of the total production of the Scottish Borders industry was sold abroad. The importance of exports extended beyond Borders-based firms, for example, Harrison notes that in the 1860s Johnstons of Elgin began selling to Italy and France and by the 1870s they had also increased their exports to Germany, Belgium, Japan and South America. In 1882, they began selling to customers in the USA and like many Scottish manufacturers they experienced the severe impact of the McKinley tariff of 1890 and the Dingley tariff of 1897.[18] These powerful trade protection measures resulted in high levels of duties being levied on Scottish tweeds. For example, Gulvin argues that the McKinley tariff "effectively placed a 90 per cent duty on woollens sent from Scotland."[19] The *Glasgow Herald* only slightly overstated the impact of these measures when it reported on August 24, 1909 that the Dingley tariff had "practically severed the commercial intercourse between the Scotch Border towns and the United States."[20] Gulvin puts the impact of these American and also European trade restrictions on the export of woolens from Scotland into context by stating that:

> Scotch tweeds found a ready sale in temperate countries with a sizeable upper and middle-class market – in the nineteenth century mainly France, Germany, Austria and the United States. After the erection of the American tariff system in the 1890s tweed producers concentrated increasingly on their European trade, which in some areas at least was growing quickly before 1914 despite growing commercial restrictions.[21]

TWEED PRODUCTION: CHANGE, COMPETITION, AND MODERNIZATION

By the mid-nineteenth century, tweeds had become the most widely made product in the Scottish woolen industry. Locke summed up these developments, as follows: "Reviewing the Scotch tweed trade … in Galashiels in 1832 the whole did not amount to £2000 or £3000. In 1862 we find it in, if not more than, £1,200,000." He also argued that the growing fashion from the early 1850s for tweed lounge jackets and suits to be worn in town helped to account for the decline in the ladies shawl trade. [22] At that time, many mills in the Borders and Hillfoots regions of Scotland, which had hitherto predominantly made shawls, were changing to tweed manufacturing.[23]

The dynamic geographical and cultural mixing of rural and urban influences and contexts continued to be important as tweed production and markets developed after 1851. For example,

Craig discussed Scottish tweed manufacturing in 1874, as follows: "The trade is now wonderfully increased, and firmly established beyond … expectations, and the goods are made all over the country from Shetland, Harris, and Skye … to Galashiels, Hawick and Langholm."[24] Between 1851 and 1918, the Scottish Borders region continued to develop as the main center in Scotland for tweed manufacturing. The small textile towns in that semi-rural area experienced major expansion between 1811 and 1881, which was primarily linked to agricultural workers being recruited to the woolen industry. Tweeds also continued to be produced in scattered locations throughout Scotland including the Hillfoots district, the city of Aberdeen and its environs, Dumfriesshire and Inverness.[25]

Jenkins and Ponting argue that between the 1830s and 1914, the Scottish industry established its position as the leading British center for the manufacture of high class woolens, thus superseding the position of the West of England.[26] Gulvin notes, however, that this industry also experienced problems toward the end of the nineteenth century. He argues about key trends within Scottish tweed production that the 1880s and more especially the 1890s were "marked by low prices and falling demand, at least until around 1900. Thereafter production expanded greatly, especially just before World War I."[27] Gulvin posits that the severe decline in Scottish woolen manufacturing of the 1890s was principally caused by the impact of American, but also European tariffs, as already discussed, and the related intensification of competition from English and foreign producers. European woolen producers benefited from the impact of trade protection measures on their domestic trade and their competitiveness was also enhanced by improvements in skills and capital equipment that had been made toward the end of the nineteenth century.[28]

In the British market of the 1890s, however, Scottish firms principally suffered from increased competition from Yorkshire manufacturers.[29] An article in *The Times* of June 24, 1907 commented that "for a considerable time" cloths had been woven in England, particularly in Yorkshire, to imitate Scottish cloths and these were largely sold under the name "Scotch tweeds." This text also stated: "These imitations so closely resemble the genuine article in design and finish that to detect them would almost require an analysis of the thread. This cloth is made of inferior materials and as it can be produced at very much less cost than the genuine article this 'substitution' trade has grown to great dimensions."[30] Gulvin argues that this imitation was so widespread that "by 1906 it was estimated that about three-quarters of the 'Scotch Tweeds' produced in Britain were made in England."[31]

In the late nineteenth and early twentieth centuries, Yorkshire was by far the largest center for woolen and worsted manufacturing in Britain and production there was focused on cloths for the middle to lower levels of the mass market.[32] The Scottish industry broadly focused on the upper end of the woolen trade, but many manufacturers attempted to spread risk by including medium qualities of simpler designs in their ranges and it was that trade which was most affected by Yorkshire competition. Gulvin also notes that a shift in the 1890s toward the fashionability of lighter cloths incorporating worsted yarns largely benefited the Yorkshire, rather than the Scottish trade.[33] Notably, the Yorkshire woolen industry chiefly focused on using shoddy and combinations of cotton and wool between the mid-nineteenth century and the onset of the First World War. In that era, Jenkins and Ponting clarify that the area around Guiseley and Yeadon also developed a reputation for making tweeds from the coarser qualities of new wool.[34]

Exploring developments within the manufacture of British mill-woven tweeds reveals the importance of modernization and a surprising persistence of hand weaving after 1851. Mechanized weaving advanced much more slowly in the woolen industry than in worsted production, as noted in Chapter 3. After the mid-century, however, the rate of adoption of power looms notably increased. Jenkins and Ponting clarify that in 1850 there were 247 power looms in Scottish woolen manufacturing and by 1889 there were 9,836. In Yorkshire, woolen producers also greatly expanded their use of mechanized looms in this period, with 3,849 being recorded as employed in 1850 and 37,626 in 1889.[35] These changes relate to the comments of Jenkins about European woolen production. He states that "When competition became so much fiercer from the 1870s and 1880s even the small savings that the power loom could permit became crucial, hastening its introduction."[36]

Along with these shifts toward modernization, hand weaving showed a surprising persistence within the fancy woolen trades of mainland Scotland and Huddersfield in Yorkshire. Jenkins and Ponting note that by 1886, the number of power looms in Galashiels had increased to 1085, but even by that late date there were still 402 hand looms.[37] A small proportion of these looms might have been used for making samples, but the large numbers recorded indicate that the vast majority were used for weaving full lengths of cloth. The most likely explanation for these developments is the focus of most Galashiels manufacturers on producing short runs of fancy tweeds. By the end of the nineteenth century the hand weaving of woolens was mainly practiced in Scotland within the domestically based industry of the Highlands and Islands.[38]

Between 1914 and 1918, the production of woolen cloths in Britain was dramatically affected by the First World War. Jenkins states: "Some exports were maintained but many firms had to convert their production from traditional specialisms to war needs; particularly to the manufacture of khaki and other service cloths. Wool supply was allocated centrally to regulate price increases and to ensure necessary supply."[39] The impact of the War on exports was felt particularly keenly by Scottish tweed manufacturers, although this was to an extent alleviated by government contracts for uniform cloths, including tartans, khaki and flannel. For example, in the company history of Henry Ballantyne & Sons Ltd of 1929, it stated that the "mills worked day and night to meet the demands of the Quartermaster-General."[40]

HOME INDUSTRIES AND SCOTTISH HANDWOVEN TWEEDS, 1851–1918

The handwoven tweed industry in the Highlands and Islands of Scotland chiefly developed from the late nineteenth century onwards. Between the 1850s and the 1870s, encouraging the manufacture of domestically woven tweeds and organizing their sale was primarily the preserve of a handful of aristocratic, or upper-middle-class women, most of whom were from local landowning families.[41] The best known cloth related to these developments was Harris Tweed and Catherine, 6th Countess of Dunmore, played a central role in encouraging the early production of these woolens, as confirmed in Chapter 3. The book *Scottish Home Industries* of 1895 contains an essay by Mrs MacDonald who discussed that lengths of tweed were sent from Harris to the Countess's main residence at Dunmore in Stirlingshire and that she soon established an "extensive connection" with leading merchants in Edinburgh and London.[42]

A further essay in the same book by Lady Alice Leslie clarifies the important work done by Mrs Thomas in encouraging the production and sale of Harris Tweed. She became involved after 1857 when she first visited Harris with her husband, Captain Thomas, R. N. who was then Nautical

Surveyor of the island.[43] Leslie presents the contribution of Thomas as significant and wholly inspired by philanthropic desires to help alleviate the effects of poverty among the islanders. These views were echoed by the Rev. Roderick Mackenzie of Tarbert in Harris when he gave evidence to the Napier Commission of 1883. After thirty years of selling Harris Tweed from her Edinburgh house, Mrs Thomas opened a small depot in Berners Street, London. For a few years before she re-married, Thomas successfully sold these homespuns to the metropolitan retail and wholesale trade.[44]

The Hebridean isles of Harris and Lewis are often known as the Long Island, because they are physically joined together. By the early 1880s, "Harris Tweed" was being made on Lewis, where the islanders were also in need of additional income.[45] Toward the end of the nineteenth century, domestically produced tweeds were also being made in other places in Scotland including the Shetland Isles, Ross-shire and Sutherland.[46] Hunter clarifies that "While Harris weaving was generally acknowledged to have been superior to that of most other districts … hand-made tweeds from other places were certainly providing competition in the textile markets of the south."[47]

In the closing decades of the nineteenth century the promotion and sale of home-woven tweeds underwent significant change. Key developments were the setting up of the Scottish Home Industries Association (1889), Highland Home Industries and Arts Association (1890) and the Crofter's Agency (1896). Significantly, the running of these selling agencies continued to be intimately bound up with the patronage and philanthropic work of royal and aristocratic women. For example, H. R. H. Princess Louise was the patron of the Scottish Home Industries Association and Hannah, Countess of Roseberry (1851–90) was its first President.[48] The objectives of this Association were to "find a market for the products of home industries, to improve their quality by providing instruction and to pay a fair price for the labour involved in making the products."[49] The activities of these agencies and the lifestyles of their patrons meant that Scottish rural and English, metropolitan contexts were closely intertwined in the making, promotion and sale of domestically produced tweeds.[50]

Another key change from the late 1870s onwards in Harris was that local merchants began to buy tweeds from the weavers, which they subsequently sold on to wholesalers. Tensions later developed between the agencies and the merchants. The main source of conflict was that individuals representing the agencies were concerned that weavers were not being paid sufficiently well by local merchants.[51] MacDonald argued in 1895, for example, that since Lady Dunmore's death in 1886 the local people had sold Harris Tweed for less profit. She stated:

> when needing the necessaries of life, they will accept very low prices from dealers, who, in their turn, have to part with the goods at a low rate to the great city dealers, in order to cover their own expenses. This has reduced the price per yard below its true value. From 3s 6d to 3s 9d per yard is not too much to give the workers, for tweeds so durable and so excellently coloured with healthy dyes.[52]

Despite these problems, Harris Tweed weaving had a significant social and economic impact in the Outer Hebrides from the 1880s onwards. Evidence given by the Rev. Roderick Mackenzie of Tarbert to the Napier Commission in 1883 included his view that in the previous three years local people had accumulated the greatest proportion of their income from making Harris Tweed, which was more profitable than either crofting or fishing.[53] Furthermore, in 1918, Ormerod posited that there were "no fewer than 1,500 spinners and 200 weavers in the island of Harris alone."[54] Given the low levels of population on these islands, these figures represent an important source of employment, which supplemented the only partial subsistence that was available from crofting.[55]

Significantly, the efforts of patrician women to promote home industries followed a time of considerable political unrest in the Highlands, which prompted unprecedented government intervention in relation to land rights. Devine states that "A series of popular disturbances in the 1880s, which have come to be known as the 'Crofters War', came together with an effective political campaign of land reformers, Gaelic revivalists and radical liberals to force the hand of government. A Royal Commission chaired by Lord Napier and Ettrick, was soon followed by the passage of the Crofters' Holding (Scotland) Act." This legal and political intervention of 1886, which was largely prompted by a "breakdown of public order" radically improved the land rights of Highland crofters and effectively curtailed the former level of power held by landowners.[56]

Janice Helland, in her book of 2007, *British and Irish Home Arts and Industries 1880–1914: Marketing Craft, Making Fashion,* discusses the fact that Millicent Sutherland (1867–1955) was a "devoted advocate of home arts, particularly the weaving and marketing of tweed" and that "her connections with the world of wealth and eminence served her project well."[57] Her husband, the 4th Duke of Sutherland was one of the wealthiest members of the traditional British elite and he owned extensive tracts of land in England and Highland Scotland. Millicent was the first President of the Highland Home Industries and Arts Association and in 1896 she took over the key role of President of the Scottish Home Industries Association.[58] Helland argues in relation to the home industries exhibitions organized in Sutherland in the late 1880s that "the Sutherland committee astutely lavished its attention upon the weaving and selling of tweeds produced in the poorest and most politically restless area of Scotland. Millicent Sutherland's motives may have been philanthropic, but her focus upon weaving rather than upon 'art' embroidery proved to be shrewd."[59] These philanthropic activities were clearly not simply inspired by benevolent desires to support her tenants to raise additional income, but were influenced by the complex political contexts that Highland landowners had to negotiate in that period.

Notably, the purpose of the selling agencies was also influenced by the cultural contexts of the era. The objectives of the Highland Home Industries and Arts Association stated about home-made fabrics that "the revival of such industries would greatly promote thrift and add to the comfort and to the self-respect of the poorer classes of people … the artistic faculty of the race would be revived and stimulated."[60] These aims have clearly been influenced by ideas about social, industrial, moral and aesthetic reform, which emerged in the second half of the nineteenth century. Gillian Naylor stated in relation to John Ruskin that he "passionately believed that beauty was as necessary to man's survival as food, shelter and a living wage, and that this essential could only be achieved in a society in which all men would work, take pleasure in their labour and share their delight in its results." Ruskin also insisted that objects should "unashamedly reveal their man-made origin, and reflect man's essential humanity, with all its roughness and individuality."[61] The distinctive visual and textural characteristics of handwoven tweeds certainly reflected these aesthetic qualities.

Domestically produced Scottish tweeds were mainly worn by men in the late nineteenth and early twentieth centuries. In 1918, for example, Ormerod discussed that they were "most popular with … sportsmen and for golfing, walking, cycling, motoring, mountaineering, and other outdoor sports they are unrivalled."[62] The fact that rural-inspired colors and small, discreet patterns were the prevalent taste of tailors and merchants at the turn of the century is revealed by the Scottish Home Industries Association publication of 1895, which discussed the woolens they sold, as follows:

There is a constant demand for homespun tweeds of good quality and pattern. A difficulty the Association has daily to face, however, is the one of getting new and original patterns. The greys and drabs which the workers persistently adhere to are now almost unsaleable. What customers ask for are the new green, brown and heather mixtures of small pattern, and, in fact, as soon as an original and good pattern comes in it is eagerly bought up. Tailors and cloth merchants are now regular customers, and give occasionally large orders for tweeds.[63]

This quote reveals that because these tweeds were made by weavers working independently in their own homes, design was organized in a somewhat haphazard fashion. Urban-based merchants clearly had much less direct influence on the appearance of domestically produced homespuns than they did on tweeds produced by the main Scottish woolen industry.

In an era of increasing mechanization, the hand-crafted character of Harris Tweed, the fact of its limited supply, and the wealthy elite lifestyles of the consumers who wore it, meant that these textiles were highly desirable. The commercial success of these homespuns led to extensive copying of them by mainland British manufacturers using power looms and mill-spun yarn. The term homespun therefore also became widely used to denote factory-woven, coarse or coarse-looking tweeds made with machine-spun yarn. Hunter confirms that because of these commercial challenges a successful campaign was mounted to secure trademark certification for Harris Tweed.[64] In October 1910, the Harris Tweed Trade Mark was registered and by early 1911, cloth had begun to be stamped on Harris with the Orb Mark. The definition of that textile enshrined in this Trade Mark was as follows: "a tweed handspun and hand-woven and dyed by the crofters and cottars in the Outer Hebrides."[65] This pivotal development formalized and protected the intrinsic relationship between these textiles and the remote Hebridean islands and underlined their powerful associations of authenticity and place.

TWEED, SOCIAL CONTEXTS, AND MALE SARTORIAL IDENTITIES, 1851–1918

The place of tweeds in the male wardrobe and a range of social and cultural meanings linked to their consumption will now be explored. As already noted, from the early 1850s, tweeds were strongly linked to the development of modern male attire in that they became one of the most popular textiles used to make the newly fashionable lounge, or lounging, jackets and suits. The term lounge suit was used to describe outfits that comprised a matching jacket, trousers and waistcoat. Breward confirms that by the early twentieth century the alternative name of business suit had also come into use.[66] At the mid-century, the frock coat was the acceptable option for formal daywear and compared to earlier in the nineteenth century it was worn relatively short, a few inches above the knee, as confirmed by an illustration of 1857 in the *Gazette of Fashion*.[67] Men's upper outer garments that were shorter than this length were associated with social and sartorial informality. For example, a previous study of the Savile Row tailor, Henry Poole and Co. revealed that even when lounge jackets and suits became well established in the male wardrobe during the 1860s, this was only for informal morning, sporting, and other leisure wear.[68]

Locke stated about the early 1850s that "Up to this time, with the exception of shooting coats, there was little thought of for gentlemen's lounging coats in our public walks and streets."[69] His text

Figure 4.1 Brooke Boothby, 1889. Photograph by W. & D. Downey. © National Portrait Gallery, London.

Figure 4.2 Young man wearing a tweed lounge suit in a garden, Paisley, Scotland, c. 1900. © National Museums Scotland, Edinburgh.

indicates that the term coat was often used to denote a short jacket at this time of stylistic change. The quote from Locke, and trade journal articles, also reveal that tweeds became increasingly widely worn in urban contexts in the form of lounge suits and jackets in the 1850s and 1860s.[70] A feature in *The Tailor and Cutter* of October 2, 1869, for example, stated that "for Suits, Check and Mixed Tweeds have been much worn this summer and we think there will be the same tendency through the autumn."[71] The popularity of these informal styles within the uppermost levels of the menswear market became highly significant to the success of the Scottish tweed industry from the 1850s onwards. Furthermore, the extensive production of cheaper tweeds by Yorkshire manufacturers indicates that these hard-wearing cloths were also widely worn by middle-middle-class and lower-middle-class men within urban contexts from the 1880s onwards.[72] From the mid-century, tweeds also continued to be worn within the country and the city in the form of capes and overcoats, including the new styles of the Inverness cape and the "Ulster."[73]

The tweeds that were used for lounge jackets and suits were notably different in appearance from the plain, dark woolens that were employed for men's formal coat styles at this period. For example, Locke discussed that although he had asked Border manufacturers to make tweeds in colors such as light gray, in the 1830s, these cloths were only for rural sporting wear. He confirms that by 1863, these pale shades were commonly worn in urban settings.[74] An example of a light-colored, checked tweed suit, worn as urban, informal morning attire by Brooke Boothby, who held the typically upper-middle-class position of Second Secretary at the British Embassy in Vienna in 1889 is illustrated in (Fig. 4.1).

Articles and fashion plates in the trade press indicate that light shades of gray remained popular for informal suits in the late 1890s, but that darker colors of Cheviots connoted a greater degree of social formality. In October 1896, for example, *The Tailor and Cutter* commented that it was "struck by the popularity" of lounge suits that were typically made of "a very dark grey cheviot." The article further stated that "Many of those who wore them were professional gentlemen, moving in the best circles of Society, and their garments were neatness personified."[75] This example illustrates the turn of the century trend toward democratization in menswear, which Breward argues continued into the early years of the twentieth century. The sportswear-inspired shift toward a greater informality in dress was exemplified by the adoption of the lounge suit for an increasingly wide range of activities, particularly by younger men (Fig. 4.2). Significantly, Breward and Ugolini's research about menswear and class reveals that although these changes raised the level of informality and ambiguity linked to male dress codes, finely demarcated distinctions of clothing and textiles remained socially important. For example, although an upper-middle-class businessman might have abandoned the frock coat as formal daywear by 1912, this is likely to have been replaced by the morning coat, rather than a lounge suit.[76]

Tweed in Male Bohemian Dress

The fact that the contexts within which tweeds were worn remained socially significant and that different types of tweeds connoted varying levels of formality is further underlined by the clothing habits of men who consciously adopted an unconventional appearance. These sartorial strategies were often linked to the political, or more usually artistic or intellectual tastes of the wearer. Horwood notes that in the closing decades of the nineteenth century, the Irish playwright and socialist George Bernard Shaw (1856–1950) became renowned for wearing, regardless of

Figure 4.3 Edward Wadsworth in front of Rotterdam (1914–16). Photograph by Alvin Langdon Coburn, London, 1916. Courtesy of George Eastman House, International Museum of Photography and Film, Rochester NY.

Figure 4.4 Roger Fry, February 28, 1918. Photograph by A. C. Cooper. © National Portrait Gallery, London.

social context, a brown tweed suit, which by mainstream dress codes was primarily for country and sporting wear.[77] This example reveals that the tweed clothing worn by some bohemian men was not markedly different from that adopted by individuals of more conventional appearance. Contemporary sartorial and social codes were, however, deliberately ignored, by the wearing of usually the rougher types of tweeds in contexts that were not "appropriate." Peter Brooker has highlighted the continuities between Romanticism and bohemianism of the late nineteenth and early twentieth centuries. He states:

> the bohemian inherits much from the figure of the Romantic artist in English and European traditions, as well as from Edgar Allan Poe and perhaps especially from ... Theophile Gautier, Gerard de Nerval and Charles Baudelaire, in pitting a personal style and aesthetic against the codes and priorities of industrialising societies. This opposition could take different aesthetic, social and sartorial forms and express different alliances – with students and the demi-monde, peasants and proletarians, gypsies, tramps, insurgents and conspirators.[78]

Brooker argues that what he terms the "bohemian modernist" emerged as the "very expression" of the period of "seismic" change that occurred in the cultural sphere in the early twentieth century.[79] In that era, male bohemian appearances that incorporated tweeds ranged from outfits that were decidedly avant-garde to those which flouted established conventions about class and occasion-specific dressing through a simple, relaxed casualness. For example, in 1909, the London-based American poet Ezra Pound bought a "suit," which was the outfit "by which he became known: a broad, loosely knotted tie worn with an open-necked shirt, a gray velvet 'suit' jacket or the tweed coat with the lapis lazuli buttons, Italian trousers and spats. Thus attired he sallied forth in his sombrero with all the arrogance of a young revolutionary poet who had complete confidence in his own genius."[80] A less eye-catching, but nevertheless, unconventional outfit was worn by the Vorticist artist, Edward Wadsworth, when he was photographed in his studio in 1916 (Fig. 4.3). In this image, he is wearing a coarse, homespun tweed jacket with a wing collar shirt, bow tie and plain dark trousers. Further evidence that homespun tweeds were favored by some avant-garde artists and intellectuals of the period can be seen in a photograph of 1918, of the painter and art critic Roger Fry (1866–1934), in which he wears a Donegal tweed suit (Fig. 4.4). His relaxed pose mirrors the fact that this type of tweed, in particular, strongly connoted a casual informality and even at that date was usually only worn as country, sporting and leisure attire.[81]

SPORT, LANDSCAPE, IDENTITY, AND THE FASHION FOR TWEED

Active sportswear, or sportswear-inspired styles in tweed were increasingly popular between 1851 and 1918. Early photographs provide revealing evidence about this type of clothing in wear. For example, an image created in the 1850s features Mr John Bell of Fife, Scotland wearing a tweed coat that is similar to the 1830s illustrations of shooting jackets discussed in Chapter 3. The fact that this outfit includes a wide-awake hat underlines its informality and suitability for country attire (Fig. 4.5).[82] Studying another photograph of 1854 gives further insights into what tweed garments of that decade looked like and how they were worn within

Figure 4.5 Mr John Bell wearing a wide-awake hat, short tweed coat, trousers, waistcoat, watch-chain and cravat, Fife, Scotland, 1850s. Courtesy of the University of St Andrews Library. ALB6-18

rural, sporting contexts by elite, male consumers (Fig. 4.6). The group depicted in this image includes W. Boothby (seated to the right) who is wearing a sporting outfit that includes a tweed coat in a large check and trousers in a different smaller checked pattern. Sir Frederick Hutchison Hervey-Bathurst (1807–81) and Washington Sewallis Shirley, the 9th Earl Ferrers (1822–59) are both specifically dressed for the sport of fishing. Lord Shirley, who is seated on the ground, is wearing a tweed suit consisting of a matching checked jacket, waistcoat and trousers worn with a checked cravat, wide-awake hat, long leather waders and a fishing bag. This image is highly evocative in encapsulating the powerful contemporary connotations of tweed. The languid, relaxed pose of the 9th Earl Ferrers matches perfectly with the informality both of his tweed suit and the social context. His elegant figure also exudes a patrician confidence, thus vividly illustrating that tweeds had acquired associations of land ownership, wealth and leisure, which meant that they had a desirable cachet and glamor. This was because before the 1870s, the adoption of tweeds for sport was primarily the preserve of men from the upper-middle classes and above.[83]

Cannadine argues that up until the 1870s, the British aristocracy "were still the most wealthy, the most powerful, and the most glamorous people in the country."[84] Furthermore, in that era these patricians formed the "unrivalled" international wealth, social and power elite.[85] The wealth of these individuals, up until the 1880s, primarily derived from the ownership of land. Because that commodity was of prime significance in relation to money, social position and power, landed field sports and the fashionable tweed garments that were worn for these pursuits formed an exclusive model of consumption.[86]

Social position had a significant impact on the extent to which men participated in sports, the type of sports they engaged in and what they wore for these activities. By the mid-nineteenth century, sports such as grouse shooting, deer stalking and salmon fishing were fully embraced within the rituals of the "season" and tweeds became an ever more integral part of the elite sporting wardrobe between 1851 and 1918.[87] The popularity of Scottish field sports continued to expand in the late nineteenth century, particularly after 1880, which confirms that these pursuits had a powerful, aspirational appeal whether individuals were in a position to buy or rent shootings. In 1892, Lt. General Henry Hope Crealock commented in a sporting handbook about the expenditure of non-hereditary wealth. He stated that "as soon as a man has amassed a fortune in any way his first desire seems to be to buy or hire a deer forest in Scotland and there to gather his friends to enjoy his hospitality and sport."[88] Significantly, Cannadine argues that from the 1880s onwards the carefully structured "social pattern of aristocratic and genteel living," known as the season began to break down. As the aristocracy entered a period of decline and the international elite was reformulated to include newly wealthy plutocrats the field sports that had formed an integral part of traditional British patrician lifestyles increasingly took place at ostentatious weekend, country-house parties.[89]

Although some sports, such as cricket or rugby required highly specific clothing and textiles, an increasingly wide range of sporting and leisure activities entailed the wearing of tweeds between the late nineteenth and early twentieth centuries. From the 1860s, a tweed shooting or Norfolk jacket worn with matching knickerbockers were typically adopted for field sports (see Fig. 4.7). However, as the range of middle-class pursuits expanded through the later nineteenth century to include, for example, cycling, golf, rambling and mountaineering this style increasingly functioned as a more generic, sporting or leisure outfit.[90]

Figure 4.6 Washington Sewallis Shirley, 9th Earl Ferrers (seated on ground), left to right: Frederick Keppel Craven, Sir Frederick Hervey-Bathurst, W. Boothby, William Craven, 2nd Earl of Craven, photograph by William Craven, 2nd Earl of Craven, 1854. Courtesy of private collection.

Figure 4.7 Party at Drumochter Shooting Lodge, Scotland, 1882: the men are wearing shooting or Norfolk jackets with knickerbockers. © National Museums Scotland, Edinburgh.

Tweeds had other powerful connotations in the late nineteenth and early twentieth century apart from those of land ownership, wealth and leisure. Exploring the associations of tweeds with masculinities, landscape and Scottish and British identities within the era of modernity, yields insights into why the growing popularity of these cloths for sporting and leisure attire was not simply about middle-class men emulating elite appearances and lifestyles. Research within the study of landscape has focused on it as a process linked to the formation of social and subjective identities. In 2003, Anderson, Domosh, Pile and Thrift argued that "the idea of a fixed identity unambiguously belonging to one group and unambiguously expressed in space has been replaced by notions of more fluid identities."[91] These ideas show clear links with recent developments within multidisciplinary work on fashion and identity. In addition, W. J. T. Mitchell in his book *Landscape and Power* argues that "Landscape is a dynamic medium, in which we 'live and move and have our being,' but also a medium that is itself in motion from one place or time to another."[92] This view of landscape does not make rigid distinctions between cities as mobile, constantly shifting spaces against perceptions of rural landscapes as "natural" and unchanging. It is interesting to consider this view of landscape in relation to historical developments within the environments that influenced Scotch tweed designs.[93]

The romantic perceptions of the Scottish Highlands discussed in Chapter 3 continued to resonate in the late nineteenth century and this encouraged increasingly large numbers of tourists to visit Scotland, for sporting and other purposes. This expansion in tourism meant that the Highland landscape continued to function as a "commodity and potent cultural symbol," as Mitchell argues.[94] Furthermore, Devine confirms that the "greatest expansion" in deer forests developed after 1880.[95] These dramatic changes in land usage continued into the twentieth century, Durie, for example, states that "in 1883 16% of the land in the crofting counties had been devoted to deer stalking, by 1911 the proportion had doubled to 34%."[96] These shifts are notable in relation to the consideration of landscape and modernity, in that in order to facilitate the modern pursuit of sport in northern Scotland, landowners continued to convert the land usage away from pasture by deliberately creating "wild" and "natural" landscapes in which grouse and deer would thrive.

The radical transformations linked to the growth of the Highland sporting economy helped to further commodify and simultaneously to idealize this landscape within the British popular imagination. These erroneous perceptions of the Highlands as a place unchanged by modernity also meant that this environment held associations with enduring ideals of masculinity. Significantly, it became one of the key British landscapes that had powerful connections with the late nineteenth-century British imperialist cult of hunting.[97] As Mackenzie states "hunting represented the most perfect expression of global dominance in the late nineteenth century. Hunting required all of the most virile attributes of the imperial male-courage, endurance, individualism (adaptable to national ends), sportsmanship … resourcefulness, a mastery of environmental signs and a knowledge of natural history."[98] The great opportunities that the Scottish Highlands presented for the imagining of these ideals of imperial masculinity were revealed by Delabere P. Blaine in his *An Encyclopaedia of Rural Sports* of 1852. He stated:

> Caledonia must indeed, from the nature of the surface of the country, long continue to offer powerful excitements to preserve the more masculine features of the chase, when cultivation and population have extirpated some of the most prominent objects of it in other localities … The stag, in a state of nature is still to be met with in this paradise of wild sports. In Mar forest, and the western parts of Ross and Sutherland, red deer yet offer to the southern traveller a realisation of those scenes which he has before only met with in story.[99]

This quote shows the continued influence of Romantic ideas about the idealization of nature and the pursuit of authentic experiences within the Scottish landscape. John Tosh argues that ideas about the virtues of sincerity and authenticity that had emerged in the late eighteenth century were from the mid-nineteenth century consolidated into the "dominant gender ideal for middle-class men."[100] That ideal of "manliness," which was introduced in the previous chapter increased in social and political significance as the nineteenth century progressed. Critically, Tosh notes that this ideal potentially applied to all men, rather than being about social status at birth. He primarily relates the ideal of manliness to the middle-class Victorian work ethic, rather than to leisured gentlemanly lifestyles.[101] However, he also argues that "Respect for martial fitness and athletic prowess" was seen as desirable within both elite and middle-class cultures of the era.[102]

In the last quarter of the nineteenth century the expansion of the British Empire was particularly aggressive and this promoted powerful associations between the pursuit of imperial gain, the warrior masculine ideal and sport. These imperialist ideas had an all-pervasive influence throughout British society and Tosh argues that there was a "striking convergence between the language of Empire and the language of manliness: both made much of struggle, duty, action, will and 'character'."[103] Patrick McDevitt notes that within the British Empire sport was used to "construct, propagate and maintain national conceptions of manhood."[104] Significantly, these popular conceptions of idealized masculinity can be strongly related to the consumption of tweeds, which were the characteristic cloths of the "manly" sportsman. These connotations of manliness meant that sport provided a safe guise within which men could experiment more freely with color and pattern than in their more formal attire.

Positive, popular perceptions of Scottish masculinities were influenced by the contemporary reputation of Highland soldiers for martial prowess in the service of the British Empire. For example, in his sporting handbook of 1852, Blaine stated that "Our accounts of the manners and pursuits of these northern inhabitants of our island ... all agree in describing them as brave, hardy, and politic."[105] These popular stereotypes of Scottish masculinity, the fashionability of sporting tourism to Scotland and the continued idealization of the Highland landscape may partly explain why those who copied Scotch tweed designs tended to keep the word Scotch firmly attached to their cloths. The widespread popularity of tweeds among British consumers was, however, also connected to a broader re-imagining of the landscape of Britain within the contexts of imperialism and modernity. As Mitchell argues:

> the discourse of imperialism, which conceives itself precisely (and simultaneously) as an expansion of landscape understood as an inevitable, progressive development in history... . Empires move outward in space as a way of moving forward in time ... And this movement is not confined to the external, foreign fields toward which empire directs itself; it is typically accompanied by a renewed interest in the re-presentation of the home landscape, the "nature" of the imperial center.[106]

Ideas about landscape were therefore pivotal to the naturalness of imperialist ideology and therefore to the imagining of the identities of British men in the late nineteenth and early twentieth centuries. This points away from the sharp, closed distinctions made between modernity, urbanization and fashion on the one hand, and the rural and the anti-modern on the other.[107] The fact that tweeds were increasingly worn by most classes of men in both rural and urban contexts from the mid-nineteenth century onwards was closely interconnected to these shifting modern notions of place, sport and identity.

CONCLUSION

Between 1851 and 1918, tweeds were strongly associated with shifting codes of social and sartorial informality. These connotations linked them to the growing, but relative, social democratization in men's fashion from the 1890s, which was exemplified by the increasing adoption of the lounge suit in both the country and the town.[108] Before the 1870s, tweeds were primarily worn for sport by elite men and this meant that they acquired strong connotations of land ownership, wealth and leisure. The powerful phenomenon of the mid-nineteenth century exclusivity of the British aristocracy and their associated glamor, as discussed by Cannadine, partly helps to explain why the shifting, social and sartorial models involved with the "season," remained influential on male fashionable lifestyles and clothing through the remainder of the nineteenth century.[109] In addition, the growing popularity of sporting tweeds among middle-class men from the 1880s was encouraged by the powerful links between these textiles and idealized modern conceptions of masculinities, sport, landscape, Scottish and British identities.

5
TWEED, FEMININITY, AND FASHION, 1851-1918

The design characteristics of tweeds worn by women, and how these fabrics were made and sold by British manufacturers, are examined in this chapter. It explores why from the 1860s upper-, upper-middle, and middle-class women began to wear woolen cloths that were so strongly coded as masculine. The evolution of tweed designs and colorings created especially for women are also investigated within the context of new developments in color forecasting within the international fashion textiles industry, which emerged toward the end of the nineteenth century. That analysis draws on new research and texts by Lou Taylor and Regina Blaszczyk.[1] Tweeds were an increasingly important element of female, informal, sporting and leisure wear between 1851 and 1918. The shifting meanings of tweeds in women's dress were shaped by a range of factors including links with travel and the growing, but limited female participation in sports, such as cycling and golf. The chapter embraces an approach to gender that moves beyond binary oppositions to examine the complex, shifting and ambivalent character of the gender coding of tweed. In particular, the text has been informed by the work of Antoinette Burton, Clare Midgely and John Tosh, which has underlined the interconnections between anxieties about Britain's position as an imperial power, idealized masculinities and conceptions of femininity in the late nineteenth and early twentieth centuries.[2]

DESIGNING, MAKING, AND SELLING TWEEDS TO THE FEMALE MARKET

Prior to the early 1850s, Scottish woolen manufacturers predominantly catered to the ladies' trade through the weaving of shawls and fine, merino dress fabrics that were known as "cloakings," as noted in Chapter 3. In 1863, James Locke described recent changes in the Scottish woolen industry, by stating:

The Scotch tweed trade then may be divided into three distinct sections- viz. tweeds, shawls, and cloakings. The last of these came to their culminating point about 1848 and have ever since declined and are now only found in a few houses. Shawls may be said to have "hung fire" since 1855. Tweeds, on the other hand are now the principal trade of many towns and are worn by nearly everybody for trousers, coats, and even entire suits, and also in a great degree for ladies jackets and cloaks.[3]

An article in *The Englishwoman's Domestic Magazine* of October 1, 1868 provides revealing descriptions of the type of "ladies jackets" described by Locke. It focuses on MacDougall and Co. of Inverness who manufactured tweeds and tartans. This firm had a shop in Sackville Street, London, which was within the upmarket, tailoring district of Savile Row. At that establishment they sold ladies' garments made up in their own cloths in styles that were described in the article as "the last Parisian." The feature of 1868 was inspired by Royal influence and it commented that "Scotia takes the lead in the walks of fashion, and will continue to do so as long as Queens and Empresses show their appreciation of her productions."[4] The arrival of colder, autumn days had prompted the author to suggest that ladies adopt the following:

> Messrs. Macdougall's jackets … really one cannot praise them too highly, both for fit and for beauty of material. These jackets, by a peculiarity of cut which I have not elsewhere seen, "show the form they seem to hide," which is, … the *ne plus ultra* of as loose jacket. Among the many autumn jackets shown, I remarked light reversible jackets of grey and violet, others of black and grey, and black and violet. The material is "lambskin tweed," and they are from £2 10s. to £3 3s.[5]

Another style is described as follows: "Thicker, and of course still warmer, are the lambskin tweed jackets with tartan and with coloured lambskin tweed revers; very stylish are these when made in scarlet and white, and scarlet and grey, and particularly adapted for country wear." The descriptions of the "jet buttons with a raised pearl centre, like a flower," which were designed specifically for these jackets underlines that these garments were being sold to the upper levels of the womenswear market.[6] It is notable that even the thicker jackets, which the author particularly relates to country attire were in fashion colorways that were not influenced by rural landscapes.

Although the Scottish trade in fine, woolen dresses declined from about 1848, due to competition from cheaper, French merino dress fabrics and Yorkshire woolen and mixed fiber textiles, as noted by Locke and Cochrane, they continued to be made by some firms, including MacDougalls.[7] The article in *The Englishwoman's Domestic Magazine* of October 1, 1868 reported that this company was selling dresses in a range of fabrics including "twill tweeds in all shades of self colours—violet, blue, brown, grey." These woolens were described as being "very soft and fine," which suggests that they were lightweight Saxony cloths.[8] The author of the article also commented about the appropriateness of these dresses for informal wear, by stating: "I must not omit naming the check shepherd's plaid in all sizes and colours for morning toilet. These plaids are very elegant in violet and white, made Princess shape, and are most convenient for breakfast dresses."[9]

It is difficult to gain a detailed picture about the extent to which Scottish tweeds were sold to female consumers in the late nineteenth century. The tweed jackets and dresses sold by MacDougalls appear to be examples of what Ponting argues were the "few cloth designs and colourings put together especially for ladies" in that era.[10] Stillie states that in the second half of the nineteenth century the trade was "almost wholly in gents' wear, and only a few select companies dealt in ladies' wear ... and this was often through sportswear cloths designed for the gents' trade."[11] Ponting, however, questions this argument by stating that "The importance of the ladies trade to the overall picture of the Scottish tweed success in the nineteenth century has probably been underestimated."[12] The adoption by women of cloths that were "masculine" in appearance, or ambiguous as to the gender of their eventual wearer does make it difficult to ascertain what proportion of Scottish tweeds were consumed by females. Samples in range books do not reveal who wore the cloths and even if information about orders is available, ladies' tweed garments were still often made by male tailors in that period. Edward. S. Harrison (1878–1977), who was employed by Johnstons of Elgin between 1904 and 1919 suggested that tweeds which were worn by women represented a limited proportion of Scottish production until after the First World War.[13] This is confirmed by an article in *The Times* of June 24, 1907, which stated, "there is no doubt that Scotch tweeds have obtained and maintain a great vogue for men's clothes and to a lesser and probably more precarious extent for ladies' dresses."[14]

English Tweeds for Womenswear

From the 1880s and particularly from the 1890s, Scottish manufacturers of tweeds faced increased competition from Yorkshire producers, as discussed in Chapter 4. Gulvin argues that the success that Yorkshire wool textile producers had in exploiting the British middle market was assisted by fashion trends of the era. In particular, he stated that the "growing ladies trade aided the movement towards lighter, more fancy fabrics."[15] The fact that Yorkshire manufacturers were more focused on the women's market when compared to Scottish producers is further endorsed by Lou Taylor. She states that the diverse range of "new, woollen fashion fabrics" including tweeds, which were designed for women from the later nineteenth century "were imported into Britain from France and were woven in English mills."[16] Significantly, Ormerod stressed in 1918 that cheap Yorkshire shoddy and union cloths were not just used for men's suits: "millions of yards" were being woven for womenswear.[17] The versatility of the Yorkshire industry in producing a large variety of designs and types of wool cloths for the mass market was a characteristic that helped to make this region the principal British producer of womenswear tweeds in the late nineteenth and early twentieth centuries.[18]

Gulvin argues that the success of Yorkshire manufacturers in the British market for tweeds toward the end of the nineteenth century was partly linked to their "great skill and enterprise" in making from low-grade raw materials "good imitations of even the most characteristic Scotch tweed patterns."[19] His study is predominantly focused on the men's trade: therefore, the chapter now investigates whether Scottish influence also impacted on the tweeds that were made in England for women. An article in *Myra's Journal* of October 1889 reveals that some English merchants were selling tweeds with Scottish names to the female market. Mr. Egerton Burnett of Wellington, Somerset, in the West of England, for example, was offering Cheviots called "Glengarry; Glencairne; Rutherglen, Kincardine and Glenlyon."[20] These tweeds may have been woven in Scotland, although it is more probable that they were manufactured in England and that Scottish names were employed because of their associations with the high quality standards of "genuine" Scotch tweeds. Not all woolen merchants adopted that strategy, however, and a further article in *Myra's Journal* of 1889 states that Messrs. Gainsford and Co. of the Borough, London were offering a "Yorkshire tweed" which was "made in several shades of grey and in dark heather mixtures" and "Bradford tweed, a light heather mixture cloth."[21] These tweeds were clearly made in England, although the heather-mixture design is of Scottish origin, as discussed in Chapter 3.

Transmission of Design Influences: Scottish and French Woolens for Womenswear

In the 1850s and 1860s, Scottish tweeds influenced the design of menswear woolens in European countries including France, as discussed in Chapter 4. At that time, London was the leading international center for men's fashion and this interconnected with the fact that the Scottish tweed industry was renowned for design.[22] In women's fashion, the pre-eminent position of Paris interlinked with the leading, design influence of France in womenswear textiles in the late nineteenth and early twentieth centuries.[23] It might be assumed from these gendered contexts that the design dialogue between Scottish and French woolens only related to menswear cloths. However, the archive of the Galashiels-based manufacturer, R & A Sanderson & Co. Ltd contains several books, which bear the name "French Patterns." Jenkins and Ponting confirm that some British manufacturers bought this type of book because it contained a varied selection of samples, which had been assembled to illustrate Paris-based fashion trends.[24] It is difficult to detect any notable impact of these French swatch books on the designs of R & A Sanderson & Co. Ltd.[25] However, studying one titled "Plaid Patterns 1886" reveals that it contains many womenswear and menswear samples, which show the interplay of Scottish and French influence in woolen cloths. These fabrics include examples where the original concept came from Scotland but it has been re-interpreted, often in finer qualities and incorporating design elements that were French specialisms.[26] For example, the book contains checked tweeds, which are similar to Harris Tweed with silk yarns through them. It also includes checked woolens for womenswear, which incorporate novelty, or *fantaisie* yarns (Plate 8). The examples illustrated are important to the investigation of the development of *fantaisie* tweeds. Along with evidence from contemporary women's journals, these artifacts reveal the existence of a late nineteenth-century design dialogue between Scottish woolens and French wool fabrics featuring novelty, or *fantaisie* yarns.[27] By the inter-war period, novelty, or *fantaisie* tweeds had evolved out of this international dialogue, as discussed in Chapter 7.

Tweeds for the Female Market: Fashion, Design, and Color

In her essay "Wool Cloth and Gender: The Use of Woollen Cloth in Women's Dress in Britain, 1865–1885," Lou Taylor explores the design and consumption of the woolen textiles that were increasingly adopted by upper- and middle-class females in that era. Her research shows that the emergence of new tailored styles of clothing for women encouraged the development of a diverse range of woolen cloths, including tweeds, that were specifically designed for the female market. She argues that from the late 1860s, the establishment of women's interest in these garments presented the question of what were suitable wool cloths for them to wear.[28] Contemporary journal articles and a surviving cloak and cape held by National Museums Scotland reveal that women often adopted tweeds that were designed for the menswear market, or which were remarkably similar to the patterns and colors worn by men.[29] Taylor argues that although wool cloths of "masculine" colorings and design were still being worn by women in the 1880s, from that decade onwards many of these textiles began to be made in lighter weights for the female market.[30]

Regina Blaszczyk has identified the evolution from the 1870s of French color, or shade cards that by the early 1890s had developed into forecasts, which further strengthened the global style influence of French fashion.[31] These changes influenced the shades used within the diverse range of woolen fabrics for women that developed from the 1870s. As Taylor states: "Fabric colours were rapidly feminised too by linking them into the existing system of seasonal colour and texture change which was diffused internationally from Paris."[32] An article titled "Paris Fashions", which appeared in *The Queen* on March 28, 1891, revealed that these changes affected some tweeds for womenswear. It stated that "Redfern, Rue de Rivoli, has some charming novelties. For costumes he is using a light make of homespun, woven expressly for him. The principal colours are beige, cream, vieux rose, pale grey, smoke-grey, abricot rose, &c, for the ground; these are striped lengthways with a deeper shade, or a different colour, for instance, black stripes on pink."[33] This text shows that the English tailoring house of John Redfern and Sons, which by 1881 had established a branch in Paris, was using tweeds in patterns, weights and shades that were designed specifically for the highest level of the female market internationally.[34]

The tendency for some tweeds aimed at the female market to come in a larger range of colors than men's cloths and for those shades to have feminized names is also evident within *The Tailor and Cutter* in the early twentieth century. By that date, this journal remained predominantly focused on the men's trade, but it also ran articles on ladies' tailoring. This meant that the regular feature the "Weekly Woollen Market" often had a small section on tweeds and other wool cloths for women. Notably, these articles sometimes involved explaining to their readership some rather impenetrable fashion color names. An article of January 26, 1911 about the merchant, Dugdale Bros. of Huddersfield discussed their tweeds, which were "specially adapted for ladies garments" and particular mention is given to the fact that "The new colours appear to be Esterbazy and amethyst. The former is a kind of wine colour and the latter is a dark heliotrope."[35]

Domestically Produced, Handwoven Tweeds and Womenswear

In the closing decades of the nineteenth century, women wore home-produced, handwoven tweeds within specific social contexts. Some of the homespun tweeds sold by the Scottish Home Industries Association in 1895 were described by that organization, as follows: "There is a growing demand for light tweeds for ladies' dresses and summer suits, and a new maker of these, with exceptionally good patterns, has lately been discovered … the soft and regular texture of the cloth being a feature in these tweeds."[36] This quote suggests that these light tweeds were a special product and that women primarily wore the heavier weights that were typical of these handwoven cloths. This is commensurate with the fact that homespuns were most often worn by elite women in rural, sporting contexts, whether the female wearer was participating in, or observing field sports. Helland's research confirms that in the 1890s handwoven Scottish tweeds were also promoted as female attire for traveling, yachting, playing golf and cycling in urban or rural contexts.[37]

An article in *The Tailor and Cutter* of February 16, 1911 reveals that Harris Tweed was copied and sold to the women's market by manufacturers using mill-spun yarn and power looms. In that journal, woolens sold by the merchant Messrs Firth & Co. Of 15 Cloth Hall St, Huddersfield were described as follows:

> If any ladies tailors reside near a golfing course or other sporting centre they will find the range of Imitation Harris Tweed offered at 2s 9d per yard, 54 inches wide, a profitable investment. These are all of a twill design, similar to the best selling men's designs and the shades are steel grey, Oxford grey, brown, grey etc. Strong wearing but not too weighty.[38]

It is notable that there has clearly been no attempt made to "feminize" the colors of these tweeds, which were most likely made in Yorkshire. Thomas Carlyle's early description of his tweed coat as "uninjurable apparatus" is relevant here, because it appears that in certain, sporting or traveling contexts, it was perfectly acceptable for women to wear shades that were more practical in dirty, muddy, or otherwise challenging environments.[39] These "Imitation Harris Tweed" cloths lacked the luxurious appeal of uniqueness and authenticity, yet they clearly appealed to middle-class consumers who were not able or willing to pay the price of the genuine article. The fact that in 1911 these textiles were clearly described as "Imitation" is a sign of the impact of the Harris Tweed Trade Mark, which came into operation in that year, as clarified in Chapter 4.

TWEEDS IN FEMALE FASHIONABLE DRESS, 1851–1918

The consumption of tweeds by women will now be explored, which includes examining the shifting gender relations and codes of social and sartorial etiquette that had to be negotiated when buying and wearing tweed garments. A photograph of the 1850s depicts Miss Jackson, who lived at Strathtyrum, a large house near St Andrews, Scotland, which indicates that she was upper-middle-class.[40] In this image, she is wearing a medium-weight, woolen tweed riding habit in a small checked pattern with a broad-brimmed hat that has a low crown (Fig. 5.1). Byrde notes that this style of headwear became fashionable among younger women in the 1850s as informal attire, particularly to be worn at the seaside and in the country.[41] In the mid-nineteenth century, riding habits were usually tailored from plain, dark, woolen or worsted fabrics. The light-colored, patterned tweed Jackson's garment is made from is therefore much less typical of the era.[42] Nevertheless, this outfit is significant because the choice of textile makes it a transitional style that links with the later extensive use of tweed for women's tailor-made costumes. Riding habits were made by male tailors from the seventeenth century onwards and from the late eighteenth century they were also worn for traveling and walking. For these reasons Arnold argues that they were the "forerunners of women's tailored suits" of the late nineteenth century.[43]

Tweeds started to be more widely adopted by females from the late 1860s onwards, mainly in the form of outer garments such as capes, paletots, cloaks, walking costumes, ulsters and coats. Significantly, there was a continuity with the established trade in riding habits, because many of these garments were made by male bespoke tailors, or by the ready-to-wear tailoring houses of the era. The shift toward women wearing heavier tweeds that were in the same, or similar patterns and colors to those worn by men was linked to the emergence of new, more functional outer garments, such as the "waterproofs" that were adopted from the late 1860s in Britain and France. Taylor notes that these "seem to have been accepted with little social comment and were simply worn as a protection over the top of normal fashionable dress. They were strikingly plain and serviceable."[44] Examples of this type of garment featured in an article in *The Englishwoman's Domestic Magazine* of June, 1870, which commented that "waterproofs of tartan, tweed, or heather mixtures are most necessary for English or Continental travellers."[45] These practical garments were strikingly different in appearance from most female attire of the era, which predominantly featured complicated styles and fine, decorative fabrics with extensive trimmings.[46]

Researching the female adoption of tweeds reveals the strong masculine coding of these textiles, but also the complexity, ambivalence and change linked to their meanings within women's dress

Figure 5.1 Studio portrait of Miss Jackson wearing a tweed riding habit, Fife, Scotland, 1850s. Courtesy of the University of St Andrews Library. ALB-6-49-4.

between 1851 and 1918. It shows that these woolens were associated with activities and social contexts, which were either largely gendered as masculine, or that had shifting relationships with established gender roles and behaviors. These areas included travel, work, education, leisure and sport. Tweeds had a notable presence within women's attire of the 1870s, but it was not until the following decade that these woolens were more widely worn by females. In the 1880s, tweeds became popular for simple, modern, tailored dresses as well as for tailored outer garments. The adoption of tailor-made dresses and costumes appears to have grown significantly by the mid-1880s.[47] Furthermore, an article in *Myra's Journal of Dress and Fashion* of October 1886 indicates that although tweeds were still adopted solely within the specific contexts of informal morning, leisure or sporting attire by females from the middle classes and above, these textiles were markedly more popular than previously. It states:

> Striped and checked tweeds and cloths are employed for the ever-popular tailor-made costumes; the stripes are narrow rather than wide, many of them being mere hair lines of colour on a different ground; the chequers are small and in mixed colours ...That the rage for various tweeds for costumes is universal is proved by the fact that enormous stocks of these fashionable materials are held by our principal drapers and ladies tailors."[48]

Tailor-made costumes initially comprised a separate bodice and skirt, but by the later 1880s when they had become more popular, this term increasingly implied a tailored jacket worn with a skirt and often a waistcoat.[49] From their emergence in the 1870s, tailor-mades were linked to the new development of English ladies tailoring houses, which included most famously John Redfern and Sons. By 1884, this firm had successfully expanded by opening branches in London, Paris, New York and Newport, Rhode Island.[50] A traveling coat of 1888 made by John Redfern in a brown and yellow checked tweed survives in the collections of the Chicago History Museum (Plate 9). This practical garment was made in America and worn by Mrs Henry Nelson Tuttle when she departed for her honeymoon following her wedding, which was attended by the uppermost levels of Chicago society.[51]

Susan North argues that the tailor-made was the garment for which John Redfern and Sons "gained their reputation." She also states that Redfern was the "first to exploit its fashion potential."[52] The influential work of English tailoring houses inspired comment about tailor-mades in an article of February 19, 1885 in *The Lady* magazine. The author stated that these were seen as "essentially an English garment, both in make and origin ... our productions in this especial line have so enhanced our reputation that English tailor-made costumes are eagerly bought by Americans and foreigners of distinction."[53] The 1890s saw the increasing adoption of these garments by upper- and middle-class females for traveling, sporting, leisure and informal day wear. An example of a middle-class woman wearing a checked tweed tailor-made features in a photograph of 1893 (Fig. 5.2). This outfit is a fascinating example of how women's adoption of "masculine" tailoring, woolen textiles and accessories such as the tie and straw boater were often mediated by elements that feminized the overall outfit. In this example, these elements included a style of jacket sleeve that only featured in women's dress, tight corseting and the all-important continued adoption of the skirt.

The tailored costume was also adopted as urban-based work attire from London to New York by lower-middle-class and middle-class females who held jobs such as clerical work, particularly from the 1890s. From that decade into the early twentieth century, the less formal and still more

Figure 5.2 Woman in checked tweed tailor-made, 1893. Cabinet photograph by Hellis & Sons, London. Manchester City Galleries.

modern outfit of a tailored skirt worn with a contrasting blouse became popular as daytime wear. These tailored women's garments were created from a variety of textiles including tweeds, serge, flannel and diagonal cloth.[54] From the 1890s, slightly decreased levels of social formality meant that a greater informality in dress also developed. For example, an article in *Myra's Journal* of January 1, 1900 reported on fashions in Paris, as follows: "The real tailor-made costume, plain, but always correct, is worn generally for constitutional walks in the Bois, or shopping in town. If by chance some ladies prefer above all to be comfortable and want to keep these gowns for afternoon wear, nothing is easier than to add a little feminine elegance, which will change the masculine appearance sans façon of this too ordinary costume."[55] This quote suggests that tailor-made costumes in a range of wool fabrics, including the finer tweeds began to be considered appropriate for all-day wear in urban contexts by 1900.

Between 1900 and 1918, tweeds were still popular for costumes, skirts, jackets and coats, however, the cut, length and use of these garments changed in ways over that period that further underlined their inherent modernity. These design developments also reflected broader, radical shifts in women's fashion, whereby from around 1907 onwards, the S-bend corset was abandoned by the more avant-garde Paris couturiers in favor of a straighter, more modern silhouette that involved less restrictive underwear.[56] Furthermore, Steele argues that French fashion illustrations from 1914 reveal that "the sight of ankles and even calves was becoming more common."[57] A series of illustrations in *The Tailor and Cutter* of autumn 1917 feature tailor-made costumes in tweed and other wool textiles, which were influenced by earlier Paris couture fashions. These women's outfits feature jackets with a loose cut along straight lines above the waist, with a self-belt that draws attention to an un-corseted waist. All of the tailor-mades illustrated are mid-calf in length, which in 1900 would only have been socially acceptable for sporting dress.[58]

FEMININITY, SPORT, AND TWEED

Mike Huggins and Neil Tranter argue that between the 1850s and 1914 there was a transformation in the scale and character of sports participation in Britain, although that development of a modern sporting culture principally involved men.[59] Women's involvement in sport remained limited, but that period also saw important changes in the scale and nature of their direct involvement. The principal sports that females took part in up until the 1870s were archery and croquet, but between 1870 and 1914 women increasingly participated in lawn tennis, golf, badminton, hockey, ice-skating and cycling.[60] The limited, but growing involvement of females in sport from the 1860s and especially from the 1880s was influenced by both reactionary and progressive debates about women's health and social roles. Tranter notes that these contradictory ideas included the

> growing realization that physical fitness was essential ... to the ability of upper and middle-class women to produce healthy babies ... Reinforced by the teachings of Social Darwinism and eugenic anxieties about the cultural, political and social implications of the especially rapid decline in levels of fertility among the "superior" social classes, adequate standards of physical fitness among upper- and middle-class females were increasingly seen as vital.[61]

Clare Midgley argues that these debates were fundamentally influenced by imperialist ideologies. She states: "Darwinian evolutionary theory and eugenics, while often deployed to buttress anti-feminist arguments, were also taken up by British feminists, who argued that the further development of civilisation and regeneration of race and nation was dependent on middle-class Anglo-Saxon women's moral leadership." These arguments about the importance of physical fitness for women existed alongside opposing viewpoints put forwards by many prominent medics and scientists of the era, which comprised a focus on the biological distinctions between the sexes. Jennifer Hargreaves notes that these views essentially legitimized widely held social ideas that because women's bodies were suited to reproduction this "naturally" limited their abilities to take part in vigorous physical activity. These arguments were highly influential in the latter half of the nineteenth century, although by 1900 there was a notable growth in the participation of young middle- and upper-class females in sport. However, the extent and scope of their engagement with organized physical activities remained very limited compared to men.[62] By 1914, the proportion of upper- and middle-class women participating in sports was significantly more than it had been in the 1880s. However, Tranter argues that codes of gender behavior still had a powerful restraining impact on the relationships between women and sport. He states:

> the ideal of female sport remained much the same in 1914 as it had been on the eve of the late Victorian and Edwardian boom: segregated from that of men or, where integrated, always subordinate to men's control and priorities; recreational rather than combative and concerned more with the pursuit of better health, social intercourse and courtship than with honing the competitive instincts; and sufficiently restrained and ladylike in its demeanour to enhance femininity and avoid any challenge to masculinity."[63]

This quote reveals that women's daily lives involved negotiating a complex mix of conformity and accommodation to, or contestation of, the dominant masculine culture. For the majority of women, these tensions related to the public presentation of the body, as John Hargreaves states, "The body then, constitutes a major site of social struggles and it is in the battle for control over the body that types of social relation of particular significance for the way power is structured – class, gender, age and race- are to a great extent constituted."[64] His arguments are pertinent to the consideration of the relationships between tweeds and the expression of gender identities through fashionable dress. Studying the newly fashionable "masculine" tailored dresses and costumes of the late nineteenth century reveals that these presented considerable, practical freedoms compared to other forms of female attire.[65] However, from the 1880s, these garments in tweed were adopted by significantly larger numbers of women for traveling, walking or informal morning activities than for taking part in sports. The widespread adoption of clothing suitable for relatively more active lifestyles represented a highly mediated and significantly less radical contestation of existing gender codes than the reality of women taking part in active, competitive sports.

WOMEN, LEISURE, SPORTSWEAR, AND TWEED

The evolution of women's tailored costumes from the riding habit meant that sportswear had an increasingly important influence on women's dress in the late nineteenth and early twentieth century, whether or not individual consumers directly participated in organized, physical activities.

Although some sports, such as tennis, required increasingly specific clothing and textiles, a wide range of leisure and sporting activities involved wearing tweeds. The social position of women had a notable impact on the extent to which they participated in sports. It also influenced the type of leisure and sporting activities that they took part in. For example, Durie notes that by the later nineteenth century sporting tourism to Scotland had become less of a bachelor preserve, because families often went to stay at shooting lodges. This meant that elite women required appropriate clothing for traveling and for other activities such as walking and sightseeing.[66] Upper-class and upper-middle-class women also participated to a limited extent in field sports. In his book *Going to the Moors,* Ronald Eden stated about women of the landed class that there were "many who were skilled practitioners with a fishing rod, a number stalked and fewer used a shot gun."[67]

In addition to taking part in field sports, women also went to the moors with shooting parties to observe the activities of male participants.[68] For example, an image of a deer-stalking party at Glen Finnan in the Scottish Highlands in the 1890s, includes women who are wearing tweed cloaks as protection from the elements (Fig. 5.3). A similar ladies tweed cape from the last quarter of the nineteenth century in the collections of National Museums Scotland features a checked pattern and colors that were initially associated with Scottish sportswear designs for men (Plate 10). These colors are inspired by rural landscapes and sporting handbooks of the era emphasize the significance of dress in providing an essential sporting camouflage for gentlemen in a country setting.[69] If women were participating in, or merely observing field sports then it would have made sense for

Figure 5.3 Deer-stalking party, Glen Finnan, Scotland, c. 1890s. © National Museums Scotland, Edinburgh.

them to also be dressed to blend into that environment. Making significant changes to the colors used in the type of tweeds that were intended for wear in rural, sporting contexts to "feminize" them would have negated the practical purpose of these cloths.

In the late nineteenth century, the powerful gender associations of sport were central to the masculine connotations of tweeds, as discussed in Chapter 4. However, that gender coding also related to an apparent contradiction whereby from the 1860s tweeds and most especially sporting tweeds were the most colorful of non-military woolen cloths worn by men. The strong masculine connotations of these textiles provided a safe guise within which men could experiment more freely with color and pattern than in the wool textiles worn in more formal contexts.[70] That ambivalence, which particularly related to the autumnal, rural colors that featured in sporting tweeds, may also have helped the increasing acceptance of their adoption by women within highly specific social contexts.

Articles in *The Queen* confirm that for upper-class and upper-middle-class women, lifestyles that centered on the model of the "season" entailed that tweed garments designed for country and sporting wear were more prevalent than in the wardrobes of middle-middle-class females. In the edition of January 17, 1891, this journal discussed a "walking dress for muddy weather" made by Mrs Charles Hancock, 125, Queen's-Gate, London, which was tailored from "thick, soft, brown

Figure 5.4 Woman in shooting costume, Scotland, 1890s. © National Museums Scotland, Edinburgh.

tweed." Furthermore, a "Fishing Costume" in checked homespun created by Mr Scott Adie of 115, Regent Street, London also featured in *The Queen* of May 23, 1891.[71] An 1890s photograph of a woman wearing a tweed shooting costume in Scotland shows that these outfits commonly featured a shorter skirt than was otherwise considered socially acceptable (Fig. 5.4). That brevity of cut was related to the fact that country walking and sports often entailed challenging environments, although it also reveals the inherent modernity of that type of female sporting costume.[72]

From the 1890s, tweeds were often worn by women while taking part in golf and cycling.[73] Tranter discusses the participation of women in cycling, by stating that "it was only from the 1890s … that the popularity of cycling among middle-class women dramatically increased. Thereafter, although rarely participating in competitive events, women remained numerous in the membership of cycling clubs, either in separate sections of predominantly male clubs or, less frequently, in clubs restricted to their own sex."[74] Specific forms of cycling dress were enthusiastically discussed in several articles in *The Queen* of 1896. In the January 25 edition, for example, a tweed costume was described as follows "Cycling dresses abound and one of the newest is … by Messrs Samuel Brothers of 65 Ludgate-hill. It is quite simple apparently an ordinary walking dress, but on the machine it is converted into a bifurcated garment by some easily adjustable fasteners."[75] Female cyclists in Hyde Park are described in the same issue as wearing "sensible short skirts and smart, tight-fitting little coats of tweed, serge, or cloth, with a neat toque or hat to match." It is notable that women's adoption of tweeds for cycling was considered much more socially acceptable by this elite journal than wearing any kind of bifurcated garment.[76] Furthermore, in January 1895, females were lampooned in a *Punch* cartoon for wearing bicycling suits that included knickerbockers instead of skirts.[77]

Tranter confirms that women's participation in golf grew substantially in Britain between the early 1890s when under 2,000 women played this game and 1912 when the numbers involved were about 40,000, which formed about 20 percent of the total number of players.[78] An elite woman's tailored costume that was worn for golf survives in the collections of the Victoria and Albert Museum (Plate 11). The matching tweed jacket, skirt and cap of about 1908 were made for Heather Firbank by Frederick Bosworth the "Ladies Tailor and Court Dressmaker" of Mayfair, London.[79] These garments are made from a handwoven, heavy-weight homespun tweed, which is in a warm brown color with a black stripe and it incorporates lots of rough, kemp fibers. Significantly, this coarse woolen outfit is lined with cream silk satin and the luxurious femininity of its interior would have transformed the experience of the wearer of this masculine-style sporting costume. The combination of the tweed and cream satin provides an extreme textural contrast, but owing to the likely cost of the handwoven tweed these textiles shared powerful contemporary associations of wealth, glamor and luxury.

By the First World War era, middle-class women were adopting the more modern and informal options of tweed skirts worn with either a blouse or knitwear to play golf. Tweeds also became more widely popular for skirtings in the early twentieth century, as revealed by two catalogs, of 1914 and 1916, produced by the upmarket Edinburgh-based retailer Greensmith Downes. These skirts were available either ready-made, or to order in a range of Scottish tweeds, including Shetlands and Saxonies. The example of 1916 illustrated shows that these woolens came in a range of subtle shades, including gray, heather and lovat mixtures and "self-colors" (Fig. 5.5). A photograph of a group of women golfers in Millport, Scotland of about 1912–1914, shows they are wearing outfits that are very similar to those depicted in the two catalogs (Fig. 5.6).

Scotch Tweed Skirt   Model 23 A

Full width, smart pockets as illustrated.   Waist, 25 inches.   Length,
38 inches.   In grey, heather, and lovat mixtures.   Price **29/6**.

Made to order in real Shetland Tweed, self-colours.   Price **37/6**.

27

Figure 5.5 Illustration from Greensmith Downes catalog, 1916. By kind permission of Scottish Borders
Council Museum Service, Hawick Museum Collection.

It is particularly revealing to look at these images together, because although only one of
the ladies in the golfing group photograph is obviously wearing a checked tweed, many of her
companions are wearing skirts that are extremely similar to the versions in subtly colored tweeds
that were sold by Greensmith Downes. The catalogs of 1914 and 1916 also reveal that this era is
the beginning of the pairing of tweed skirts and knitwear as outerwear together, a highly modern,
sporty combination that was to have a significant influence on women's popular fashions, particularly from the 1920s to the 1960s.[80]

Figure 5.6 Group of female golfers, Millport, Scotland, c. 1912–1914. © National Museums Scotland, Edinburgh.

FEMININITY, IMPERIALISM, AND TWEED

A range of men's clothing styles, accessories and textiles, including tweeds began to be adopted by women in the closing decades of the nineteenth century. Diana Crane posits, however, that "trousers, when worn by women, constituted a greater symbolic challenge to the system than most middle-class women were prepared to make."[81] In contrast, from the 1880s, tweeds were worn by large numbers of women, which shows that these originally "masculine" textiles were considered more appropriate for females than the adoption of trousers. Furthermore, Taylor argues that women began to wear practical tailored clothing in woolen textiles such as tweed before the dress reform movement had any notable influence. She states "the dress reform movement, which reached a peak of activity in Britain in the 1883–1900 period, built upon, rather than created, the success of already established tailored styles."[82]

Research by Antoinette Burton, Clare Midgley, Philippa Levine and John Tosh has shown that imperialism had a powerful impact on gender relationships within Britain and its Empire in the late nineteenth and early twentieth century.[83] The all-pervasive influence of imperialist ideas in British society is demonstrated by Burton's discussion of their impact on feminist campaigns of the era. She states that, "In a cultural climate where claims for women's equality were met with repeated hostility, liberal bourgeois feminists … conceived of empire as a legitimate place for exhibiting their fitness for participation in the imperial nation-state."[84] The female adoption of tweeds formed similarly complex responses to the dominant ideologies of gender and imperialism, whereby, as Mangan argues "an imperial masculinity consonant with empire building became a sexual imperative."[85] The wearing of tailored garments in tweeds constituted on the one hand the appropriation of powerful signifiers of manliness. However, that adoption was highly mediated by the fact that tweed outfits were always "feminized" in some way through, for example, restrictive underwear, hairstyling and the continued adoption of skirts.[86]

CONCLUSION

Because tweeds were worn by both men and women, researching these textiles yields new perspectives about the relationships between woolen design and gender. By the 1880s, tweeds were embraced within mainstream, fashionable, female attire and the variety of the tweeds worn reflects the complex, shifting and ambivalent character of gender identities of the 1851 to 1918 period. In that era, imperialism helped to shape contemporary debates in Britain about sport, femininity and women's health.[87] These debates reflected contemporary anxieties about masculinities and the Empire, which Tosh argues "played off each other in mutually reinforcing ways."[88] This chapter has shown that the numbers of women engaging in active sports had increased, but remained limited by 1914. Activities that were more socially acceptable for women, such as travel and countryside walking were therefore more significant than competitive sports in encouraging the widespread adoption of tweed garments. Nevertheless, in the late nineteenth century sportswear began to have an increasingly significant influence on women's fashion. Furthermore, toward the close of the nineteenth century a modest expansion in education and employment opportunities for women entailed that the tailored costume in tweed or other wool cloths was adopted as suitable daytime attire by limited numbers of independent, middle-class and lower-middle-class women.[89]

6
SUITS YOU: MEN AND TWEED, 1919-1952

In the contemporary fashion media, tweeds are often associated with heritage and tradition. However, an exploration of fashionable menswear garments made from these textiles in the inter-war period reveals how they were incorporated into the new and evolving, male modern image. In medium weights, tweeds were widely used for men's lounge suits and, particularly from the 1920s, they were a popular element of what was known in the USA as sportswear, as *Garment News* noted in 1922.[1] By exploring the design and consumption of tweeds, this chapter interrogates the links between those textiles and changing notions of conventional masculinities, class, respectability and sex appeal. That investigation draws particularly on the work of Peter Brooker, David Cannadine, Catherine Horwood and Laura Ugolini.[2] Furthermore, the chapter explores how the relationships between tweed and local Scottish and British identities developed within a period of major international political and economic upheaval. Key developments in the design, manufacture, promotion and selling of tweeds for menswear, primarily in Britain, but also internationally between 1919 and 1952 will now be examined.

MANUFACTURING, DESIGNING, AND SELLING TWEEDS FOR MENSWEAR

Following the First World War, as Jenkins clarifies, there was an immediate boom in the wool textiles trade, which for a brief period generated high profits and labor demand.[3] In the company history of J. & J. Crombie of Aberdeen these developments are described as follows:

> there was a tremendous increase of business in the autumn of 1919. Prices went sky-high till many of Crombie's cloths were three times what they had been before the war. It was a short and disastrous boom followed by a terrible slump in 1920 that caught the woollen merchants when they were over-extended. They had made a great deal of money during and immediately after the war, but their profits were used to finance new purchases.[4]

The more significant and long-term trend was that throughout the inter-war period Britain's output of wool textiles failed to reach the levels attained before 1914. Furthermore, Jenkins argues that between 1919 and 1939, "Foreign markets provided a continual struggle for the British manufacturer as well as his continental competitors."[5] The Nuffield College Social Reconstruction Survey, a major economic study, which was undertaken on behalf of the British government between 1941 and 1944, published its research into clothing and textile manufacturing in 1946. A chapter of that publication was devoted to a detailed study by Jean S. Pattison on "The Tweed Section of the Scottish Woollen Industry," in which she states:

> until 1939 the industry was primarily interested in export, but the volume and proportion of the foreign trade in the inter-war period were considerably less than they had been before 1914. The deficiency of the foreign trade made it imperative for the manufacturers to pay more attention to the home market... . In the opinion of representative manufacturers the crux of the industry's inter-war problem was the decline in the foreign trade.[6]

It is clear that from the 1920s, concerted efforts were made to overcome this problem by promoting and protecting the trade in Scottish tweeds, both in the UK and internationally. The extensive copying of Scotch tweeds in the late nineteenth and early twentieth centuries discussed in Chapter 4 eventually led to the setting up of the Scottish Woollen Trade Mark Association (SWTA). In 1921, that organization consisted of thirty-five members who were woolen manufacturers and five associate members who were yarn spinners. According to an article of December 1921 in the British trade journal *The Clothier and Furnisher* this Association was primarily formed in order to pursue the granting of a trademark.[7] A Cuttings Book of 1921–47, which appears to have been assembled for the SWTA by the public relations firm of Byron G. Moon Company Inc. 65 Fifth Avenue, New York, includes a press release of December 30, 1921. That document is headed "British Empire Chamber of Commerce in the United States of America," with the sub-heading of "The Scottish Woollen Trade Mark Association." It states:

> In order to protect the reputation of Scottish woollens and Tweeds, which was menaced by placing on the market cloth purporting to be Scotch tweed but composed largely of shoddy and cotton, this Association applied for and received two years ago from His Majesty's Board of Trade a National Trade Mark, the use of which is a guarantee that the cloth upon which it is stamped is "Made in Scotland, of Pure New Wool."[8]

It is notable that this trademark refers to the use of pure new wool, which was a key characteristic of tweeds produced in Scotland. The reference to low grade tweeds with shoddy wefts and cotton warps, primarily relates to competition from the poorer quality sections of the Yorkshire woolen industry, as already discussed in this volume. Significantly, this trademark was entirely distinct from the one related to Harris Tweed. The Cuttings Book of 1921–47 also contains newspaper and trade journal articles that document a visit of members of the SWTA to the USA and Canada in November and December 1921. On that trip they visited New York, Washington, Philadelphia, Boston, Buffalo, Rochester, Cleveland, Chicago, Hamilton, Montreal and Toronto. The aims of their visit were to study the markets of the USA and Canada in an effort to increase sales, including looking at climactic conditions, sports tendencies and other aspects of lifestyle.[9] It is likely that these attempts to revive export sales to North America were encouraged by what the *The Clothier and Furnisher* described in 1921 as the "increasing vogue for sports clothes and the growing favour of tweeds and homespuns."[10] On December 1, 1921 the *Daily News Record*, an American newspaper, quoted W. Thaw Munro, Chairman of the delegation from the Scottish Woollen Trade Mark Association as stating:

> If all the tweeds sold in the United States as Scottish tweeds were Scottish tweeds, our business today would be six times greater than it is. In offering our product to this country we have several difficulties to overcome, such as credits and tariffs and shipping, but one of the greatest obstacles to fair merchandising and legitimate business is the misrepresentation of our product.[11]

It is difficult to gauge the effectiveness of the trademark and the overall success of the promotional strategies of the 1920s and 1930s. Certainly, for some Scottish firms trips to the USA were highly significant to their fortunes in the inter-war era. For example, Edward S. Harrison, the Chairman and Managing Director of Johnstons of Elgin, was part of a delegation to America on behalf of the National Association of Scottish Woollen Manufacturers. During the trip he became aware that there was a "demand for cloths lighter and looser than those normally supplied by the Scottish woollen mills and on his return he started to experiment with the production of lightweight cloth." That trip also began the firm's trade in scarves to the USA and according to E. P. Harrison it was mainly through these research and promotional initiatives that Johnstons "survived the years of recession in the 1920s and 1930s."[12]

Design and Sampling of Tweeds for Menswear

Pattison's study covered the inter-war period, as well as the years between 1941 and 1944. Her research clarified that across most of the Scottish woolen industry cloths were designed for the two distinct seasons of spring and autumn. She also demonstrated that the sampling processes involved with producing a range of cloths each season still formed a relatively high proportion of the final cost of the woolens sold. This was principally because of the highly speculative character of these sampling and selling processes and the labor costs involved with designing and making up a full seasonal range of sample designs.[13] Pattison also noted in 1946, that "The heavy pattern expenses in the Scottish woollen industry are often justified on the ground that the very existence of the industry depends on its ability to produce distinctive and highly individualized fabrics, and in some cases exclusive novelties. A highly standardized demand can be more cheaply met by Yorkshire."[14]

Significantly, Pattison's research showed that following the First World War Scottish manufacturers placed an increased emphasis on novelty cloths. However, examination of surviving swatches also reveals notable continuities in the design of menswear woolens.[15] An order book of 1933 from G. & G. Kynoch Ltd of Aberdeenshire, which is held by National Museums Scotland contains a large range of woolen samples, most of which are tweeds.[16] These cloths include everything from fine suitings to rough homespuns and coating fabrics in a wide variety of designs including stripes, windowpane checks and Glenurquhart checks. Notably, these tweed swatches of 1933 feature more urban style colorings than explicitly country ones and many samples contain small areas of brightly colored yarns, including shades of orange, red, blue and green. This book also contains a notable amount of twist suitings and some swatches with silk stripes through them, which both remained noted specialities of the Scottish mainland tweed industry, as discussed in Chapter 4. In fact, Ponting commented that twist suitings were the "biggest success" of Scottish woolen design.

The variegated color effects that are characteristic of these cloths were produced by twisting yarns of different colors together to create a double yarn.[17] A detail from the Kynoch's order book of 1933 shows some twist suitings of that era, which feature gray urban-related main colors and small areas of bright, contrasting yarns (Plate 12).

THE HARRIS TWEED INDUSTRY: CHANGE AND EXPANSION

Following the First World War, Harris Tweed was still predominantly worn by men as sporting attire.[18] However, the market for these woolens had expanded to include a broader social strata, including individuals who engaged in an increasingly wide range of sports and leisure activities, as Hunter states:

> That market was no longer composed of the benevolently-minded friends of Lady Dunmore or the Duchess of Sutherland. The customers of the post-war years were not simply the aristocracy and minor aristocracy who ... spent their autumns on the Highland grouse moors, but the reasonably affluent middle classes, teachers, doctors, lawyers and businessmen who at weekends became golfers, hillwalkers, or anglers.[19]

The growth in demand for Harris Tweed provided an incentive to develop new ways of increasing output, while retaining the distinctive characteristics of these cloths and their intrinsic relationship to the Outer Hebrides.[20] In particular, Hunter clarifies that the greatly superior efficiency of machine-spinning compared to hand spinning created pressure to change the definition of 1910 enshrined in the Harris Tweed Trade Mark. From 1934 and after much heated debate in the industry, this trademark was amended to allow the use of mill-spun yarn. Despite this significant change, in the 1930s a good proportion of Harris Tweed was still made from handspun yarn, or at least had a handspun weft.[21] A further major development from 1919 was that the Domestic Hattersley Loom began to be introduced into the Harris Tweed industry by Lord Leverhulme who had purchased the island of Lewis in 1918. In contrast to the large wooden loom known in the Hebrides as the *beart mhòr* the Hattersley model was driven by the feet and it was also capable of weaving more complex patterns. Significantly, the new type of loom enabled a faster rate of output than the *beart mhòr*.[22]

Prior to the 1930s, hand-dyeing methods using crotal and other natural substances were widely used to make Harris Tweed. By 1934, however, almost all of these tweeds were colored with chemical dyes in a mill, as Hunter confirms. This was because dyeing at home was too time-consuming and once the industry had expanded it was important to get consistency of color across a big order. The Harris Tweed Trade Mark was amended accordingly but it continued to stipulate that all dyeing had to be done in the Outer Hebrides.[23] The revised definition of 1934, stated that "Harris Tweed means a tweed made from pure virgin wool produced in Scotland, spun, dyed and finished in the Outer Hebrides and handwoven by the islanders at their own homes in the Islands of Lewis, Harris, Uist and Barra and their several purtenences and all known as the Outer Hebrides."[24]

The Scottish Council on Industry set up a Committee of Enquiry in 1943, which published its *Report of The Committee on the Crofter Woollen Industry* in 1946. Significantly, that text reveals that following the introduction of the revised trademark, output of Harris Tweed markedly increased.

Figure 6.1 Advertisement for S. A. Newall & Sons Limited, cover of *The Tailor and Cutter*, April 22, 1949. © National Museums Scotland, Edinburgh.

It also shows that a significant proportion of sales between 1938 and 1942 were to international, export markets. In 1938 about two and a half million yards were sold to the British market and about half a million yards were exported. By 1942, almost two million yards of cloth stamped as Harris Tweed were sold in the UK and exports had reached about one and a quarter million yards. In the Report of 1946, these early wartime sales to the home market are related to the fact that "For a considerable period after the general introduction of coupons for clothing, many types of Hebridean tweed production remained virtually free from effective coupon control." However, this text also clarifies that "since 1943 coupon and price control have ... been in effective operation."[25] Pattison noted in 1946 that the changes of the inter-war period had achieved a successful compromise between increasing output and retaining the distinctive characteristics of Harris Tweed. She stated:

> The particular circumstance favouring the Hebridean section was the outstanding individuality of the native product.... The efforts of the Harris Tweed Trade Mark Association along with the introduction of the carding and spinning mills have, it is maintained, brought about a greater uniformity in the yarn and finish of the cloth. While retaining its distinctive appearance, Harris tweed is now more varied in design and more pliable in handle than it was before the introduction of the Trade Mark.[26]

The front cover of *The Tailor and Cutter* of April 22, 1949 featured an advertisement for S. A. Newall & Sons Limited, a Harris Tweed mill in Stornoway, Lewis (Fig. 6.1). This image depicts the port of Tarbert in Harris, the surrounding sea and Hebridean landscape, which are all made from cut-out shapes of Harris Tweed. The imagery and text in this advert vividly depict the integral connections between these textiles and a specific, remote rural landscape, while also proudly proclaiming that Harris Tweed is "Shipped to every corner of the World." The urban and international connections of the Harris Tweed industry are further underlined by the fact that contact details include addresses in London and New York.

TWEED MASCULINITIES, FASHION, SPORT, AND LEISURE, 1919–1939

In her book *Men and Menswear: Sartorial Consumption in Britain 1880–1939,* Laura Ugolini argues that following the end of the First World War, there was a notable tendency toward greater informality in male dress. This was accompanied by shifts in the finely delineated codes of acceptable dress that men had to negotiate successfully in order to protect themselves from social disapproval. She also notes that most men tended to observe these boundaries, rather than risk wearing clothes that were not "respectable" or "appropriate." This usually involved treading a very narrow line that was shifting and therefore precarious, as influenced by changing models of masculinity, class and social formality.[27] Despite the notable shift toward informality in men's dress, the codes of what might be acceptable in different social contexts and for certain activities remained sufficiently important that they form a useful model through which to discuss the place of tweed in the male wardrobe. The chapter will now explore the three main categories of clothing that were made from tweed at this period, including suits, active sportswear and sportswear or "sports" clothing, along with the key social contexts in which they were worn.

Tweed and Tailored Suits

Tweeds were widely worn by men in the form of lounge suits between 1919 and 1939. The quality of cloth and tailoring, the design of the wool cloth used and when these suits were worn varied according to the social standing and occupation of the wearer. Catherine Horwood's research shows that by the early 1930s most middle-middle-class and lower-middle-class men wore a dark, three-piece lounge suit for work. By that time, the more formal combination of black jacket and striped trousers was mainly worn by professionals such as solicitors, bank managers and doctors. Ugolini indicates that before the First World War this attire was also considered appropriate for the more lowly position of a clerk.[28]

Contemporary accounts of the post-First World War period confirm this picture of a move away from formality in men's dress, even in the workplace. The ex-serviceman R. H. Mottram, observed in his autobiography that after returning to his position as a bank clerk in 1919 he was now "dressed in 'tweeds' with a soft collar, for we never resumed the black coat and starched shirt of perfect clerkdom."[29] By looking at this quote alongside other evidence of male clerk's dress of that era, it is clear that Mottram is referring to a lounge suit made from tweed. His description clearly suggests these textiles were still a marked signifier of informality, compared to the plain black, smooth-textured, woolen cloths that dictated his pre-war working appearance. Mottram's observations record a significant shift in the codes of acceptable work attire for lower-middle-class men in white collar jobs. His account of this change toward wearing a lounge suit in tweed as acceptable working dress to be worn all day signals an important stage in the gradual, but pivotal, shift in the history of men's dress, toward the widespread adoption of the modern business suit.[30]

Lounge suits in tweed for weekday work attire were usually in dark, sober colors, such as gray or navy and subtle designs.[31] Horwood argues that many men opted for "more relaxed clothing when they were not working," which meant that some individuals from the better off sections of the middle class also owned tweed lounge suits in sportier patterns and colors for weekend leisure wear.[32] The light- and medium-weight categories of tweed known as Saxonies and Cheviots, in particular, were widely used for men's suits. An advertisement for the Scottish Woollen Trade Mark Association titled "Scotch Tweeds" reveals that these cloths were a popular element of 1930s men's tailoring. It includes depictions of a business outfit, which was a striped lounge suit worn with a bowler hat and a more informal, double-breasted lounge suit worn with a soft, felt hat.[33]

Horwood argues that despite the major shift by the 1920s toward the lounge suit as everyday work attire for most middle-middle class and lower-middle-class men. The "perception of increased job insecurity" among the middle classes during the harsh economic climate of the 1930s "led to the re-embracing of formality."[34] This view is, however, contested by some contemporary evidence, such as the following article in *Empire* magazine of April 1933. It states:

> The average man is deplorable in his attitude towards clothes. Where, before the War a middle class man would order six suits, he now orders three, complaining that he cannot afford more, and he spends the money on motor cars and amusements ... . There is no doubt that men are growing less and less formal in their attire. The sloppy uniform of the Oxford and Cambridge undergraduate – tweed jacket, pullover and grey flannel trousers – can be seen parading even in Bond Street."[35]

Tweeds in Male Active Sportswear

Between 1919 and 1939, sport continued to have powerful interconnections with idealized masculinities and British imperial identities, as discussed in Chapter 4. The historian, Martin Pugh argues about the broad position of sport within British society during and after the First World War that "Victorian ideas about sport as a means of maintaining manliness and national spirit, and fostering the British qualities of discipline, team spirit, endurance and fair play were still widely endorsed … . The foundation of the British Empire Games in 1930 symbolized the importance attached to the connections between sport and empire." These factors meant that "during the interwar period sport continued to be crucial to the British self-image."[36] This cultural and political climate inter-connects with the significant popularity of "manly" tweeds for a range of active sports between 1919 and 1939.

Field sports continued to play an important role in the British social calendar, which involved people from an increasingly wide spectrum of the international wealthy in the 1920s and 1930s.[37] These changes are discussed by Longrigg as follows: "Since 1918, England has been full of rich people disporting in the countryside … But a decreasing proportion of them have been hereditary owners of land or sporting rights."[38] This quote points to fundamental shifts in wealth, class and land-ownership within Britain in the inter-war period, which Cannadine clarifies as follows: "Between the onset of the Great depression and the outbreak of the Second World War, the traditional British territorial classes ceased to be the wealth elite, as new rival, and gigantic non-landed fortunes proliferated; and they also ceased to be the landed elite, as the great estates were gradually broken up and dispersed."[39]

These changes meant that an increasing proportion of the British upper classes had to take up occupations, such as those linked to business, finance or the Empire, which took their time and focus away from landed interests and pursuits.[40] Cannadine argues that the process of the "decay and fragmentation of London society was exactly paralleled by the decay and fragmentation of the county community" and these shifts identified in Chapter 4 continued into the inter-war period. He further states that "In the shires, as in the city, the new elite of money bought their way in at the very time that the old elite of birth was in decline … . the new rich disported themselves in indulgent and ignorant opulence, with their ostentatious weekends and their sumptuous shooting parties."[41] These dramatic changes meant that field sports such as grouse-shooting remained popular, but they often took place at weekend country-house parties.[42] It also meant that clothing for country sports made from tweed was consumed by an increasingly wide section of the British and international wealth elite in the inter-war period. The decline of the established lifestyle of the British aristocracy encouraged a greater propensity for frequent travel among those individuals who retained the necessary level of wealth, as Lee states:

> A greater threat to the established pattern of behaviour … was the alteration in the standard of manners which opportunities for travel had brought to the upper classes. The next generation of young aristocrats … were accustomed to new habits of leisure; and were emancipated from the routine of the London season and country-house responsibilities. The age of the motor car and the private yacht, the weekend in Paris and the polo season in Monte Carlo, did not breed the solid worth which the … previous generation had expected.[43]

These shifts meant that British patricians were increasingly internationalized.[44] From the 1920s onwards, among those socially elevated or simply rich enough to be part of the worldwide elite there was a fashion for health and fitness, as well as a major impetus to travel for leisure and pleasure.[45] Wealthy individuals increasingly flocked to fashionable continental resorts, as Josephine Ross states: "for Vogue's readers in the 1920s and '30s, the tennis courts of the Riviera, the 'winter playground' of St Moritz and the golf-courses of Le Touquet offered the ideal settings for the sporting life."[46] Clothing appropriate for various sports was therefore an essential part of the fashionable wardrobe of those who could afford international travel and a leisured existence. In the inter-war period tweeds still formed an important element of the clothing worn by these individuals for traveling and for sports, such as golf. Furthermore, the newly fashionable sport of skiing entailed novel styles of clothing such as ski trousers, which in the 1930s were made from a range of woolen fabrics, as shown by a men's pair in blue tweed held by National Museums Scotland.[47]

In the inter-war era, tweeds also continued to be worn by the middle classes for a wide range of sports including cycling, golf and the newly popular activity of hiking.[48] A key change at that time was that golfing wear became a particularly important market for tweed manufacturers. This was because by the 1920s, golf had become the most fashionable sport practiced by the British upper and middle classes.[49] British Vogue commented on these developments in October 1930, as follows:

Figure 6.2 Group in golf attire: the men are wearing tailored jackets and plus fours, Scotland, early 1920s. © National Museums Scotland, Edinburgh.

Figure 6.3 H.R.H. Edward, Prince of Wales in a checked tweed golf outfit, c. 1915. Photograph by Keystone/Getty Images.

Golf is *the* week-end sport. To one who muses on the great and growing popularity of this game, the following thoughts inevitably occur: that it is surprisingly well adapted to both old and young: that it is the greatest boon to the hostess in occupying and entertaining the week-end guest; that it is admirable for pairing-off couples with matrimonial prospects in a discreetly casual manner; that it gives men unexampled opportunities for the exercise of imagination in their attire."[50]

This quote raises the question of what men wore to play golf in this era and how that clothing provided them with "unexampled opportunities" for sartorial expression. In the 1920s, golf wear for men often involved a tailored jacket, plus fours and a soft peaked cap, all of which were usually made from tweed. These garments were generally accompanied by a shirt and tie, and knitted woolen stockings. Outfits of this kind worn by two men at Ballantrae in Scotland may be seen in a photograph of the early 1920s (Fig. 6.2). The most high-profile, international exponent of male adventurous dressing in the inter-war era was Edward, Prince of Wales (1894–1972). This prominent royal has been renowned for helping to popularize golf in the 1920s and 1930s through his enthusiasm for the sport.[51] A photograph of about 1915 depicts him taking part in his first golf lesson wearing light-colored checked tweeds (Fig. 6.3). This image was subsequently published in the company history of the Scottish Borders tweed manufacturer, Henry Ballantyne & Sons Ltd of 1929, along with the claim that "The Prince of Wales's suit is made of H. B. & Sons cloth."[52] In his memoir of 1960, *A Family Album,* the Duke of Windsor, as he was known by then, described the relationships between his wardrobe and golf as follows:

> my favourite sport was golf, and here I found more scope for indulging my freedom of taste in dress. There was nothing new about plus fours, though I was given the credit for making them popular. They had become the regulation service dress for officers in the Brigade of Guards, and before that both my father and my grand-father had worn a baggy type of knickerbockers … Possibly, however, my own fell a fraction lower than plus fours hitherto had done and it was this that attracted so much attention.[53]

By the 1920s, knickerbockers had largely been replaced by the similar style of plus fours, which differed in that they were generally longer and wider in cut than the former style. Horwood notes that the "four" in their name refers to the fact that they were usually cut to fall that number of inches below the knee.[54] The Duke of Windsor attracted attention for wearing plus fours in an exaggerated cut. However, only minor variations in cut and stylistic detail typically applied to plus fours and tailored jackets, so those elements are unlikely to have provided the significant scope for male fashion experimentation described by *Vogue*. From the early 1920s, however, some fashionable men began to wear patterned colorful knitwear, instead of a tailored jacket with their tweed plus fours, which formed an informal sporting outfit that was more adventurous in pattern, texture and color than most other menswear of the period.[55] For example, in 1926 the golfers Jesse Sweetser from the USA and A. F. Simpson from Scotland were photographed at the British Amateur Championship wearing fancy patterned knitwear (Fig. 6.4). These developments indicate that it was primarily the textiles used, rather than the style or detail of garments, which meant that golf attire provided more scope for male fashion experimentation than the majority of the male wardrobe in the inter-war period.

Figure 6.4 Golfers Jesse Sweetser and A. F. Simpson at the British Amateur Championship, Muirfield, Gullane, Scotland, 1926. Photograph by Kirby/Getty Images.

The types of outfits worn by men for golf in the inter-war period are popularly perceived today as a rather comical reminder of outmoded styles of English, upper class life. These connotations partly derive from the humorous, satirical characters in the novels of P. G. Wodehouse.[56] However, these perceptions form a stark contrast to the social and cultural meanings of sporting outfits including tweed in Europe of the 1920s. The modernity and contemporary fashionability of this type of male golf outfit is revealed by the costumes that featured in the Diaghilev ballet *Le Train Bleu*, which debuted in Paris in June 1923. This production was also rapturously received in London a year later. Owen states that *Le Train Bleu*, was "uncompromisingly modern, both in its scenario, devised by Jean Cocteau, which celebrated sport and outdoor life amongst fashionable young people on the French Riviera, and in its setting." The talents of Pablo Picasso were employed to design the curtain, the set was designed by Henri Laurens and the costumes were created by Coco Chanel.[57] Lydia Sokolova, the female principal dancer was attired in a striped swimming costume and the male principal dancer Leon Woizikovsky wore an outfit that was based on fashionable golf clothing, which included a colorful striped sweater and knitted stockings, along with tweed plus fours (Fig. 6.5).

Figure 6.5 Lydia Sokolova as Perlouse and Leon Woizikovsky as the Golf Player in *Le Train Bleu*, 1924. Photograph by Bassano Ltd. © National Portrait Gallery, London.

Male Sportswear, "Sports" Clothing, and Tweed

Tweeds were particularly popular for what was known as sportswear, or "sports" clothing, which was a category distinct from clothing worn for actually participating in sports. Notably, these terms were used in different ways within the British and American trade press of the era. The following article of January 16, 1922 in the American publication *Garment News* is revealing as to the type of clothes that were included under the American term of sportswear. It states:

> When fashion is taking "tweeds" loudly, and everyone is wondering whether tweeds will end when the summer ends, the opinion of Mr Thaw Munro, spokesman for the Scottish Woollen Trademark Association is of especial note ... . Mr Munro believes that since American recreation and business life seem to be reaching a place best suited for one kind or another of "sports clothes," Scotch tweeds must certainly be an important textile used. If this turn in style is permanent then tweeds must become a staple, as they are the backbone of sportswear.[58]

This quote clearly identifies that sportswear was beginning to be an important part of the American male wardrobe around 1922. It is also significant that the author refers to Mr Munro describing sportswear as suitable for "American recreation and business life." This implies that the term embraced a range of outfits including lounge suits, sports jackets and flannels and also plus fours worn with either knitwear, or a tailored jacket. As the quote from Mr. Munro indicates, within Britain in the inter-war period the term "sports" clothes tended to be used rather than the American

Figure 6.6 Group on leisure outing, early 1930s. © National Museums Scotland, Edinburgh.

one of sportswear and this expression had a slightly different meaning. In both countries these terms implied "informal clothes not necessarily worn for a particular sport," as Horwood argues, although these clothing styles all derived from active sportswear.[59] However, in Britain these garments tended to be worn for leisure only, because unlike the American example quoted above "sports" clothes were not commonly worn for business. Horwood notes that there were exceptions to this broad picture, for example, some male teachers wore flannel trousers and a sports jacket to work.[60] She also confirms the wider popularity of this clothing by stating that in 1939 "Virtually all the men questioned by Mass-Observation mentioned 'sports' jackets and flannels in their wardrobe listings."[61] The respondents to the Mass-Observation survey came from a range of social levels, although they were mainly middle class.[62]

A snapshot of the early 1930s from the Scottish Life Archive of National Museums Scotland shows a lower-middle-class group enjoying their leisure time, with the two men both wearing sports jackets and flannels (Fig. 6.6). The jacket worn by the man on the left of the image is made from a checked tweed. Sports jackets were most usually made of tweed, although other woolen cloths were sometimes used and some men wore their gray or cream flannels with a navy woolen blazer. Furthermore, plus fours were almost always made from tweed.[63] These textiles were therefore a key element of the appearance and social and cultural meanings linked to men's dress for leisure between 1918 and 1939. Sportswear, or "sports" clothing, including tweed was also very fashionable in continental Europe during the 1920s and 1930s. Farid Chenoune discusses the popularity of clothing made from that textile in France, as follows:

> The tweed myth, inextricably linked to British gentlemen-farmers and sportsmen, produced a new generation of imitation Englishmen in the 1920s, particularly in France. These heirs to nineteenth-century imposters ranged from highly visible to discreet, and from run-of-the-mill to distinguished, depending on the nature of their Anglomania. The former favored an orgy of checks and plaids that sometimes betrayed poor-quality cloth. This was also true of fashion-conscious hunters who, decked out like scarecrows, prompted Andre Daligault de Beauregard, an advocate of subdued, harmonious shades, to complain in 1930 that, "the fallacious excuse of Anglomania is being used to produce brash suits that splatter the russet hues of nature with bad taste."[64]

The sartorial Anglomania of the period, also spread to Italy where in 1923 Curzio Malparte, observed the appearance of "smartly-dressed young attaches … in that delightful style of very, young Italian civil servants who wear tweed and flannel to the office as though heading for a weekend in Scotland."[65] An example of how the influence of London as the international center of men's fashion and its strong focus on British wool cloths intermingled with other local and national tastes to form new styles can be seen in (Fig. 6.7). This photograph features Alfonso Teofilo Brown (1902–51), otherwise known as Panama Al Brown, who is the first Hispanic world boxing champion.[66] He is wearing a long, American-style jacket in the Glenurquhart check. Brown's outfit is distinctively different in style, compared to the very short French-style jacket worn by Jean Cocteau who is holding the sunshade and the five other men in suits of a more conventional cut of about 1937. This image demonstrates that the Glenurquhart check, which became known in the USA as the "Glen check" was widely used internationally as a modern, sporty, tailoring cloth.[67]

Figure 6.7 Boxer, Panama Al Brown (center left) with Jean Cocteau and five other men, c. 1937. © LAPI/Roger-Viollet.

The modernity, glamor and sex appeal associated with sportswear for men is revealed by the fact that Hollywood stars of the inter-war era were often photographed wearing tweed garments. These new developments meant that particularly from the 1930s tweeds began to be incorporated into the evolving male modern image of the period.[68] Errol Flynn (1909–1959), a leading male Hollywood heart-throb, was photographed in about 1933 wearing a sports jacket in a fine checked tweed, with flannels and a silk cravat (Fig. 6.8). Furthermore, the American actor Gary Cooper (1901–1961) wore a double-breasted suit in a small checked tweed pattern in a publicity shot of 1934, which has the smoldering title of "A Suave Star" (Fig. 6.9). Significantly, a photograph of 1935 shows the influence of American Ivy League style on the dress of the popular star James Stewart, who graduated from Princeton University in 1932 (Fig. 6.10). Tweed sports jackets were a signature feature of that look, which was largely based on re-interpretations of British tailored garments.[69]

Key reasons why tweeds were present in imagery of these male fashion leaders are simply the international fashionability of these textiles and their prominence in modern sportswear of the era. In addition, a survey of a wide range of inter-war photographs of male Hollywood stars, suggests that the contrasting shades in tweed patterns helped to create more visually interesting images than could be achieved by depicting individuals in plain-colored textiles.[70] As Jane Gaines stated in relation to early black-and-white films, these required "screen costume to exhibit a sufficient contrast of light and dark and a strong line in order to make an interesting photographic composition."[71]

Figure 6.8 Errol Flynn wearing a checked tweed sports jacket, c. 1933. Photograph by John Kobal Foundation/Getty Images.

Figure 6.9 Gary Cooper in a checked tweed, double-breasted suit. Photograph by Clarence Sinclair Bull, April 17, 1934. Getty Images.

Figure 6.10 James Stewart in a tweed sports jacket, v-neck sweater and flannels, 1935. Hulton Archive/ Getty Images.

TWEED AND BOHEMIAN MEN'S DRESS, 1919–1939

Although the broad trend was toward increased informality in men's clothes after the First World War, the precise characteristics of menswear cloths were still associated with particular levels of social and sartorial formality. The tendency for some men with artistic or intellectual leanings to consciously adopt an appearance that flouted conventional dress codes also persisted into the inter-war period. An article in *The Tailor and Cutter* of May 15, 1931, commented on the dress of artists attending a private view at the Royal Academy, London, by stating that they "revelled in tweedy roughness of garb, illuminated by barbaric splendour of shirt and collar. There was a suggestion of defiance in their rococo style, as if they were not merely aesthetic rebels but also sartorial ones."[72] This quote clearly illustrates that the adoption of garments made from the coarser types of tweed in the formal social context of this private view was regarded as highly unconventional, because in Britain these cloths were still only considered acceptable for country, sporting or urban leisure wear for the middle classes upwards. This meant that rough homespun tweeds remained suitable attire for those who preferred to challenge, or ignore, the accepted codes of social and sartorial behavior, by wearing clothing made from them within "inappropriate" social contexts, as discussed in Chapter 4. Brooker places the shaping of a non-conformist appearance as one of many possible outcomes of life as a bohemian modernist. He states:

> The creative outcome was various – a magazine or masterpiece perhaps; or no more and no less than the length of a man or woman's hair, the cut of a jacket, the shape of a hat, the fall of a dress, an earring, a cane, the choice of one café rather than another. For the bohemian is the figure in whom aesthetic and cultural style, artistic strategy and personal bearing, male and female, come together."

Brooker also discusses how bohemian modernists knowingly expressed the tensions within the evolving modern, commodity culture.[73] The complex meanings of tweeds, which were ephemeral fashionable commodities that also possessed connotations of authenticity, meant that they were ideal materials through which to express the tensions between social conformism in dress and more radical, cultural stances. Furthermore, the relaxed, sometimes saggy quality that the more loosely woven tweeds developed in wear assisted bohemian desires to create a casual, or calculatedly disheveled appearance. Owen discusses that the Oxford contemporaries of the poet W. H. Auden "remembered him as an untidy exhibitionist in appearance, wearing unconventional combinations of garments, all of which were creased and uncared for."[74] In 1928, when Auden came down from Oxford, he was photographed wearing a tweed sports jacket, flannels, a crumpled dark-colored shirt and a badly knotted, "artistic" tie. A contrasting example of how the characteristics of some tweeds helped to connote an informal elegance is provided by the dandified bohemian wardrobe of the British writer Aldous Huxley. Sybille Bedford, his biographer and friend described Huxley's clothing of around 1930 as follows:

> He was then and always mildly, idiosyncratically dandified. His suits were made by a good London tailor; they were never blue or pinstriped or a solid colour, they were speckled, softly patterned, snuff coloured, cinnamon coloured or … a nice brownsey-grey. He wore a waistcoat and a watch and chain. His shirts, soft collars, were usually white and his socks always white. His ties often verged on the cubist or the floral. Sometimes he wore a snake-skin tie, or was it a lizard tie?[75]

Bedford's description of Huxley's suits indicates that they had the type of patterning and colorings that are typical of medium-weight tweeds. The fact that his suits "were never blue or pinstriped or a solid colour" is pivotal is distinguishing Huxley's clothing from the more conventional urban attire of other upper middle class men of the period. As already discussed, professional dress for many men of Huxley's class was a dark suit or a black jacket and pinstripe trousers and certainly a stiff collar.[76] It was therefore still the case in the inter-war period that the open texture, elasticity and soft draping qualities of most tweeds connoted informality, as did the tendency of these textiles to incorporate color and pattern. The characteristics of the type of cloths that Huxley wore made a significant contribution to what Bedford called his look of "casual elegance."[77]

A more extreme version of artistic dress involving tweed was adopted by Norman Parkinson, the renowned photographer who recalled about the 1930s that "I had the mistaken idea around that time that I was a bit of an artist ... I affected sandals, rather a lot of leather and suede, and a mid-calf cape affair made from blood-red Harris tweed." Parkinson's bohemian appearance was challenged by Noel Coward who after having a portrait photograph taken by him in 1936 stated: "you are a very good photographer, but you will learn that people who have talent dress like stockbrokers."[78] In this quote, Coward tartly mocks Parkinson's bohemian attire and re-iterates the dress codes of Society, whereby homespun tweeds were still principally worn in rural or sporting contexts, as already noted in this text. The chapter will now briefly explore the design, production and consumption of tweeds for menswear both during the Second World War and in the immediate post-war period.

WOOL, WAR, UTILITY, AND AUSTERITY, 1939–1952

The Second World War (1939–45) had a highly significant impact on the production of wool textiles in Europe. From 1941, in Britain the Utility Scheme and clothes rationing were put in place by the government and these measures had a lingering influence in the years immediately following the war.[79] In April 1940, Edward S. Harrison wrote a pamphlet for the National Association of Scottish Woollen Manufacturers titled "A Scottish Woollen Mill in War Time." In that text he writes evocatively about his impressions on entering the weaving shed of his firm Johnstons of Elgin, which by then was predominantly producing uniform cloths. He stated:

> Work and seeming prosperity have come, but for the most unwished-for reasons.... . Glance along row after row of busy looms – where are the bright colours and varied designs of other days? Nothing but khaki, khaki, its neutral shade fading into the distance. Here and there, however, the monotony may be broken by a patch of Air Force blue or a spot of colour indicative of what is now familiarly called "civilian work," which must be put through as time and material permit.[80]

Harrison's comments reveal that government contracts for service cloths dominated the production of mills in Scotland that formerly had predominantly woven tweeds. They also show that some weaving of woolens for civilian wear continued. Furthermore, Harrison noted in October 1940: "The Treasury is now conscious of the fact that, without exports, it will not be easy for us to pay for our needed imports of all sorts of munitions and raw materials. So export is helped in every possible way, and our slogan, 'KEEP THE QUALITY UP' is as binding a command as ever."[81] The importance of exports led to the establishment of the National Wool Textile Export Corporation (NWTEC) in December 1940. This organisation's main purpose was to promote and protect the British export trade in the products of the wool industry. The NWTEC continued to operate after the war ended and it played a central role in the substantial efforts made in the immediate post-war era to encourage international exports from Britain of wool textiles, including tweeds.[82] Other developments included the launch of *The Ambassador*, a new British export journal in March 1946, which prompted an editorial in its sister publication *International Textiles* to state that it aimed to "show the world what British creative ability and craftsmanship can offer in the field of textiles, fashions and allied goods."[83] In the early post-war period that journal contained many articles that featured tweeds and other wool textiles for men's dress. A feature of January 1951, for example, identified:

> a definite trend towards the more conservative. Shepherd checks, Glen Urquharts and tartans are in good demand, some with variations ... Old favourites – the herringbone, block check, etc., have new variations. There are broken twills, herringbone diagonals and broken basket weaves.... On the whole the general effect is one of neatness with a tendency towards plainer styles and simpler patterns.[84]

This emphasis on design continuity within wool textiles echoed the limited clothing choices for men between 1939 and 1952. British men who were not in uniform during the Second World War had the options of continuing to wear their existing wardrobe, buying second-hand clothing, or purchasing new Utility garments using their coupon allowance under the rationing measures. The fact that rationing continued until 1948 and the Utility specifications lingered on until 1952 also meant that for some men their government issue "Demob" suit continued in their wardrobes for rather longer than they had envisioned.[85]

CONCLUSION

An important shift following the First World War was that tweeds in the more sober colors and quieter designs became acceptable as everyday work attire for some middle-class and lower-middle-class male occupations. Significantly, many tweeds also retained powerful associations of sport, manliness, imperialism and Britishness, as discussed earlier in this volume. The sporting connotations of these textiles were central to their strong links with modern, male fashionable identities of the period within British and international contexts. Furthermore, the modernity of tweeds was underlined by their embrace within the evolving sartorial language of American sportswear. A new and inter-related development was that tweeds were prominent in imagery of male fashion leaders of the inter-war era, such as Hollywood actors, which led to their association with new forms of male glamor. All of this encouraged the international, fashionability of these textiles and their role as the "backbone" of modern sportswear.[86]

7
SPORTSWEAR CHIC: TWEED IN WOMENSWEAR, 1919-1952

The explicitly modern and more emancipated, female appearances of the inter-war era often incorporated tweed. In particular, these textiles were integrally linked to new conceptions of sportswear for women, which emerged from the 1920s. The chapter examines the relationship of these fashions to actual female participation in sport, which continued to provoke controversy and debate in the inter-war period. That analysis draws on publications by Fiona Skillen and Catherine Horwood, as well as surviving garments in the Chanel private archive.[1] These shifting developments are also considered within the contexts of the fraught, economic, political and social climate that dominated the 1919 to 1952 period. The chapter now focuses on the considerable impact that changing conceptions of femininity had on the design, production and sale of tweeds to women in the UK and internationally. In particular, key shifts in the design of tweeds, which were created especially for womenswear, are explored. The ideas presented are informed by original research, including the study of the Otterburn Mill Collection, held by National Museums Scotland.

DESIGNING, MANUFACTURING, AND SELLING TWEEDS FOR WOMENSWEAR

Detailed statistics about the proportion of British tweeds, which were consumed by women, or made specifically for the female market between 1919 and 1952 are not available. However, estimates from key Scottish woolen industry bodies and a government study give a useful indication about the picture within Scotland up to 1946. The visit of the Scottish Woollen Trade Mark Association to the USA and Canada toward the end of 1921 prompted an article in *Garment News* of January 1922, which stated that "Only 25 per cent of the cloths promoted by the Association were originally intended for women's apparel."[2] An estimate and comments from members of the National Association of Scottish Woollen Manufacturers (NASWM) suggests that the proportion of tweeds that were designed and made specifically for women increased substantially between the early 1920s and the mid-1940s. Edward. S. Harrison wrote a pamphlet for the NASWM titled "The Ladies Trade," which was published in November 1946. In that text, he discussed the proportion of the output of the Scottish woolen industry that was made for women and how that had changed since 1921. Harrison stated: "probably the estimate of one of our most experienced members is pretty near the mark when he suggests half, and that is a remarkable development for say twenty-five years. It is proof of that ... adaptability which we have always claimed for Scottish Woollens."[3] In her study on "The Tweed Section of the Scottish Woollen Industry" of 1946, Jean Pattison stated:

> The Scottish woollen industry is traditionally a man's trade and men's suitings still form the bulk of its products. Some of the larger firms turned to the women's trade as a sideline after the last war and a few of the smaller firms now specialize in that branch. The prosperity of the industry as a whole, however, is still bound up with the men's trade.[4]

This suggests that the estimate of 1946 from the NASWM may be on the high side at around 50 percent. Significantly, however, Harrison and Pattison concur that there was an increased focus on cloths for women following the First World War. In his pamphlet of 1946, Harrison discussed the changing contexts that encouraged some Scottish manufacturers to diversify by making more cloths for the female market. He notes, for example, the impact of increased competition from English woolen producers from the end of the nineteenth century onwards. Harrison also cited the influence of structural changes in the British clothing industry, whereby after 1918 the ready-to-wear section "took a great bound forward and at the same time—spurred on by the example of America—gradually improved the qualities they worked. Thus they came up into the price category which brought Scottish Woollens within their reach."[5] In addition to these shifting contexts, he identified that the commercial links between Scottish manufacturers and womenswear designers, including couturiers, increased after the First World War. He stated:

> a few of the great designers, seeking after new effects and ideas discovered that in ... the "set-up" of the Scottish Trade lay the possibilities of a most useful development. They saw that the small size of the firms went far to guarantee exclusiveness.... in the Scottish Woollen Trade, the owners of the businesses recognise that designs and specialities are their goodwill and they are usually their own head designers and devisers of cloths.... Still further there is a very tough core in Scottish folk – we hate to be beaten, and will go almost any length before we admit some idea submitted to us is impracticable. The combination of all these features has made the Scottish Woollen Trade of great value to those sections of the Ladies' Trade that appreciate quality and originality.

Significantly, Harrison also noted the importance of dialogue about design at the couture level of the ladies' market for tweeds. He stated: "It is a type of trade that calls for co-operation between the dress designer and the cloth designer.[6] In addition to the factors identified by Harrison the greater interest from leading womenswear designers in Scottish tweeds after the First World War was strongly linked to trends within women's fashion. That international shift was described in an article of October 1927 in American *Vogue,* titled "Scotch Tweed: The Latest Godchild of the French Couturiers." It states:

> Scotch tweed as a fashionable fabric is a comparatively new thing. Only a few years ago, the world of fashion had not awakened to its possibilities. Then, the Scotch tweed, in fact all tweed, was employed to build men's clothes and if used for women's clothes it was confined to sports things of the most rugged type. And only the British wore these... The War changed many things and the mode is always influenced by the spirit of the times. Post-War dress declared that the beautiful and the practical must be reconciled: then the French couturiers adopted the tweed. This acted like a magic wand; the tweed blossomed into a new versatility of design and colour. Today, tweed is one of the most important woollen fabrics; new designs are created every season and guarded jealously before their appearance.[7]

The significant change identified in this article was the widespread adoption by Paris-based couturiers of tweeds in their collections. However, this quote overlooks the fact that the fashionable women's sportswear of the inter-war era evolved from earlier tailored styles in tweed by British houses, such as John Redfern and Creed both of whom had branches in Paris, as Chapter 5 of this volume has shown. The text of the *Vogue* article of October 1927 reflects the dominant international influence of Paris as the leading center for women's fashion. It also demonstrates the influential role of individual, French designers, such as Coco Chanel and Jean Patou, who are described as having used Scotch tweed in their recent collections.[8] Significantly, the enthusiasm of Paris-based designers for tweed would also have encouraged the popularity of these textiles with the better quality, ready-to-wear manufacturers of women's fashions and with female consumers.[9] The prestige of making cloths for leading designers was therefore of real commercial value to textile companies, particularly if the customer was a top, Paris-based house. These exclusive sales made a mill's cloths considerably more attractive to high-class makers-up, who placed orders that were substantially larger than those given by couture houses, as Pattison clarifies.[10]

Design and Color in Tweeds for Womenswear

The characteristics and colorings of tweeds designed especially for women and sold by the agents of Scottish Borders manufacturers to the American market were discussed in an article in *Women's Wear* of January 14, 1922. That feature was prompted by the visit of the Scottish Woollen Trade Mark Association to the USA and Canada in 1921. It stated:

> Bright colors will be used in woolens, according to Lionel Phillips, representative of Sime, Williamson & Co., in the United States. The mills of this firm are producing, in addition to the regulation Scotch tweed that is familiar, gay colored sports materials in various weaves ... Saxony in orange, rose, red and other bright colors has four-inch two-color stripes. These exceedingly gay woolens, it is thought will be much favored for sportswear and are specially designed for the separate skirt ... Scotch tweeds in unusual weaves are featured by Martin B. Lippman, who represents P & R Sandersons in this country. These mills, which are, according to Mr Lippman the largest tweed mills in Scotland are offering most original textiles ... This house, which has never carried women's apparel before, expects these novelty weaves to be very popular for sports wear. The same weaves will be used for men as well as women.[11]

The Tailored Suit, Style C. 12, shown below is in fine CHECK SUITING in a beige and brown mixture. Single-breasted semi-fitting coat with plain wrap-over skirt. Price 8 gns.

Above is an example of many styles of smart inexpensive Three-piece Cardigan Suits. This is Style C. 14, in a fawn with red mixture CHIFFON TWEED. The tuck-in blouse is in fine stockinette to tone with the tweed, finished red pipings and buttons. Medium size. Price £6 : 12 : 6.

Figure 7.1 Chiffon tweed suit and tailored checked suit, Fashions for Summer 1930 catalog, Jenners Archive. © National Museums Scotland, Edinburgh.

This quote suggests that although in some cases the same patterns were being produced for both genders, there was a tendency for some Scottish manufacturers to make woolens in brighter colors for the female market. In the 1920s, the design of fashionable tweeds for womenswear was still also influenced by colors from rural landscapes, as shown by an article in the October 1927 edition of American *Vogue,* which stated: "For autumn, the tendency is for very large, or very small rather indefinite designs. The colours seem to have been produced to melt into the landscape; there are beiges, browns, dull reds, blues, bottle-greens and various combinations of grey and blue, black and white and beige and brown."

In addition to these aesthetic connotations of landscape, the author makes strong associations between the place where these textiles were made and their quality and desirability. The article of 1927 refers principally to "Scotch tweed" and it states that: "The weaving of tweed seems to be something that the British Isles can still do better than the rest of the world."[12] Tweed designs listed in that *Vogue* feature included those described as "Black and white flecked with colours; spot motif enclosed by orange cross lines on dark brown" and "Diamond motif in white on dark red." The fact that by 1944 womenswear tweeds still often, but not always, featured a brighter range of colors than in menswear woolens is shown by samples within a VIP Order Book from the archive of R & A Sanderson & Co. Ltd of Galashiels. The page illustrated includes a red and gray mixture tweed "selected by H. M. The Queen for HRH Princess Elizabeth" and a colorful yellow tweed "Selected by HRH The Duchess of Gloucester for wear in Australia" (Plate 13).

In his discussion of the particular challenges and opportunities offered by the womenswear market, Harrison stated in 1946 that "The light weights needed in the finer part of the Ladies' Trade have always been a real difficulty, for yarn spun on the Scottish Woolen system cannot be made so small as is possible on the English or Worsted system.... . This has largely been overcome by the extended use of English Worsteds along with our own Woollen yarns."[13] By the inter-war period wool textiles for women's suits often had a softer, more supple handle than the firmer cloths that were typically used in tailored menswear. Harrison noted an important related shift after the First World War, whereby ready-to-wear clothing manufacturers had "ceased to demand firm cloths and have learned how to use open, soft, fine, draping fabrics."[14] A catalog of women's fashions for summer 1930 produced by Jenners, an Edinburgh-based department store, reveals the wide range of tweed garments that were sold to their female customers, who were predominantly middle class. A cardigan suit in a lightweight Chiffon Tweed by Munrospun illustrates the type of soft, supple womenswear cloths described by Harrison. Furthermore, the use of a "fine check" to make a suit shows the lightweight tailoring cloths that were produced for the women's market (Fig. 7.1). Significantly, this catalog also reveals that women's garments in medium- and heavy-weight tweeds, such as a Harris Tweed coat "for travel or country wear," were still being sold in 1930 (Fig. 7.2).

At left is a Coat, Style M. 4, for town or country wear in fawn and brown mixture SUITING. This is a plain tailored shape with the waistline slightly defined. Lined artificial silk to tone. Price £3 : 9 : 6.

A practical Coat for travel or country wear, Style M. 3, in HARRIS TWEED. In fawn with faint overcheck in plain Raglan style with all-round belt. Lined throughout to tone. Price £6 : 19 : 6.

Travel Coats   Jenners make a special feature of really inexpensive Coats that are ample in cut and smartly tailored.

JENNERS

15

Figure 7.2 Women's tweed coats, Fashions for Summer 1930 catalog, Jenners Archive. © National Museums Scotland, Edinburgh.

Linton Tweeds and Otterburn Mill Ltd

These English firms both sold tweeds to the upper levels of the womenswear market between 1919 and 1952. In his book of 1954, *Just So Far*, Hardy Amies commented that "Miss Agnes Linton, of the famous Linton Tweed Mills in Cumberland" provided financial support to his business. He then stated:

> Old Mr Linton, Miss Linton's father, the founder of the firm, worked in close collabo-
> ration with the great Chanel, and a little later with Schiaparelli. Together they devised
> many wonder-fully coloured tweeds, which delighted and startled the world of fashion
> in the late 'twenties and early 'thirties. Mr Linton is now dead, but Miss Linton and her
> cousin George still continue the tradition of taking a trunk full of tweed patterns twice
> a year to New York to show the big manufacturers there. They have never bothered to
> advertise their name in England but it is a household word in dressmaking circles in
> America.[15]

The history of Linton Tweeds has been published by Patricia Hitchon in her 2012 book *Chanel and the Tweedmaker*, but company archive material from the 1919 to 1952 period has unfortu-nately not survived.[16] This underlines the significance of the Otterburn Mill Collection, which is held by National Museums Scotland. That archive documents the history of a comparable firm, which by the 1920s specialized in the design and manufacture of tweeds and other woolens for womenswear.[17]

The Otterburn Mill was established in 1821 within the village of Otterburn, Northumberland in the north of England by William Waddell who came from a family of Scottish Borders woolen manufacturers. By 1888, Messrs Waddell and Son had also purchased a large mill at Warwick Bridge, near Carlisle for the production of tweeds.[18] The history of the Otterburn Mill is connected to and shares many characteristics with that of Linton Tweeds, in particular, these firms both had strong personal and business links with the woolen industry in Scotland. William Linton came from Selkirk and he worked in the Scottish Borders tweed industry before moving to Carlisle in 1912. In that year, a new private company called Waddell's Limited was registered and the joint Managing Directors of this firm, which was based at the Warwick Bridge Mill, were Cranston Waddell and William Linton.[19] In 1917, Cranston Waddell died, which precipitated William Linton setting up business on his own, a venture that was the real beginning of Linton Tweeds, although the company initially had the name of Linton's Cumberland Homespuns Ltd. Mr William Waddell bought back the Warwick Bridge Mill for Otterburn Mills Ltd, and that firm continued to produce tweeds in Carlisle and Otterburn until it closed in 1976.[20]

The Otterburn Mill Collection consists of around 1,000 objects dated between the 1920s and 1976, which includes order books, range books, bunches of samples, novelty yarn samples, pattern blankets and advertising material. A typical order book of 1926 provides written information about each customer and what they ordered, along with a fabric swatch.[21] The wide range of Otterburn Mill customers listed in that artifact of 1926 includes the upmarket British department store Fenwicks; the Leeds-based wholesale clothier Hepton & Co.; the Wisconsin-based Bradley Knitting Company who made knitwear and sportswear; the New York high-class, ready-to-wear manufacturer Davidow; and the British tailoring houses of John Redfern and Creed.[22] It is notable that the Paris-based couturiers Heim, Molyneux and Drecoll were also listed as purchasing woolen cloths from this British firm. There are also several orders from the French cloth merchant, Dormeuil Freres who had been importing English fabrics to France since 1842 and which had branches in London and New York. Notably, by 1920, this large merchanting house had opened a ladies division.[23]

Surveying the swatches in the order book of 1926, reveals the astonishing variety of tweeds woven by the Otterburn Mill Ltd. Most samples are in the twill weave and many of the designs are fancier in appearance than menswear tweeds of the era, which is primarily because of the use of color, rather than complex weaves. Notably, the types of district check patterns that were popular for men are not present. A wide range of shades of brown, orange, green, blue, dark red, gray and cream predominate, although quite a lot of samples also feature bright red, pink, orange and yellow yarns. Significantly, although loosely spun yarns are used in some samples to create texture, novelty yarns are not evident.

The Otterburn Mill Collection also includes a group of womenswear tweed samples from 1934, which are held together by a leather mount thus forming what is known in the wool textile and tailoring trades as a bunch. This method of displaying groups of samples in bunches is still used today as a way of tailors showing cloths to their customers and then ordering from the stock of a manufacturer. The Otterburn Mill bunch of 1934 includes eight different medium-weight tweeds and a sample in every colorway for each pattern.[24] These samples have a strong, visual relationship with earlier tweeds and some patterns are the same, or virtually the same, as those for men's cloths, particularly the shepherd's checks and another district check-type designs. The colors used are mostly rural-influenced shades of brown, gray, cream, dark red, green and blue, although there are also some black and white, or blue and gray designs that have a more urban appearance.

The majority of samples in the Otterburn Mill bunch of 1934, however, differ from men's cloths. For example, the swatch illustrated demonstrates that in the mid-1930s some womenswear tweeds featured enlarged versions of long-established menswear patterns and the use of brighter colors than were commonly used in men's tweeds (Plate 14). Furthermore, most of the yarns used in the bunch of 1934 have been selected to create highly textured effects in the finished cloth. These subtle effects are created by using, for example, different thicknesses of yarn in the one cloth, or slubs along the length of a yarn, also some yarns are more loosely twisted than with most men's cloths. Apart from the slubbed yarns, there are no novelty yarns in this bunch, although in a coatings bunch from the same year all but one design have fancy, novelty yarns in them and the resultant textured appearance is a key thing that distinguishes them from menswear cloths.[25]

Novelty, or *Fantaisie* Tweeds

Significantly, the Otterburn Mill Collection contains evidence about an important development within the nomenclature and design of the "family" of textiles known as tweeds. Studying that Collection strongly suggests that how novelty, or *fantaisie* woolens became known by the term tweed was that the same companies who had previously made the well-established categories of tweeds, such as Cheviots and homespuns began to modify their products for the womenswear market, principally by introducing more highly, textured yarns. As discussed in Chapter 5, a design dialogue between Scottish and French wool textiles had existed since the late nineteenth century. By the inter-war period tweeds, which had developed as a Scottish design speciality had evolved by incorporating the novelty, or *fantaisie* yarns that had been a long-established specialism of French manufacturers of womenswear textiles.[26]

Owen notes that since 1934 "pronounced texture had … been established as an important feature" of a wide range of woven, knitted and embellished womenswear textiles.[27] This development meant that novelty or *fantaisie* yarns such as boucle, slub, knop, gimp and loop featured prominently in highly textured tweeds for the womenswear market. These fabrics typically featured a simple weave and they relied on often-colorful yarns in order to create appealing visual and textural effects. An article of 1934, in the British journal *The Wool Record and Textile World* stated that "Manufacturers who specialise in the women's wear section of the trade have to carry a large variety of novelty yarns to cope with the orders for model lengths, as these have to be delivered quickly."[28] These fashion trends and commercial contexts still had huge organizational and cost implications for producers of womenswear tweeds in 1946, as Harrison stated: "Fashion changes in the ladies trade are rapid and somewhat bewildering to the cloth maker trying to plan his programme of production. His stocks are expensive and the variety of his raw material astonishingly great."[29]

LONDON COUTURE, SPORTSWEAR, TAILORING, AND TWEED, 1919–1939

Tweeds were an intrinsic element of the new, modern conceptions of sportswear and feminine appearances that evolved in the inter-war era. These developments were integrally connected to the work of London couture houses, such as Lachasse, Digby Morton and Hardy Amies. Ehrman comments about the continuities within the relationships between French and British couture, as follows:

> Paris remained the dominant influence on womenswear design in Britain during and after the First World War. However, English tastes informed much of the clothing made in London. These were dictated by the lifestyle of the upper classes who moved from town to country according to the social calendar. Considerations of suitability and practicality guided their choice of fabric and cut as much as fashion.[30]

This quote indicates that although the traditional lifestyle of the British aristocracy continued to decline in the inter-war era, as discussed in Chapter 6, the social season still had a lingering influence on social and sartorial practices. From the 1920s onwards there was an expansion in the number of London-based designers who sought international success. Two of the most successful new houses were Isobel, and Norman Hartnell. Ehrman confirms that Isobel "was best known for her furs and sportswear, which she exported to America and designed with her American clients in mind."[31] These designers faced difficulties in promoting their businesses, because of the huge bias of the British fashion press and women's magazines aimed at the middle classes toward French couture. Furthermore, London-based couturiers did not have the support available to their counterparts in Paris whereby, as Ehrman states: "With the encouragement of the Chambre Syndicale de la Couture Parisienne, designers and textile manufacturers co-operated, providing each other with mutual inspiration and the raw materials for a well-designed product."[32]

The turbulent, economic conditions of the inter-war period presented further challenges for British couturiers. Christopher Price argues about the position in Britain, following the boom in the American stock market and the subsequent crash of 1928 to 1929, that "The British depression represented a worsening of the 1920s pattern of economic disappointment … . when the pound was forced off in September 1931, it seemed as if the British economy was on the verge of an inflationary collapse to rival that of Germany in 1923."[33] This catastrophe did not happen and although the crisis in global trade had a significant, negative impact on the UK's export industries, the home economy was "less badly affected and had considerable potential for growth."[34] Significantly, Ehrman notes that the economic difficulties of the period led to the government encouraging consumers to "Buy British."[35] That strategy influenced the commercial activities of British couturiers who "wisely built on the city's reputation for fine tailoring and quality sportswear made in British fabrics," which effectively encouraged their use of tweeds. That increased focus on the home market, as British *Vogue* reported in April 1930, led to them designing:

> for the very practical life of Englishwomen, as opposed to the more luxurious existence led by that limited section of society, the cosmopolitan … Consequently the London dress collections show many tweeds, suits for town and country, dresses with short capes or three-quarter coats, little dresses in fine wool or heavy crepe or tie silk, the simpler dressmaker suit; and not so many of the ultra formal afternoon-dress or ensemble that Paris delights in.[36]

These comments reveal how designers responded not just to the global economic crisis, but also to major changes within the British aristocracy and upper classes who comprised their main clientele. Between the late 1920s and the beginning of the Second World War, these sections of British society were no longer the wealth, nor the landed elite, as discussed in the preceding chapter. These fundamental changes in wealth, class and landownership meant the decline of the traditional lifestyle of the British aristocracy. Those individuals who retained the necessary level of wealth assumed new habits of frequent international travel and they effectively became part of a "cosmopolitan," international, wealthy elite, whose "luxurious" tastes had since the close of the nineteenth century tended more toward French, rather than British couture.[37] In contrast, the quote from *Vogue* of April 1930 suggests that members of the British upper classes who were relatively less wealthy than these "cosmopolitan" individuals formed a significant proportion of the clientele of London couturiers.

The overall picture of decline in the fortunes of the British elite and minor aristocracy meant that many individuals were obliged to go into business, or otherwise work for a living, which encouraged the phenomenon of the society dressmaker. One such individual was Christabel Russell, the daughter-in-law of the second Baron Ampthill, who in 1920 established an elite dressmaking shop in Mayfair, London.[38] An article titled "Tweeds Acquire a New Significance," in *Harper's Bazaar* of October 1929, features an illustration of a fur-trimmed coat by Christabel Russell, which reveals how the pronounced patterns or twill weaves of some tweeds were used in a modern way at that time. This garment was made from "Soft brown and fawn tweed with diagonal stripes ingeniously arranged to form a geometrical design."[39] Methods of cutting tailored garments, which made a feature of the graphic qualities possessed by many tweeds became a signature element of clothing by British couturiers. These design developments were encouraged by the popularity of striped textiles in the 1930s, whereby in 1932, Vogue reported on: "Light woollen fabrics that … give scope for smart diagonal cutting and much variation of treatment by using the stripes running in different directions."[40] A further example is a checked, tweed jacket by the high quality

Figure 7.3 Anne Paget in a checked tweed jacket, photographed by Norman Parkinson, 1939. © Norman Parkinson Ltd/courtesy Norman Parkinson Archive, London.

Figure 7.4 Miss Georgina Wernher; The Hon. Deborah Mitford; Miss Virginia Brand; Miss Kenyon-Slaney; Lady Margaret Ogilvy and Lady Jean Ogilvy (left to right) at the Perth Hunt Races, 1937. © National Museums Scotland, Edinburgh.

ready-to-wear firm Matita, in which the patch pockets are cut on the bias, thus giving a contrasting visual effect (Fig. 7.3). This photograph of Anne Paget was taken by Norman Parkinson for a Matita advertisement, which ran in the January 1939 edition of *Harper's Bazaar*.[41]

Ehrman argues that "London couture flourished in the 1930s. It was revitalised by a group of talented young designers ... Under their direction tailoring became more sensitive to fashion change."[42] One of these young designers was the Irishman, Digby Morton (1906–1983), who began his London-based fashion career in 1928, when he was appointed as the first Designer at Lachasse, a British couture house, which was a newly established sportswear offshoot of Gray and Paulette Limited.[43] Hardy Amies stated in 1984 that this new venture, an "immediate success ... specialized in women's suits made to measure, mostly in tweed. It was a tremendous innovation showing a *couture* collection which did not include a single evening dress, and barely one suitable for wearing in the afternoons. This was the heyday of the tweed suit, and the customers belonged mostly to the rich racing set, who wore suits all day long."[44]

The social milieu linked to horse racing at this period is described by Pugh, who states that this "highly exclusive sport … was controlled by a group of self-appointed, wealthy, aristocratic owners."[45] The November, 1937 edition of *S.M.T. Magazine and Scottish Country Life*, reported on the fact that "The younger set was well represented at the Perth Hunt Races."[46] This article was accompanied by a photograph that features Miss Georgina Wernher, The Hon. Deborah Mitford, Miss Virginia Brand, Miss Kenyon-Slaney, Lady Margaret Ogilvy and Lady Jean Ogilvy (Fig. 7.4). These upper-class women are mostly wearing either a tweed suit, or a coat in that textile along with fine knitwear. Notably, the tweed clothing considered appropriate for Perth Hunt Races and local race meetings would not have been worn at high profile events such as Ascot.[47] In 1984, Hardy Amies credited Digby Morton as having a major role in stimulating the adoption of the tailored, tweed suit. He stated:

> Morton's philosophy was to transform the suit from the strict *tailleur*, or the ordinary country tweed fit only for the moors, into an intricately cut and carefully designed garment, so fashionable that it could be worn with confidence at the Ritz. Such clothes have become so much a part of the fashion picture in all parts of the world during more than the last fifty years that it is hard to realize how much they owe to Morton's original ideas.[48]

Tailoring in tweeds also featured strongly in the journalist Linda Watson's account of Morton's career. She noted that, "His skill with tweed was legendary, as was his ability to tailor. Morton was instrumental in encouraging Scottish weavers to switch from neutral tones to pastels. With an intense dislike of vivid colours, he preferred black, half-tones and pastels."[49] In 1933, Morton left Lachasse to set up his own couture house and Amies succeeded him the following year.[50] Amies noted that when he first started at Lachasse he followed the creative lead set by Morton. In particular, his design methods began with the selection of the tweeds that had been established as a central element of that house's tailored suits. He stated:

> Firstly there was the tweed. This the designer chose with great care. It had to be firm enough for the jacket to be moulded into a defined shape: and able to withstand the pressures of a beautiful behind wriggling in a sports car. It had, however, to be soft to the touch and have enough wool at the surface to mute the colours.[51]

The popularity of the tweed suit in the 1930s was a sign of increased informality and social democratization in women's fashion, as well as being indicative of the growing influence of sportswear. For example, Amies gives the following account of what type of clothes his customers at Lachasse in the 1930s wanted and how these fitted into their changing lifestyles of the period. He stated: "Although we were ostensibly a sportswear shop, a customer bought a new suit to wear not only for luncheon parties in the country, but also on shopping expeditions to London … she would only wear such a suit for real sporting occasions, such as local race meetings or at shooting parties, when it began to look slightly old and shabby. The clothes that sold best were those that were good for town and country. I realized that the day of the lady's maid was waning, so clothes had to be easy to look after."[52]

WOMEN, SPORT, AND SPORTSWEAR

Harrison argued in 1946 that the increased demand for Scottish tweeds for womenswear since the 1920s was hugely influenced by the greater popularity of sports and sportswear. He also posited that the demand for woolens from Scotland in particular was encouraged by the inter-linked fashion for knitwear. Harrison stated: "Knitting has come in for outerwear and our Scottish Woollens blend better with knitted garments than the more dressy types in which Roubaix and Bradford excel."[53] He is referring to the fact that Bradford, in Yorkshire and the Roubaix-Tourcoing area in Northern France were major centers for the manufacture of worsteds.[54] Harrison's comments that the textured, colorful surface of Scottish tweeds complemented the fashion for knitwear better than smooth-faced worsteds, make sense in both aesthetic and contextual terms, as both were key elements of sportswear. As discussed in Chapter 5, women had begun to wear fine knitwear as outerwear before the First World War. The informal combination of knitwear with a simply cut skirt in tweed became more prominent in the 1920s and it epitomized the new, modern, female image of the era, as described by the American, fashion designer Claire McCardell. She stated:

> The big change came in the twenties. Novelists of the time talked about it. Ernest Hemingway describes Lady Brett in *The Sun Also Rises*: "She wore a slipover jersey sweater and a tweed skirt and her hair brushed back like a boy's. She started all that." The interesting fashion point is just where Brett wore this "look" she had started. On a brisk, breezy day at the Yacht Club? No. On a golf course? No. In a country setting? Anything but. At the exact moment the narrator describes her she is sitting in a bar in Paris.[55]

The wider adoption of sportswear garments, outside of sporting contexts was a key development in fashion of the inter-war period. Wilson, for example, argued that sporting styles, many of which were made from tweed, were "adapted for modern city life."[56] This begs the question of how sport related to ideas about femininity and female appearances in the inter-war period. There was a significant increase in women's participation in sport within the UK in that era. However, Fiona Skillen argues that this "boom" stimulated a "frenzy of discussion in the British media," which centered around opposing viewpoints. She states that "while one camp praised women's newfound ability to play a variety of sports, the opposing camp made frequent protestations about the potential hazards such activities could wreak on the delicate female body, to say nothing of the immorality of allowing women to compete against each other in frequently rough sports." This meant that although the reaction against women's participation in sport was not as strong as that of the late nineteenth century, female engagement in sports still involved a "complex process of negotiation."[57] This was principally because sport was still seen as a key sphere in which dominant discourses of masculinity were reinforced and maintained. Sports that were especially vigorous, aggressive or competitive were seen as potentially threatening to established conceptions of women as "naturally docile and submissive."[58]

The controversy and public debate about women's participation in sport influenced social perceptions of female clothing for sport. Skillen argues that women potentially faced strong moral criticism when wearing sports attire and this encouraged experimentation about what constituted socially acceptable female active sportswear. She states about the inter-war period that "There was a fine line between practicality and respectability, and it was this invisible, yet powerful, boundary

Figure 7.5 British golfer, Henry Cotton (right) with (left to right) Miss Enid Wilson, Madame R. Lacoste and Lady Heathcote-Amory at a charity golf match, Essex, England, 1938. Photograph by J. A. Hampton / Getty Images.

which influenced the innovations in women's sportswear."[59] In the 1920s a new, more athletic, streamlined body ideal became an important symbol of fashionability and modernity. Thus, physical activity became an intrinsic element of feminine modernity, which was expressed through this body ideal and fashionable sportswear, as well as through actual participation in sport.[60] This had a political dimension, as Skillen states: "many people regarded women's involvement in sport as fundamental to their new independence."[61] These social and political changes were reflected in the clothing industry: as from the 1920s there was an increase in the availability and range of sports-specific clothing for women.

Women participated in a wide range of sports in the inter-war period, including tennis, hockey, swimming, golf, skiing and netball.[62] A key sport that had a wider influence on women's fashion and which often involved wearing tweed was golf. Horwood notes that "*Vogue* acknowledged the popularity of the sport among its readers by according it the unique accolade of a regular column on the game itself, rather than just its clothing, in the mid-1920s. Advertisements for the new sportswear shop to be opened in Paris by the couture house Lanvin featured female golfers, confirming the international popularity of the game."[63] The female adoption of bifurcated gatments continued to be highly controversial in the 1920s, as shown by an article titled "Should Woman Wear Plus Fours?" in *Golf Illustrated* of January 23 1925.[64] The first woman to wear trousers to play in the English Ladies Championship was Gloria Minoprio. *Golf Illustrated* reported on this sartorial event of 1933 by arguing that this was "only officially frowned upon" and that as well as giving increased warmth and comfort, trousers "emphasise in the woman's mind the sense of her complete emancipation."[65] Horwood argues that despite these developments, the vast majority of females continued to wear skirts to play golf in the inter-war era.[66] A photograph of a charity golf match of 1938 in Essex, England shows that these garments were often made of tweed (Fig. 7.5).

TWEED AND THE RURAL IN INTER-WAR BRITAIN

In addition to its continued close relationships with notions of sport, the fashion for tweed was in sympathy with the greater emphasis on the rural within English culture of the period. As Amies states about the tweeds he used in the 1930s, "All colours came from nature: the best from the earth. The greeny-brown of upturned furrows could have little flecks of green like wheat shoots."[67] Pugh argues that the international, political and economic turmoil of the era may have encouraged these desires to "retreat to a timeless and more secure world."[68] However, Matless contests the idea that the new visions of landscape, Englishness and preservation that emerged in the late 1920s may simply be related to nostalgia. He stated that the "desire for preservation must be understood as expressing a particular modernism, committed to order and design, whether in country or city." Matless and Pugh concur, however, about the important relationships between landscape and "senses of Englishness" in the 1920s and 1930s.[69] Pugh, for example, stated:

> Paradoxically, while the younger country-dwellers looked for ways of escaping to the towns, the urban population increasingly celebrated the countryside as a refuge from town life... . During the nineteenth century the romantic appeal of rural life was associated with writers and pundits, but there are indications that it became a pervasive element in English society after the war. Not only was the countryside regarded as healthy and visually appealing, it was increasingly seen as a key element in English national identity.[70]

This cultural mood of a preoccupation with the rural was reflected in several books of the era, such as J. B. Priestley's, *English Journey* (1933) and *In Search of England* (1927) by H. V. Morton.[71] Its influence can also be seen in a photograph by Norman Parkinson of 1938, which features a model wearing a fine sweater and a herringbone tweed suit (Fig. 7.6). Parkinson has annotated the print of this photograph with the words "double exposure against my cottage in Elmley Castle."[72] The focus of this image on juxtaposing the textured tweed, the thatched cottage and sheaves of wheat eloquently illustrates that although that textile was widely worn in urban contexts in the 1930s, it also retained strong cultural associations of the rural.

TWEEDS, FRENCH COUTURE, AND CHANEL

The use of tweeds within French couture and sportswear will now be explored. In particular, the notion that Coco Chanel played *the* leading role internationally in popularizing the tweed suit

Figure 7.6 Model in herringbone tweed suit, photographed by Norman Parkinson at his cottage in Elmley Castle, Worcestershire, 1938. © Norman Parkinson Ltd/courtesy Norman Parkinson Archive, London.

for women in the twentieth century is investigated. That discussion will be continued in the next chapter, because tweed only became a core signature element of the Chanel house style following the re-opening of her business in 1954. Valerie Steele in her essay, "Chanel in Context" states that "The popular image of Chanel is of a creative genius who created her personal style in isolation from the work of other fashion designers. Yet style is a social phenomenon ... Clearly we cannot simply take Chanel's word that she originated all the important new sartorial ideas of the twentieth century."[73] The difficulties in separating myths from facts in relation to Chanel's work are relevant to researching the use of tweed within French couture of the 1920s. Bonnie English states that, "As an innovator in textile usage, Chanel also introduced British tweeds into the female fashion domain. She procured her fine tweeds from Linton Tweed Ltd of Carlisle, and in 1927 opened a boutique in London where she sold tweed cardigan suits."[74] An article of October 1927 in American *Vogue*, however, stressed that Scotch tweeds had in recent years been adopted by Chanel and a wide range of other French couturiers. It states:

> Chanel, an important influence on the mode, whose clothes are invariably simple, practical and beautiful, is making a feature of models of Scotch tweed in her recent collections. Some of these appeared in the summer, and still more are shown in her autumn collection... . Vionnet also showed a considerable number of tweed models last season, and outstanding for smartness among these was a coat in black-and-white tweed rather loosely woven. It had a fur collar to match, shading from grey into white. O'Rossen is using Scotch tweed for a large number of his tailleurs. Patou is making many of his sports costumes of this material. In fact, nearly all Paris is godmother to the Scotch tweed.[75]

An example that illustrates the use of tweed within French couture of the era is a photograph by Edward Steichen of a two-piece dress by the house of Drecoll, which featured in the November 1, 1926 edition of American *Vogue* (Fig. 7.7).[76] In addition, an article titled "Tweeds Acquire a New Significance," in *Harper's Bazaar* of October 1929, described a "Scotch tweed ensemble" by the French couturier Paul Caret. This outfit called "Sel et Poivre" was "lightly flecked with scarlet and orange, which note is repeated in the scarlet and orange binding to the hem of the unlined coat. The circular skirt is composed of small godets attached to a pointed yoke and is the new length."[77] Chanel was therefore not the only, or even the principal, French couturier to use tweeds from the mid-1920s, but her influential work in those textiles remains significant to a study of their design and consumption in the inter-war period. This designer opened her first couture house in Biarritz in 1915 and in 1919 she took larger premises at 31 Rue Cambon, Paris where she was allowed to open a couture salon.[78] Chanel met her lover the Duke of Westminster in 1923 and Amy de la Haye argues that this relationship was a pivotal influence on her subsequent use of tweed. She states:

> The inspiration for Chanel's garconne look was to a large extent the simplicity of men's everyday and sporting apparel, especially that worn by the fashionable Duke of Westminster and his circle. Menswear combined function, comfort and durability and in this instance had the added kudos of an aristocratic design source. Chanel's blazers, waist-coats, cardigans, shirts with cuff links and her famous tweeds were all inspired by the Duke and his friends. Following her fishing trips to Scotland with the Duke, she introduced tweeds and knitted Fair Isle designs into her fashion collections.[79]

Figure 7.7 Model wearing a hat and two-piece tweed dress by Drecoll, 1926. Photograph by Edward Steichen/ *Vogue*. © Condé Nast.

Figure 7.8 Coco Chanel with Vera Bates, both wearing men's tweed jackets, Lochmore Estate, Scotland, 1920s. © Private collection.

Significantly, de la Haye also notes that "The versatile clothes of Chanel collections became hugely popular and were much copied, as they appealed to the contemporary woman who wanted to look sporty, even if she did not participate in any form of physical exercise."[80] An extremely rare, haute couture, tweed jacket and skirt, which date from about 1927 to 1929 are held by the Chanel private archive in Paris (Plate 15). This jacket is highly reminiscent of the clothing in a photo of Coco Chanel with her friend Vera Bates, which was taken on the Duke of Westminster's Scottish sporting estate, Lochmore in the 1920s (Fig. 7.8). In that image, both women are wearing men's oversized checked, tweed jackets with the cuffs unbuttoned and turned back.

The garment in the Chanel archive was clearly inspired by a man's shooting, or sports jacket, however, its design also forms a distinctive re-interpretation of that style for women. It has the typical menswear features of a loose, straight cut with no bust shaping, a back vent and just below the waist seam on each hip are patch pockets with a flap that are fastened by buttons, a detail that derives from men's nineteenth century shooting jackets.[81] In addition, the jacket cuffs are folded back in a similar fashion to how Chanel and Bates wore theirs in the Lochmore photograph. A further well-thought-out design feature, which again is meant to look casual, is that the collar is cut to permanently stand up, in a way that is clearly based on how a man's tailored jacket looks with the collar turned up. However, the dropped waist seam of this jacket clearly signals that it is fashionable women's attire of the 1920s. Furthermore, in contrast to a man's tailored sports jacket of that era, it has no padding or canvases in the chest or shoulders and therefore the effect is very soft and unstructured.

The tweed that the Chanel jacket and skirt of 1927–9 are made from is woven in the plain weave from yarns that are quite coarse in character. On first examination, this fabric looks rough and rustic, but it has actually been carefully designed and constructed. The yarns vary in thickness at regular intervals along their length and the wider sections of yarn create ill-defined vertical and horizontal stripes, which combine to form a subtle, checked effect. The warp yarns are beige and the weft yarns are in varying shades of brown with intermittent brown knops. It is probably French, because it is not like any cloths that I have seen in British archival collections to date. This tweed outfit provides rare and important material evidence about the much-discussed tensions between the masculine and feminine and poverty and luxury in Chanel's work.[82]

WOMENSWEAR, WAR, UTILITY, AND AUSTERITY, 1939–1952

In Britain, the major government measures and controls put in place following the outbreak of the Second World War, which impacted on the clothing and textiles industry were rationing and the Utility Scheme, both from 1941, as discussed in Chapter 6.[83] At first only the fabric and price of garments were controlled by the Utility regulations, but in 1942, the Civilian Clothing order introduced Utility clothes. In that year, the Board of Trade asked the members of the Incorporated Society of London Fashion Designers, which included Hardy Amies; Digby Morton; Creed; Worth; Bianca Mosca; Peter Russell; Edward Molyneux and Victor Stiebel to design four outfits, a coat, suit, cotton overall dress and afternoon dress. From these designs, the Board of Trade made a selection of styles that were subsequently mass-produced and sold in shops from spring 1943. Many of the prototype garments survive in the collections of the Victoria and Albert Museum.

Figure 7.9 Model (right) wearing a tweed suit by Sumrie. Photographed by Norman Parkinson, British *Vogue*, July 1941. © Norman Parkinson Ltd/courtesy Norman Parkinson Archive, London.

These artifacts include several women's tweed suits, which show the inventiveness that British couturiers demonstrated in meeting a brief that involved minimizing fabric use to meet the Utility regulations.[84]

The tailored tweed suit was an ideal wartime outfit because of its adaptability to different social contexts within straitened times. For example, in July 1941, British *Vogue* published a feature, which included a suit by Sumrie. That outfit was described as "the tweed you'll live in, summer and winter. Caramel and cream squared-off in sea blue-green; pockets in the high-buttoned jacket and box-pleats in the skirt."[85] This suit features the typical pared back and military-influenced style of the era, which included square padded shoulders, flapped breast pockets and a narrow skirt with shallow pleating (Fig. 7.9). The somewhat rectangular silhouette favored by many British designers and ready-to-wear manufacturers of tailored suits was not the only option worn internationally during the war and its immediate aftermath. Lauren Bacall's wardrobe in the Hollywood film *The Big Sleep* of 1946, for example, included a tweed suit that had broad padded shoulders, but also a nipped in waist. In this outfit, the contrasting light and dark shades within checked tweeds are used

Figure 7.10 Humphrey Bogart as Philip Marlowe and Lauren Bacall as Vivian Rutledge in *The Big Sleep*, 1946. Bacall is wearing a houndstooth check suit. Silver Screen Collection/Getty Images.

to excellent cinematic effect and Bacall demonstrated the potential of the tweed suit to simultaneously look everyday, elegant and sexy (Fig. 7.10).

Christian Dior's New Look created an international sensation in 1947. In contrast to typical, wartime fashions, it featured "rounded shoulders, full feminine busts, and hand-span waists above enormous spreading skirts."[86] Worldwide responses to this style veered between celebration and condemnation, for example, Wilcox states that "The amount of fabric required to create New Look garments – typically 15 yards in a woollen day dress … caused outrage, for rationing was still in place."[87] An image by Norman Parkinson published in *Vogue* of February 1950, which features his wife Wenda modeling a suit by Simpsons, reveals the muted influence of the New Look on British women's tailored suits. Compared to the Sumrie suit of 1941, it includes a narrower, softer shoulder line, some waist shaping and the box pleated skirt is longer and features more fabric than the wartime outfit, although its silhouette is still narrow. This outfit reflects the fact that although British women's tailored suits were influenced by the New Look, their styling in the immediate post-war era was also restrained by continued austerity.[88]

The close relationships between the post-war export drive, British couturiers and the native textile industry are revealed by the Annual Report of the Incorporated Society of London Fashion Designers of 1950. It stated: "The main aim of the Society is to promote the London Fashion Designers and British fabrics at home and overseas. Because of present-day conditions the Society's activities are confined almost exclusively to developing the dollar market overseas."[89] Tweeds for womenswear were a prominent category of woolen textile involved in post-war, British promotional activities, which is demonstrated by the fact that they frequently featured in articles in the export magazine, *The Ambassador*. For example, an article titled "London Spring 1951: Fashion Lines, Fabric Trends" stated "There is nothing flamboyant about the novelty weaves used in the collections. Many of them are the dotted, or birdseye variety … There are many others of the same school which, new in design, are discreet in interpretation. A neat grey 'chain' design by Otterburn Mill is used by Amies."[90]

CONCLUSION

A highly significant development of the inter-war era was the international shift toward greater interest from leading, Paris-based designers in "Scotch tweeds." Another key change was that a larger proportion of tweeds from Scotland were designed and made especially for women.[90] Although the popularity of sportswear fashions in tweed was connected to the expansion in women's sports in the inter-war period, Skillen argues that the fraught character of gender relations meant that women's participation in those activities remained controversial. Despite these tensions, physical activity became an integral aspect of feminine modernity, which was articulated through a new, athletic body ideal and fashionable sportswear, whether or not women actually participated in sport.[92] As Hollander notes "What is meant by 'modern' looks developed after the First World War with the aid of clothing that expressed (though it did not always provide) an ideal of comfort and the possibility of action."[93] During the Second World War and its immediate aftermath, the tweed suit continued to have an ever more integral role in women's wardrobes, primarily because of its adaptability and suitability for all-day wear.[94]

8
COUTURE TO POP AND NOSTALGIC FASHION, 1953-1980

The international successes and considerable challenges experienced by British producers of tweeds between 1953 and 1980 are examined in this chapter. It explores the designs associated with firms that sold high quality tweeds to the elite fashion market such as Linton Tweeds and Bernat Klein Ltd. The overall picture of decline in British tweed manufacturing is also set against wider shifts within the international woolen industry. In contrast to the preceding chapters, tweeds designed for the male and female markets are both explored here. This approach enables an investigation into the growing influence of androgynous styling on tweeds in fashion from the mid-1960s onwards.

Tweeds held an increasingly diverse range of cultural and social meanings within international fashion between 1953 and 1980. As Palmer notes, these textiles were widely used by French, fashion houses to make elegant couture suits, styles that were widely copied by American, ready-to-wear manufacturers.[1] The notion of re-interpreting and challenging the established concepts of tradition, class, gender and Britishness through the bold, innovatory use of tweed also emerged from the mid-1950s, in the youthful clothes by British designers such as Mary Quant and Jean Muir. The chapter also examines how the earlier associations of tweeds evolved within the emergent post-colonial era, when British identities were in a state of flux.

DECLINE, CHANGE, AND INNOVATION: PRODUCING, DESIGNING, AND SELLING BRITISH TWEEDS

Between the early 1950s and the late 1970s, the production of woolen cloths in Britain was still primarily concentrated in Yorkshire, Scotland and the West of England.[2] Yorkshire continued to form by far the largest manufacturing region and Brearley and Iredale concluded in 1977 that "more than two thirds" of British woolens were still woven there. By that era, the West of England woolen industry was very small in scale and there were "less than a dozen" manufacturers still in operation.[3] It is difficult to pinpoint what proportion of the output of Yorkshire and West of England mills consisted of tweeds between 1953 and 1980. This chapter will therefore primarily focus on tweed design and production in mainland Scotland, the Harris Tweed industry and by the key English firm, Linton Tweeds. Major changes within British and global wool textile manufacturing will first of all be examined in order to set these sectors and firms within their broad contexts.

Wool Textiles in UK and International Contexts

The economic historian, Jim Tomlinson argued that "what was undoubtedly the most successful period of British economic performance ever (the 1950s and 1960s)" was "followed by a period of crisis in the 1970s."[4] Developments in the post-war British wool textiles industry were linked to these broad economic trends, but did not exactly mirror them. The decline in that sector of manufacturing after 1953 was part of a general tendency toward contraction in the UK textile industries. There was a rapid decrease in the numbers employed in producing wool textiles from 195,500 in 1951, to 151,300 in 1958, as confirmed by G. F. Rainnie. Despite these changes, in 1958 the British woolen and worsted industry remained, in relation to employment, the largest in the world.[5] The leading international position of the UK had, however, changed by the mid-1960s, as Italy became the largest global exporter of wool fabrics. Between 1974 and 1978, Britain accounted for around 6 percent of world production, whereas Italy made over 16 percent and it thus retained its position as the foremost global producer.[6] Significantly, David Jenkins argues that in the post-war era Italian competition had a major impact on the UK-based wool textiles industry, impacting on sales in both the home and export markets.[7]

Broad shifts within men's and women's fashion also affected the popularity of British tweeds. In particular, the growing fashion for casual clothes from the mid-1950s onwards meant that cotton, synthetic fibers and knitted fabrics began to play an increasingly significant role in male and female dress.[8] However, the continued dominance of the tailored suit in the male wardrobe of the 1950s and 1960s, meant that wool and wool mixture cloths remained important within menswear, as Bennet-England and Jobling confirm.[9] Fashion trends in this period, however, increasingly moved toward lighter weight suitings which favored the use of worsteds, rather than woolen cloths like tweed.[10] That broad shift encouraged in the youth market by the popularity of the Italian Look, which came to Britain around 1956. The journalist, Nik Cohn confirms that this menswear style was most typically made from lightweight cloths with a crisp handle and a smooth surface such as mohair or worsted cloths.[11] The trend away from tailored clothing in British wool textiles continued into the 1970s and Jenkins notes that British sales of suits made in the UK declined from around "7 million in 1971 to only 3 million in 1980."[12]

The position of British wool textile manufacturing grew substantially worse between 1972 and 1981. Hardill estimates that the numbers employed in that industry decreased by 47 percent, figures that primarily reflect contraction in Yorkshire.[13] In addition to the factors already identified, the dramatic decline in that era was also related to internal economic problems in Britain in the early 1970s, which were accompanied by a global rise in inflation. Tomlinson argues that the quadrupling of oil prices by the Organization of Petroleum Exporting Countries in 1973 seriously exacerbated these problems and led to "a 'stagflationary' (stagnation plus inflation) crisis that adversely affected almost every country in the industrial world."[14]

The textile and clothing industries in Europe and America also experienced an intensification of foreign competition in the 1970s. The response of GATT (the General Agreement on Tariffs and Trade) to these developments was discussed by Anthony Moreton in the *Financial Times* of October 29, 1984. GATT's prime purpose was to reduce trade barriers between over 150 countries worldwide, yet this organisation took the unprecedented step in 1974 of creating a protectionist agreement called the Multi-Fibre Arrangement (MFA). Moreton argued that this represented a "desperate attempt" by GATT to "give Europe and America time to reorganise their industries" against intense and growing competition from countries such as Hong Kong, South Korea and Taiwan.[15] The limited impact of the MFA import quotas was noted in a market research report of 1982 and by Moreton, who discussed that 1.5 million textile and clothing jobs had been lost in Europe during the decade that it had been in place. These sources indicate that the complex factors that encouraged the continued contraction of the UK woolen industry after 1974 included high levels of imports, job losses due to improvements in efficiency and the impact of inflation and high unemployment, which constrained consumer spending in Europe.[16]

Scottish Tweed Production

Woolen manufacturing in Scotland changed significantly in scale and character between 1953 and 1980, although there was also some continuity in that era. For example, the Scottish Borders remained the primary locale in Scotland for the production of tweeds. The other main areas where woolen cloths were made in Scotland around 1970, were Aberdeenshire and the Highlands; Ayrshire and the South-West; Lanarkshire and the islands of Bute, Skye and Shetland.[17] The NASWM was still the main organization related to that industry and the majority of firms, apart from those who made Harris Tweed, belonged to it.[18] Rainnie argued in 1965, that the main product of Scottish mills remained high quality tweeds, and by 1970, the Scottish woolen industry still primarily made "cheviot and saxony cloths in infinite variation for both men and women."[19] A NASWM handbook of 1970 and a Scottish Woollen Publicity Council (SWPC) publication of about 1971 emphasized that Scottish firms also continued to weave homespuns and novelty tweeds for the ladies market, as well as a diverse range of other products, including worsteds, tartans, fine dress fabrics for the haute couture, scarves, blankets and upholstery cloths.[20]

In 1956, the NASWM had ninety-one member companies, but by 1970 there were only eighty-three, including spinning firms, cloth manufacturers, dyers and finishers.[21] This reduction in membership can be interpreted as a sign that the industry was beginning to contract. It may also be attributed to a trend toward take-overs and mergers to form larger companies, with the aim of surviving in the more competitive business climate of the late 1960s and 1970s.[22] This trend only had limited impact by 1970, however, because the main focus of the industry continued to be on creating individualized cloths, rather than producing standardized designs in large volumes. The NASWM handbook of that year stated: "For the most part the mills are comparatively small. This is a potent asset because it has led to specialisation. Each firm can produce cloth which in texture or content, colour or design, and above all in quality, is unique."[23]

By the early 1970s, considerable investment was required to remain competitive by embracing new technological developments. In 1971, for example, the SWPC stressed that: "New weaving machines … involve expenditure seven times that of conventional looms. The latest automatic warping machine costs one thousand times that of traditional equipment."[24] These new technological developments, such as the use of shuttleless rapier looms, were combined with a continued emphasis on maintaining a highly skilled workforce. Notably, the SWPC stated that "The traditional care, skill and craftsmanship of the people is as important as ever."[25] Significantly, by 1980, the Scottish wool textile industry was seen by the Scottish Development Agency (SDA) as having kept pace with technological improvements when compared to its international competitors.[26]

Global exports remained highly significant to the sales of Scottish tweeds and other woolens and according to the NASWM the main destinations exported to in 1970 were "North America, Western Europe, Scandinavia, Japan and the Far East."[27] In the early 1970s, the SWPC estimated that since 1945 Scottish mills had "rarely sold overseas less than 40 per cent" of their output.[28] At that time, the NASWM and the SWPC were clearly aiming to change buyer's perceptions of the Scottish woolen industry as only producing medium to heavy weight tweeds. The NASWM handbook of 1970, for example, emphasized that the industry "consistently sells considerable quantities of lightweight fabrics to countries in extremely warm zones."[29] This statement was clearly linked to an industry drive to expand export sales because of a shrinking home market and competition from synthetic fibers, which meant that wool fabrics were increasingly seen as "quality" or luxury cloths.[30]

Between 1979 and 1980, the SDA undertook research about the wool textiles industry in Scotland within its international contexts. This study was carried out because of government concerns about contraction in the manufacturing of tweeds, other woven wool textiles and knitwear. That sector was still considered a "major employer" in Scotland, particularly in the Scottish Borders where it provided about 60 percent of manufacturing jobs.[31] In the period covered by the study, the Scottish wool weaving sector had an annual turnover of over £60 million and it employed around 4,200 people. These individuals worked for over forty firms, which was a substantial drop from the sixty cloth manufacturers that were members of the NASWM in 1970.[32] The SDA report also revealed that a trend for firms to diversify into knitwear meant that over 8,000 people were employed in that sector. The reasons for contraction throughout the industry were discussed, as follows:

> It has been under increasing pressure in domestic and overseas markets because of strong competition from both low cost and high cost producers. The products of the industry are not covered to any significant extent by the Multi Fibre Agreement and so the UK and other EEC markets are freely open to competitors. The pressure is reflected in continued shedding of labour and firms, with fears that the Scottish industry would suffer as badly as the Yorkshire trade.[33]

This quote refers to the fact that the MFA restricted imports by volume, rather than by value, therefore it offered relatively less protection to high value producers, who tended to sell small quantities. The term Multi-Fibre Agreement was sometimes used when referring to the Multi-Fibre Arrangement. Although concerns were expressed in the SDA report about fierce international competition, it positively endorsed the strategy of focusing increasingly on export markets that was pursued in the 1970s. This study revealed that by 1980, over 60 percent of Scottish wool cloths were sold abroad. That emphasis on exports meant that the wool textiles industry in Scotland fared better than the Yorkshire sector between 1974 and 1979. At that time, the main export markets for Scottish wool cloths in order of scale were the EEC; rest of Europe; United States, Canada and Japan.[34] The SDA report also noted a recent trend toward increased competition from Italy, whereby "Italian manufacturers have made a rapid entry into the German market, offering distinctive designs and a look very similar to that of Scottish cloth. This has been a particular problem in the jacket and suitings trade. In general the Italians have anticipated market trends much more effectively than the Scots, largely because of their greater emphasis on research."[35]

The SDA study recognized that manufacturers had "maintained an international reputation for quality and distinctiveness of product" and it concluded that the potential for increasing exports was "very promising." The scale of the difficulties for Scottish wool textile manufacturing in 1980 were, however, made clear by the principal recommendations of the report, which were put in stark, apocalyptic terms. It stated: "firms will have to adopt a much more aggressive marketing approach involving more product design research, individual targeting of major garment makers, improvement in agent representation and more effective promotions. Failure to do this will lead to a continuing erosion of market penetration and by 1990 the industry could cease to exist on any scale."[36]

Harris Tweed: Boom, Decline, and Change

Developments in the Harris Tweed industry between 1953 and 1980 were both distinctive in character and also broadly influenced by the same UK and international contexts as the rest of the Scottish woolen industry. Hunter notes that from 1953, a challenge to the Harris Tweed Trade Mark took on a growing momentum and that culminated in important court cases of 1964 and 1965. She lays out these detailed legal and commercial developments in depth, so only the key aspects are summarized here.[37] Hunter pinpoints that the campaign by a small group of Scottish woolen manufacturers was to have "unstamped Harris Tweed recognised as a valid alternative to Orb-stamped Harris Tweed." The term unstamped Harris Tweed principally implied cloth made by woolen mills from mainland Scotland who sent yarn spun in that locale to the Outer Hebrides to be handwoven.[38] These practices were contrary to the definition in the amended Harris Tweed Trade Mark of 1934, which set out that only cloths that were made from yarn that was spun and dyed in the Outer Hebrides, handwoven in the weaver's own homes and finished on those islands could be stamped with the Orb mark by the Harris Tweed Association's Inspectors. Lord Hunter declared the judgment in the landmark Harris Tweed case of 1964 in favor of the Orb-mark producers, which confirmed the importance of the 1934 definition.[39] In his comments he stressed the importance of the meaning of the name "Harris Tweed" to consumers, as follows:

> Part of the reputation that Harris Tweed enjoys ... with the purchasing public is based on the fact that it is not only a product of the Outer Hebrides, but also the product of a cottage or home industry.... . I am satisfied from the evidence that in the mind of the purchasing public ... it is an important selling point that the main surviving hand-process should be carried out, not under factory conditions, but at the home.[40]

It is impressive that despite these highly distinctive manufacturing methods, production of Harris Tweed was at consistently high levels between 1953 and 1971, although figures prepared by Hunter show that there were also frequent cyclical fluctuations in output. Notably in 1966, the industry attained its highest ever level of production when over seven and a half million yards were made.[41]

By 1970, output was still relatively high at just over five million yards but it continued to decline significantly in the following five years and by 1975 it had plummeted to around two and a half million yards. Hunter argues that these developments resulted in major structural changes in the industry, whereby a number of firms, particularly small Independent Producers went out of business. The companies that survived tended to be the larger mills, which underwent rationalization and often amalgamation.[42]

The marked decline in Harris Tweed production between 1970 and 1975 was related to the key shifts within the global textile market already discussed, including increasing competition and the growing fashion for casual clothes in synthetic and cotton fibers. The serious difficulties experienced by that industry were also linked to the challenging economic conditions of that era in Britain and internationally. The impact of the global oil crisis on the British government's economic policies and by implication, Harris Tweed manufacturing is shown by an article in the *Stornoway Gazette* of June 1, 1974. It commented that the "three month clampdown on fuel resulting in the three day week" had caused a significant slowdown in production, which meant that the Clansman Group mills were struggling to fulfill export orders on time.[43] The decline in Harris Tweed output of the 1970 to 1975 period also had a significant social impact. It contributed to the scenario noted by the *Daily Telegraph* on March 10, 1976, whereby the Outer Hebrides had "the highest unemployment rate in the United Kingdom at 22 per cent."[44]

The difficulties experienced within Harris Tweed manufacturing in the first half of the 1970s were also related to factors distinctive to that industry. A key issue was the falling demand for single-width Harris Tweed, which was 29 inches wide and still being woven on foot-driven Hattersley looms, as discussed in Chapter 6.[45] By the mid-1970s, these developments helped to prompt radical restructuring plans that were developed by the Highlands and Islands Development Board (HIDB) in conjunction with the Harris Tweed Association (HTA).[46] *The Scotsman* newspaper reported on March 6, 1975 that the HTA were proposing to apply to the Department of Trade and Industry to have the Orb trademark amended to include double-width cloth. These proposals were highly controversial because that breadth of tweed could only be woven on power looms at that time and the plans also entailed weavers becoming employees and working in premises approved by the HTA, rather than in their own homes.[47] An article in the *Draper's Record* of February 15, 1975 revealed that the plan was linked to market research commissioned by the HIDB, which suggested that double-width cloth would better meet the needs of clothing manufacturers worldwide.[48]

In April 1976, the lengthy discussions about the proposed reorganization of the industry culminated in a ballot of the weavers who had to agree to the proposals for them to go ahead. The result was an overwhelming majority vote against the controversial modernization plans.[49] That outcome prompted critical comment in the *Glasgow Herald* of April 19, 1976, which noted that "It would be tragic if the weavers' dedication to their craft and their spirit of sturdy independence, paved the way for the disintegration and decline of their industry."[50] The highly specific history of Harris Tweed means that viewing the rejection of the restructuring proposals simply as a struggle for, or against progress is inadequate. The comment in the *Glasgow Herald* ignored the pivotal relationship between the brand name Harris Tweed and public perceptions of it as a handwoven product made in the homes of Hebridean weavers. Although the HTA's desire to respond to clear market demand for double-width cloth was entirely sensible, hindsight has shown that the vote against plans to weave Harris Tweed by power looms in small-scale factory contexts has been critical to its survival as a distinctive and protected textile.

From 1976, there was a slow but steady growth in output of Harris Tweed to reach almost four and a half million yards by 1980, although the industry was never again to reach the peak levels attained in the 1960s.[51] Hunter argues that improvements in that era included the setting up of a Distribution Centre, which allocated work to weavers. In addition, the HIDB addressed the shortage of Hattersley looms by making them available for weavers to lease.[52] From 1976, the British economy also showed signs of improvement and Tomlinson argues that by 1979 "economic growth had resumed."[53] The increase in output of Harris Tweed between 1976 and 1980 was also linked to exports. Ian A. Mackenzie, the current Chief Executive of Harris Tweed Hebrides argued that in the late 1970s the depressed value of the pound meant that these cloths became relatively cheaper to buy and that encouraged export sales, particularly to the USA.[54]

Harris Tweed: Exports, Gender, and Design

The peak outputs of the 1960s were largely linked to foreign sales, which resulted in *The Ambassador* granting the Harris Tweed industry one of its prestigious annual Awards for Achievement in 1965.[55] Furthermore, W. G. Lucas confirmed in *The Scotsman* of June 23, 1967 that 70 percent of these tweeds were exported. He also identified that America was still a key international market for these cloths.[56] Hunter confirms that since 1957, exports of Harris Tweed to the USA had benefited significantly from a preferential tariff that only applied to single-width tweed.[57] In particular, men's sports jackets in Harris Tweed sold well in America, which was linked to the boom in college students from the mid-1950s and what Mears describes as the "newly popular collegiate look."[58] By 1967–8, that post-war interpretation of the elite Ivy League style had all but come to a demise, but in the 1970s the work of American designers, including most significantly Ralph Lauren, laid the basis for its popular resurgence in the 1980s.[59]

Harris Tweed continued to be mainly used for menswear in the late 1950s and early 1960s and a feature in *The Ambassador* of August 1962 suggested that subtle colors were still favored for menswear tweeds.[60] However, in that article, a Harris Tweed sample by James MacDonald is used to show that in womenswear the "use of strong, boldly clashing colours" was "right in the forefront of fashion."[61] Furthermore, W. G. Lucas noted in *The Scotsman* of June 23, 1967 that Harris Tweed was by then available in a wide range of weights including standard (11 oz); lightweight (8–9 oz) and bantamweight (6–7 oz). He also stated that the latter was "proving very successful for ... K. J. Mackenzie Ltd who had introduced a 'Chelsea Set' range" for womenswear in that very lightweight tweed.[62] The creation in the 1950s and 1960s of a wider range of designs, colors and weights than was previously available in Harris Tweed was about encouraging a greater diversity of markets, including expanding its use in womenswear. Furthermore, Francis Thompson notes that by the later 1960s, these woolens were also being used for interiors, including upholstering "modern furniture."[63]

WOMENSWEAR TWEEDS AND INTERNATIONAL FASHION

Wilcox argues that, soon after the Second World War, Paris successfully reasserted its position as the leading international center of women's fashion and that meant it also had an important influence on fashion textiles developments.[64] In her essay about the use of fabrics by French couturiers between 1947 and 1957, Lesley Miller discusses the popularity of well-established tweed patterns, which originally derived from Scottish menswear cloths. She states: "Pattern entered the equation in woollens in a variety of checks – houndstooth, Prince of Wales, shepherd's plaid and tartans. They were particularly associated with winter and the colour ranges varied from season to season."[65]

An article of 1959 in *L'art et La Mode* focused on the new woolen fabrics offered for sale by manufacturers and agents who were almost exclusively French. It revealed that many of the key patterns, or types of tweeds, such as Prince of Wales checks, "*cheviote*" and "Shetlands" were being widely made for womenswear by high-quality French wool textiles manufacturers such as Pierre Besson, Gerondeau, J. Leonard et Cie and A. Leleu, thus reflecting the significant international design influence of Scottish tweed designs.[66] It is not surprising that French couturiers sourced most of their tweeds from native suppliers because their government offered financial incentives to do so. Jeannette A. Jarnow and Beatrice Judelle discuss these measures, as follows:

> From 1950 until 1963 couture houses received a yearly subsidy from the French government. These subsidies, ranging in total from $300,000 to $600,000 came from a tax levied against French fabric firms. To qualify for its share of them, a couture house would agree to use approximately 80 per cent of their fabrics from those of French textile producers. The portion received by individual houses depended on how much fabric was actually used.[67]

In addition to these government incentives, Miller notes that the fashion media in France focused primarily on promoting French couturiers and manufacturers in the 1950s.[68] Competition from British and other foreign textile producers continued, however, because as Miller argues "major French couturiers clearly chose textiles wherever they found what suited their standards of excellence and vision."[69] The international export and design impact of British tweeds for womenswear will now be further explored within this Paris-based context.

Exports of British Tweeds for Womenswear

Research in the private archives of Balenciaga, Dior and Chanel in Paris, has revealed that only a handful of British firms sold tweeds to those leading couture houses. For example, in a list of suppliers compiled by the archivist at Balenciaga, the only UK-based firms included were Ascher, Otterburn Mill and Ceemo. The remaining firms listed are predominantly French agents and manufacturers, although Paris-based agents also represented some British producers, for example, Robert Perrier acted for Ceemo and Dumas Maury sold Bernat Klein fabrics. A study of six books of textile samples related to the Balenciaga collections between summer 1964 and 1968, further underlined that this house overwhelmingly bought tweeds from French manufacturers and agents such as Burg, Lesur, Besson, Hurel, Gerondeau and Dumas Maury. The only British firms listed in these books as selling to Balenciaga are Ascher and Bernat Klein.[70] The Dior private archive also contains evidence that the UK-based firms that sold tweeds to that leading fashion house between the mid-1950s and the mid-1960s included Ascher, Bernat Klein, Heather Mills, Otterburn Mill, Ceemo and Linton Tweeds.[71]

Coco Chanel successfully re-launched her couture house in February 1954, after an absence from fashion since 1940. Following that comeback collection, tweeds became a core, signature element of her designs, most famously in the form of her *tailleurs* (Fig. 8.1). The tweeds used by the house of Chanel between 1954 and 1980, were predominantly the novelty, or *fantaisie,* type.[72] Unusually

Figure 8.1 Tweed suits from Chanel's, autumn/winter 1961–2 haute couture collection. Photograph by Paul Shutzer for *Life* magazine. Time & Life Pictures/Getty Images.

for a Paris-based designer, her key supplier of these textiles was a British firm, Linton Tweeds, although French manufacturers were also used, including notably the firm Malhia Kent, which began to supply Chanel from 1960.[73] This fashion house also bought woolens from Otterburn Mill, as shown by the coat of 1955, in a pinky, brown tweed, which is illustrated (Fig. 8.2).

Furthermore, Chanel was the first French couturier that bought the innovative fabrics of the Galashiels-based designer and manufacturer, Bernat Klein. A section-dyed mohair and wool tweed by him was used in her spring 1963, haute couture collection (Plate 16).[74] The womenswear tweeds designed by Klein came to international prominence in the 1960s, as Mary Brogan noted in the *Sunday Telegraph* of December 6, 1964. She stated:

> Over the last few years Scottish clothes have entered the high fashion field ... Now ...
> foreign buyers are snapping up fashion styles as well as straightforward tweeds and woollens.
> Leader of the invasion of the haute couture world is, of course, Bernat Klein, whose fabrics
> made their first big impact in Paris and look like doing so again in January."[75]

This characterization of Klein ignores the earlier success of Linton Tweeds and Ascher in selling to French couturiers, but his fabrics were indeed used by many leading London- and Paris-based fashion houses including Chanel, Christian Dior, Yves St Laurent, Hardy Amies and Norman

Figure 8.2 Chanel coat in tweed by Otterburn Mill, published in "Paris Fashions with British Fabrics," *Picture Post*, March 5, 1955. Photograph by Kurt Hutton. Getty Images.

Hartnell between 1963 and 1966.[76] Klein's vibrantly colored fabrics, which often incorporated mohair were part of international developments, whereby from the late 1950s, *fantaisie* tweeds involved increasingly experimental approaches to color and texture and a diverse range of fibers. The chapter will now look in depth at a firm that was successful in selling to French and British couturiers, namely, Linton Tweeds.

Linton Tweeds

This mill continued to focus predominantly on designing tweeds for womenswear between 1953 and 1980, having been established in 1917, as discussed in Chapter 7. The strong personal and business connections of this English firm with the Scottish Borders woolen industry continued when Leslie Walker joined it as a manager and designer in 1963. Walker trained at the Scottish College of Textiles in Galashiels and he had family links to Heather Mills, an important tweed manufacturer from Selkirk.[77] An interview with Walker, who is now Chairman of the Directors, along with examination of material in Linton's private archive, has informed the following discussion of the firm's work.

By 1953, the company was being run by Agnes Linton, daughter of the founder William, and George Stirling Linton, who was the son of her father's cousin.[78] The international focus of Linton Tweeds in the 1950s, was recalled by Agnes as follows:

> Twice each year a Director goes to North America with new designs, orders from which have to be executed with considerable speed if repeats are to follow… . There are also frequent visits to London and Europe, not only to take orders but to remain conversant with the trend of fashion… . We are proud to number a large percentage of the Haute Couture, past and present both in Paris and London, as users of our materials for their collections… . In America we sell only to the best manufacturers and stores with most of whom we have done business for thirty years or more.[79]

The re-launching of the house of Chanel in 1954, offered major opportunities for Linton Tweeds, because they had a close relationship with that designer in the inter-war era, which they successfully re-established.[80] Another significant change in that year was the appointment of their first Paris agent, Robert Burg. Walker acknowledged that the relationship with Burg was "important" in helping to facilitate the firm's trade with Paris couturiers, but he also emphasized the pivotal significance of personal interaction with customers. He stated that contact with clients was "Mostly face to face. Have an agent, yes, who can follow up after you are gone, but no you had to … I think face to face is most important." These meetings were critically important because they involved direct dialogue with the couturier about design development, which was an essential precursor to successful selling. Walker, for example, recalled that "for Chanel we had to have something that was quite different. But we worked with Chanel, Coco Chanel gave us indications. So right from '63, I would meet Coco Chanel, she would tell us what she was after, and we supplied it."[81]

Walker's professional experience means that he has a good knowledge of Heather Mills, Linton Tweeds, and Otterburn Mill. When asked why those three firms were among the very few British mills that sold to French couturiers, he stated that "These companies all had designers that were there to design new cloths. I think most of the other companies said 'this is what I do' right 'take it or leave it.' Now, definitely Otterburn, definitely Linton Tweeds, definitely Heather Mills would make what the customer wanted, or what they thought the customer wanted."[82] The interview with

Walker and the research in the Dior and Balenciaga archives already discussed suggests that British firms, which had success in selling to Paris couturiers designed fabrics that were distinguished in some way from tweeds made in France. These visual and technical distinctions were sometimes slight, but nonetheless, sufficient to attract the interest of a couture house.

The Linton Tweeds private archive contains a small group of order books from the 1950s and 1960s, which illustrate the fabrics produced by the firm at that time. All of the tweed samples in an order book of the early 1950s, for example, have a flexible and soft handle, rather than being firm and crisp like the Scottish twist suitings that were popular for men at this period. Furthermore, the majority of these swatches include novelty yarns, which rarely, if ever, featured in menswear tweeds. Almost all of the samples of the early 1950s are made entirely from wool and most of the cloths are medium weight with a small proportion of lightweight fabrics and heavier weight coatings. Notably, some of the samples in this book bear a strong relationship to *tweels* of the 1830s, with the same use of two colors with the lighter color forming the diagonal, although these cloths are much softer and of higher quality than the versions in early pattern books.[83] Walker confirmed that samples from another order book of 1956 to 1957 are typical of the type of cloths that Linton Tweeds were still making when he started with them in 1963. He described these textiles, as follows:

> The company's fabrics were all piece dyed … into a range of colours, green, pink and yellow, or whatever it was … fifty per cent of them would be all white fabrics with the surface interest, or weave interest. The others were black and whites, or grey and black and white … And they … all, could be over-dyed. So we ended up getting some very nice colours, colours you hadn't anticipated because there were mixture yarns, so, you know, if you were dying it yellow … it would come through.[84]

Tweed samples from the order book of 1956 and 1957, which show the color effects achieved through these dyeing processes are featured in Plate 17. Notably, this book contains evidence that Chanel's favorite British tweed mill, also sold fabrics to the firms of Davidow; Monte-Sano & Pruzan; Philip Mangone; Nettie Rosenstein; Anthony Blotta; Best & Company and Bergdorf Goodman. These American companies were either department stores or high-class, ready-to-wear designers, or upmarket ready-to-wear manufacturers.[85] Significantly, Walker estimated that in 1967, 70 percent of the mill's business was to the United States and France, with the former constituting the largest proportion of this figure. The remaining 30 percent was sold to the British market.[86]

The trade to French couturiers and to North American customers provided a complementary balance of prestige and profit to Linton Tweeds. Paris-based couturiers mostly bought short, model lengths that were enough to make one garment only. Miller describes the benefits of this high risk and seemingly, low profit trade, in relation to the French textiles and fashion industries between 1947 to 1957. She states that:

> Manufacturers could use sales of high-fashion textiles to couturiers as a springboard from which they could leap into export and domestic markets (comprising high-class ready-to-wear manufacturers as well as professional and home dressmakers). If manufacturers found success with couture houses, they demonstrated their standing in the fashion world and received the orders that helped them to cover their production costs.[87]

Walker discussed how these commercial dynamics operated in relation to Linton Tweeds, as follows: "Davidow … and Auckie Sanft from Canada … they made arrangements with Chanel that they would reproduce some of the models so they actually bought the models and then came to me to say this is your cloth. So we had a ready-made market for it. Because the couture houses didn't give you repeat orders."[88]

Alexandra Palmer's research further confirms that Davidow, which was a high-class, ready-to-wear manufacturer from New York, bought bonded models from Chanel in order to legally produce their own copies and adaptations of designs. She argues that bonded models were an "enormously important design resource for the North American fashion industry" and they proved to be a highly profitable trade for Paris-based designers.[89]

In 1969, Leslie Walker became Managing Director of Linton Tweeds and he described the challenging market conditions around that time, as follows: "we could have gone out of business really because, Seventh Avenue collapsed ... altogether and we didn't have orders."[90] In this quote, Walker refers to what was formerly the center of New York ready-to-wear manufacturing and Milbank confirms that this trade was suffering at that time from foreign competition.[91] Walker's response to these difficulties was to go to Japan to try to encourage Linton's export trade there, a strategy that was inspired by their most high-profile client's commercial priorities. He stated that "at Chanel I knew that it was their up-and-coming market ... I thought if Chanel can sell, we can sell as well." By the time that Walker retired in 1994, Japan accounted for about a third of the business of Linton Tweeds.[92]

CONSUMING TWEEDS IN INTERNATIONAL FASHION, 1953–1980

The shifting range of cultural and social meanings associated with tweeds and their consumption by men and women between 1953 and 1980 will now be explored. The role of these textiles within high-class menswear of the 1950s will first of all be examined.

Back to Formality: Tweeds in British Men's Tailoring

In 1952, the publishers of *The Tailor and Cutter*, launched a new fashion and lifestyle magazine for men, titled *Man About Town*.[93] The male clothing featured within this publication in the 1950s was primarily high class bespoke tailoring, therefore it provides revealing insights into the use of tweeds at that level of the menswear market. An article titled "The Shape of Things in 1953: A Military Air," focused on garments that were representative of the style, which Jobling confirms emerged about 1948 and that subsequently became known as the Neo-Edwardian look. That "revivalist" mode of dressing was originally associated with the elite young men who frequented Savile Row bespoke tailors.[94] The *Man About Town* feature of 1953 revealed that a range of different types of tweeds from medium weight, Prince of Wales, shepherd's and windowpane checks to heavier homespuns, formed part of the repertoire of wool tailoring cloths that were used to create that post-war look. Furthermore, this article suggests that these woolens were used to make Neo-Edwardian style suits and jackets for town and country wear, thus complexifying the usual portrayal of this look as exclusively urban-based.[95] Tweeds therefore formed an element of what Breward argues was "the potential for renewal hidden in the new style, its bridging of modernity and tradition."[96]

Another article in the Spring 1953 edition of *Man About Town* outlined a model of the acceptable garments and textiles to be worn for different social contexts, activities and locations.

It is notable that this new fashion and lifestyle magazine continued to promote established codes of social and sartorial formality.[97] The examples given cannot be taken as a precise indicator of actual male clothing practices, but they are nevertheless revealing as to where tweeds were situated in the early, post-war period in relation to the sartorial codes that upper- and upper-middle-class British men had to negotiate. Under the heading of "Right dress in Town," the article stated that:

> The most formal lounge suits for town wear are of worsted – but Cheviot, Saxony or Flannel are excusable – provided the accessories are formalised … . Where Cheviots Saxonies or flannels are being worn in town try if possible to tone them with black shoes – as it gives that extra touch of formality to a cloth which might otherwise appear sporty.[98]

The long-established and subtle distinctions between different types of tweed garments and their appropriateness for a range of social contexts and activities clearly continued into the 1950s. For example, the article advises that "For country town wear and slightly more formal country wear, the country suit may be single or double-breasted in tweed, cheviot, Saxony or flannel."[99] Furthermore, for active sports, such as "Shooting, shore fishing, golfing, rambling," the options of a "sports coat, wind breaker, blazer, plus four suit" were considered appropriate. The continued strong influence of late nineteenth century and inter-war sporting styles, is shown by the further detailed advice, as follows:

> Jacket … is inclined to favour bellow pockets, pivot sleeves and pleated and yoked backs. Waistcoat can match the jacket or contrast it (again no silks and brocades) or a pullover or cardigan can be utilised … . trousers can be of flannel, cavalry twill, gabardine, tweed, etc or you may prefer plus fours or knickerbockers.[100]

It might be assumed that these comments were exclusively aimed at older men of conservative tastes, or that sports clothing became less associated with modern, male fashionability than it had been between the 1830s and the 1930s. The fact that unfashionable older men would have been unlikely to read *Man About Town* and the reference to silk and brocade waistcoats, however, implies that these recommendations were primarily aimed at the young, elite consumers who adopted the Savile Row version of the Neo-Edwardian look. That predominantly urban style was nevertheless "revivalist" in character, as Breward notes, and it is likely that the mood of revivalism and formality that prevailed also had an influence on clothing for country sports in the early post-war period.[101] Significantly, that mood co-existed with a continuing post-war trend toward modern informality in sportswear, particularly for golfing. A Sceptre knitwear advertisement of 1953 in *Man About Town*, for example, featured checked, tweed golf trousers, which were simply combined with a shirt and sweater.[102]

By the late 1950s, a notable tendency toward stylistic conservatism persisted within high-class English menswear. A feature in the autumn/winter, 1959 edition of *Man About Town*, titled "Elegance: an advertisement for fine tailoring" includes outfits by bespoke tailors, most of whom were from Savile Row. The garments depicted are clearly still shaped by codes of social and sartorial etiquette, as they include lounge suits for town and country wear, a "town overcoat," a tailored Harris Tweed sports jacket and smoking jackets. This article also reveals that tweeds remained a popular choice within the established range of wool cloths used by Savile Row tailors. Surprisingly, a Norfolk jacket is featured, a sporting style, which was highly popular in the late nineteenth and early twentieth century and that was typically made in tweed. The example illustrated won a Gold Medal award in "The Tailor and Cutter Exhibition" of 1959, thus suggesting that this garment, which appears hopelessly outmoded for the era, was still commonly made by high-class, British tailors. As Sherwood argues, Savile Row had by this period lost its position as the leading, international influence on men's fashion and the dynamic of London-based menswear had begun to shift to the youth market.[103]

Tweed and Young Men's Fashion Consumption

A pivotal change in the shifting dynamics between men, masculinities and fashion from the 1950s and particularly from the 1960s onwards, was that youth culture became a new sphere, in addition to sport, where male interest in fashion became more socially acceptable.[104] Frank Mort argues that in addition to the emergence of youth subcultures "mainstream advertising and marketing also played a pivotal role" in reframing post-war male identities and appearances. He emphasizes that from the mid-1950s, UK-based menswear manufacturers and retailers attempted to "encourage the idea of fashionability" and these new commercial approaches were primarily aimed at young male consumers.[105]

The global market for men's fashion lacked a dominant style leadership in the 1950s. In particular, Italy and the USA started to have a more major role, which primarily involved fashions

Figure 8.3 John Stephen (second right) with models in Carnaby St., 1966, photograph by Terrence Spencer. The Life Images Collection/Getty Images.

for the young such as t-shirts, jeans and Italian tailoring.[106] The emergence of new, more youthful ways of self-fashioning from the mid-1950s in the UK was closely linked to London boutiques, which initially catered to a growing gay, male subculture. These outlets included "Vince Man's Shop" of Soho, opened in 1954 by Bill Green and the boutiques that John Stephen ran in the Carnaby Street area from 1957 onwards, which developed into a globally influential retailing empire.[107] This era signaled the beginnings of what became by the 1970s, a fundamental shift toward a new type of leisure clothing for men. The role of tailored garments in tweed as a key option for male, informal, or leisure wear, which had existed since the mid-nineteenth century, as this book has shown, began to be supplanted by casual clothes such as jeans, t-shirts and sweaters. This shift happened gradually, however, and significantly tweeds continued to have a place within the youth fashions of the 1960s, including those by John Stephen.

In 1957, Stephen moved his first shop to Carnaby Street and by the early 1960s his numerous boutiques attracted significant numbers of young people. His clothes for men often incorporated unconventional fabrics such as corduroy, leather, satin and velvet, which were made up into casual styles.[108] The journalist, Geoffrey Aquilina Ross argues that Stephen also appropriated elements from the established language of men's dress and subtly subverted them to create fashionable, youth-orientated styles. For example, tweeds in checked patterns were used by Stephen to make hipster trousers, a style that Cohn argues was originally worn in the south of France (Fig. 8.3).[109] Furthermore, Phil May of the rhythm and blues group The Pretty Things wore a double-breasted jacket by Stephen in green, white and red houndstooth checked tweed in *The Sunday Times*, of June 6, 1965 (Fig. 8.4). The pattern of this tweed follows well-established design precedents that originate in the nineteenth century, as this study has shown. However, the cut of the jacket distinguishes it from conventional menswear of the mid-1960s and the established codes of men's dress are further subverted by the fact that May has long hair and wears a shirt with an unusual collar. Ross discussed how Stephen re-interpreted men's tailoring in tweed for the youth market, as follows:

> He updated traditional styles by slimming the fit and changing the fabric slightly. If a suit was in a Prince of Wales check, for example, it might look traditional but the jacket would have wide lapels and fit tightly, shaped at the waist, with two deep vents at the back. Its armholes would be high, the sleeves narrow. And the fabric, probably lightweight and found in a range destined for women's fashion, would have an unusual, fine line of colour running through the check.[110]

The expansion of Stephen's retailing empire was partly fed by the growth of the mod phenomenon, which developed from about 1960, first of all into a small subculture comprising individuals who only wore bespoke suits and subsequently into a major and increasingly meaningless trend in youth fashion.[111] Cohn discusses an early London mod, Bernard Coutts who stated that "I was never casual. Even in summer, I'd look just as good, in tweeds and waistcoats. No matter what the heat, I'd suffer, because I wanted to be perfect."[112] By 1965, the original identity of mods as individual stylists had dissipated, but some acutely clothes-conscious young men continued to wear tweeds. A television documentary of that year about Rod Stewart, who was then a little-known singer and working class mod from North London, features him entering a tailor's shop. Stewart then stated that "I like tweed you know; the country gentleman appearance appeals to me a lot." Subsequent footage shows him singing in a London nightclub sweating heavily in a thick tweed suit.[113]

Figure 8.4 Phil May of The Pretty Things in a jacket by John Stephen, *The Sunday Times*, June 6, 1965. Photograph: Mike McGrath/Fashion Museum, Bath.

The example of Bernard Coutts shows that some mods wore tweeds as an expression of narcissistic perfectionism. Stewart's desire to dress like the landed classes may also be linked to the instability of class relationships of the era and can be seen as challenging, rather than aspiring to, the stereotypical image of the British upper classes in tweeds. Cannadine argues that the post-war decline of the British Empire had a profound impact on traditional social structures within Britain. He states that "The late 1950s and early 1960s witnessed both the end of the British Empire and the end of the British aristocracy's claims to be the national and imperial ruling class." In Britain itself, these developments resulted in a "decline of deference" and in the 1960s "a less hierarchical, less 'moral' and more open society" emerged.[114] Furthermore, Mort argues that post-war affluence and the related "upsurge of consumption" made class categories more fluid than previously in Britain.[115]

Britishness was a key cultural meeting point between the old world of Empire and fixed social hierarchies and the new world of affluent consumption and youthful individualism. As the Empire came to an end and British identities entered a state of flux, important relationships developed between significant symbols of Britishness and male pop fashion of the 1960s. Breward notes, for example, a "nostalgic preference for the louder elements of the nineteenth-century dressing-up box" and patterned tweeds amply fulfilled these cultural and aesthetic requirements.[116] In addition, Robert Orbach, director of the store, I Was Lord Kitchener's Valet recalled that Mick Jagger bought a "red Grenadier guardsman drummer's jacket" in 1966.[117] This fashion for second-hand imperial military jackets subsequently spread more widely and Nigel Whiteley argues that:

> the appeal of uniforms was not only due to their colour, decoration and extravagant detail, but also due to their campness.... The essence of camp, as outlined by Susan Sontag in 1964, is its love of the unnatural, of theatricality, of artifice and exaggeration. The older generation did not understand camp, and the wearing of uniforms was considered to be an insult to Queen and Country. A similar reaction occurred when Pete Townshend of The Who wore a jacket made from a Union Jack.[118]

Imperial uniforms and the Union Jack were deeply significant symbols of the British Empire and their adoption by rebellious young people may be seen as part of wider developments, whereby, as Cannadine states, the "whole culture" of imperialism "fell victim to satire and scepticism and scorn."[119] The historian Stuart Ward discusses that following decolonization even films that involved the "disavowal of imperialist ambition" often "indulged in the most striking forms of imperial nostalgia" including evoking "the glamour of the masculine hero."[120] These arguments suggest that the adoption of significant symbols of British imperialism by young men was not simply part of the visual eclecticism within 1960s pop fashion.[121] Neither was it merely about wearing garments and textiles that were provocative to members of the older generation. The embrace within youth fashion of textiles and garments that were emblematic of Britain's imperial past was also part of what Ward argues was the "fundamental ambivalence of the end of Empire as a theme in post-war British culture."[122]

Tweed as a significant cultural symbol of Britishness was not as profoundly iconic as the Union Jack or militaria, yet from the 1960s it became an element of how shifting and ambivalent notions of British national identity were played out through the global consumption of fashion. For example, the cover of the 1968 album "Dance To The Music," by the American, funk band, Sly & the Family Stone features the African-American lead singer, Sly Stone wearing a re-interpretation of

Figure 8.5 Tommy Nutter in a houndstooth and Glenurquhart check suit, 1973. Central Press/Getty Images.

garments that derive from the era when British imperialism was at its height. This outfit includes a jacket with a self-cape and knickerbockers, which are both made from thick, brown checked tweed. [123] Paradoxically, Stone's sartorial choices were linked to the worldwide popularity of British pop culture, which communicated a new, young image of Britain internationally in the 1960s.[124] The strong relationships between Victorian menswear and Stone's outfit are linked to the cultural contexts identified by Kelly Boyd and Rohan McWilliams, namely that from the 1950s in Britain a "dialogue was established between the post-war present and the Victorian past."[125] They also state that:

> Although the notion of the "swinging sixties" has been overplayed, sexual liberalism, moral relativism and the pleasures of consumerism defined themselves against the Victorian inheritance which many felt still held sway.... Paradoxically, this gave the Victorians even greater importance; they served as a vehicle against which fashionable people could define their identity as peculiarly modern. Yet it also became possible to find the Victorians sexy.... Victorian clothing became fashionable once more.[126]

As this quote indicates, cultural tensions between innovation and historical revivalism were vividly expressed within 1960s fashion. In the late 1960s and early 1970s the strong associations of tweed with men's tailored garments from earlier historical eras such as the 1930s and a wide range of cultural stereotypes from the British landowning classes to Hollywood gangsters, inspired designers to create new designs that evoked, but also re-interpreted past styles for the present.[127] This cultural mood influenced English tailoring, principally through the work of Nutters of Savile Row, which opened in 1969. That establishment, which was led by Tommy Nutter and the cutter Edward Sexton soon became renowned for injecting bespoke tailoring with much-needed fashionable ideas. The Nutter look typically combined historical references, daring new styling and the use of eye-catching textiles such as patterned tweeds.[128] Tommy Nutter was photographed in 1973 wearing a three-piece suit of his own design, which features a re-interpretation of 1920s Oxford bags and a jacket with wide notched lapels that are reminiscent of 1930s and 1940s styles (Fig. 8.5). This flamboyant outfit is made from houndstooth and Glenurquhart checked cloth used to contrasting effect, which was a signature way of employing tweeds within Nutter's work.

Tweeds in French Couture: Elegant and Correct?

The use of tweeds by French couturiers continued to be influenced by codes of social and sartorial formality between the early 1950s and the mid-1960s. Based on her study of the 1947 to 1957 period, Lesley Miller confirms the debates already established in this book, namely, that there was an "etiquette of textiles," which significantly influenced couturiers' choice of fabric for specific garments. She notes that this etiquette: "observed the season ... the time of day ... and the wearer's age, as well as the nature of the event" and that "Fibre, colour, structure and embellishment all played a part." Based on her analysis of the views of Genevieve Antoine Dariaux, the *directrice* of Nina Ricci, Miller further states that in the winter season:

> tweed suits in brown, autumnal shades were suitable for morning (not black), and a woollen suit in a solid colour (not black or brown) for lunch, a wool dress and contrasting

town coat in a vivid colour for afternoon... . A wool or crepe dress could be worn for early evening, and a silk, velvet or coloured brocade cocktail outfit for theatre openings and black-tie dinner parties."[129]

Miller acknowledges that Dariaux showed a notable preference for plain-colored fabrics, which may have influenced her advice that tweeds were only for morning wear in both the winter and spring seasons.[130] It is therefore worth examining further evidence about the use of tweeds within the sartorial and social codes that elite, couture customers still had to negotiate between the early 1950s and the mid-1960s. Leading Paris-based designers such as Christian Dior and Cristobal Balenciaga had a dominating influence on international, women's fashion in the 1950s.[131] In his book, *The Little Dictionary of Fashion: a guide to dress sense for every woman* of 1954, Dior states under the entry for "Tweed," that they are:

> The most popular of all the British materials. They have been copied in every country but have never been made better than in Great Britain. In the last few years tweeds have extended their use even for dressy suits. I think they are extremely elegant. To wear them in the country is a "must." At one time you could only get tweeds in a rather heavy weight but now you can get them in all weights and qualities and colours.[132]

Dior further states under the heading of "Holidays" that "You can wear skirts, or slacks, tweeds or cottons, sweaters or blouses; all the comfy, gay and casual clothes you wish."[133] He is therefore clear about the continued appropriateness of wearing tweeds within the informal contexts of the country and holidays. Notably, Dior also strikes a more ambiguous note than Dariaux, by acknowledging that some tweeds can be used to make "dressy suits" that are "extremely elegant."[134] Among the tweeds used by Dior, he repeatedly employed the dogtooth pattern, which is known in France as "*le pied de poule*" in his collections. This checked, tweed pattern was also engraved on the bottles that held his first perfume "Miss Dior" which was launched in 1947. The Prince of Wales check, which is an adaptation of the Scottish estate tweed the Glenurquhart check, was another cloth associated with masculine tailoring that was often used by Dior for female garments.[135]

Tweeds were widely used to make suits, or *tailleurs* by Paris couturiers in the 1950s and they were also employed to create coats, jackets, skirts and dresses. That versatility and the huge diversity of weights, textures and colors available meant that these textiles were not solely used for informal, morning wear. For example, Palais Galliera has in its collections a Dior dress of autumn/winter 1953, which was designed for early evening and that is made from a pale blueish, gray, mixture tweed. In that year, this dress was worn with long satin evening gloves in a French *Vogue* feature titled "Au diner: une robe de tweed."[136] An article in American *Vogue* titled "Six Pages of Tweed: An International Fashion" suggests that these textiles were particularly widely used in the autumn/winter 1953, collections. It stated:

> No word in the fashion vocabulary has worked harder this year than – tweed. From the town suit to the little dinner dress, tweed's the fabric most often seen; designers in Paris, America, Italy, Ireland and London tweeded practically all of their most important clothes. It's hard to imagine a smart winter wardrobe in which tweeds don't play a starring part ... and it wouldn't have been much of a surprise the way things went in the collections, to have come across a tweed ball dress. There were pailletted tweeds ... wonderful turbans of draped tweed, tweed coats with sumptuous linings of mink.[137]

This quote reveals that although an "etiquette of textiles" was important within the elite couture market, couturiers did not always strictly adhere to these shifting codes in the early 1950s. A description of Coco Chanel's wardrobe in American *Vogue* of September 1963 reveals the continued tensions and ambiguities between the tweed suit as a symbol of modern informality and the persistence of the sartorial etiquette codes that still influenced elite French couture. The article commented about Chanel that she "lives in her offhand tweed suits, her underplayed late-day clothes, which are, for many, the chosen uniform of the twentieth century."[138]

Tweed and Women's Fashion for the Youth Market

Young British designers of womenswear turned to the innovative use of tweeds between the mid-1950s and the 1960s. The chapter now offers an analysis of tweed garments by the new, dynamic designers who emerged in that era such as Mary Quant and Jean Muir. In 1973, the London Museum (now the Museum of London) held a retrospective exhibition called "Mary Quant's London," which featured garments made from a diverse range of textiles, including linen, georgette, PVC and crepe. The exhibition catalog shows that in her early designs, Quant appropriated British woolen textiles associated with men's tailoring, such as flannel, striped suitings, striped tweed and Harris Tweed. These cloths were sometimes combined with historical stylistic references used in new ways and they were always re-interpreted to form a modern image of youthful femininity.[139]

A woman's outfit of 1957–8 was described in the "Mary Quant's London" catalog as follows "Rust-red Norfolk-style jacket; matching Harris tweed knickerbockers with camel, black and white checks; worn with pinafore dress."[140] Although Norfolk jackets and knickerbockers were still made for some male customers of Savile Row, by 1959, as discussed earlier in this chapter, they were no longer widely worn by men.[141] In the late 1950s, it was truly radical of Quant to seize on these outmoded symbols of British masculinity and to re-interpret them for young women in a fun and witty way. Notably, the Harris Tweed jacket and knickerbockers were inspired by a similar historical era to the revivalist designs of Dior's New Look, which had a lingering influence on the fashions of the late 1950s. Quant, however, approached this nostalgia in a completely new and different way by taking styles from men's sportswear and making them youthful and contemporary. These comfortable, masculine clothes formed a stark contrast to the mature, formal styles and restrictive underwear typically associated with Paris and London couture in the 1950s, as shown by the Hardy Amies suit illustrated (Fig. 8.6).[142] Another Quant design in tweed of 1960 that typified her simple youthful look is held by the Victoria and Albert Museum (Plate 18). This red tweed dress epitomized Quant's new approach to dressing the female body, which she recalled, as follows: "I wanted everyone to retain the grace of a child and not to have to become stilted, confined, ugly beings. So I created clothes that worked and moved and allowed people … to retain this precious freedom."[143]

In October 1963, the American magazine *Life*, featured an article, "Brash New Breed of British Designers," which focused on young creators of womenswear, including Jean Muir, Mary Quant, Sally Tuffin and Marion Foale. The easy-fitting and informal clothes featured were made in a range of textiles, although tweeds and knitted fabrics were predominant. A garment by Kenneth Sweet, for example, was described as follows: "Race track checks … are newly bright in wrap-around tweed coat" (Plate 19). The vivid colorway of this checked tweed was, in fact, not new because in

Figure 8.6 Enid Boulting wearing a Hardy Amies tweed suit. Photograph by Norman Parkinson, British *Vogue*, February 1954. © Norman Parkinson Ltd/courtesy Norman Parkinson Archive, London.

the 1930s the Otterburn Mill was producing similar cloths for the womenswear market in only slightly less vibrant shades.[144] This outfit shows, however, that tweeds were often re-interpreted by young designers by incorporating them into an overall look that was innovative. The Kenneth Sweet coat, for example, is short and unstructured in style and it is worn with a hairstyle, make-up and accessories that together epitomize the "irreverent" British youth style of the era. Furthermore, in the photograph by Norman Parkinson this outfit is framed by two iconically British red phone boxes, which echoes the strong emphasis throughout the *Life* article on symbols of London, including Chelsea street signs. These images exemplify the media developments that led Breward to comment that "By 1966 the whole of London appeared to dominate the fashion consciousness of the world."[145]

Harris Tweed featured in the mid-1960s collections of the London-based company Jane and Jane, which were designed by Jean Muir and aimed at young women. Mary Brogan wrote on December 6, 1964 in the *Sunday Telegraph* that "Harris tweed, probably the best known of all, was used this autumn for a complete collection by … Jane and Jane."[146] A *Vogue* feature of September, 1964, "Young Idea's top export the nifty English look," which was shot by David Bailey in outdoor, country environments included a dress from that collection. This fashion spread stated that "Nowadays from Zurich to San Francisco, the English look means clothes that are dashing, daring, dynamic."[147] Significantly, the Jane and Jane dress in Harris Tweed was the visual and textural antithesis of the expendable pop textiles such as shiny PVC, synthetic fibers and paper, which are stereotypically associated with London fashions of the 1960s. This outfit was described as "A yoked smock for a bright yokel, in tough olive homespun tweed for mollocking in pastures and for harvesting compliments. Here it looks most demure."[148] Muir's work had an emphasis on quality of cut and materials, which set it apart from much of the British fashion for young women of the era. Nevertheless, the fact that the setting of this Vogue feature of 1964 and Muir's designs have a strong rural influence, complexifies the popular image that the young "English look" of the mid-1960s was exclusively metropolitan in inspiration.

It is notable that in the examples researched for this chapter, young British womenswear designers tended to use tweeds, which historically have an explicitly Scottish, or British provenance and that derive from the more "masculine" types of tweed. By contrast, as already noted, the more "feminine" *fantaisie* tweeds, which even if made in Britain derived from an Anglo-French design heritage, were highly popular with Paris-based and London couturiers. This issue of gendered tweed design and the related play on menswear styles for women was a significant element of the androgynous styles that emerged in Britain and internationally between the mid-1960s and the late 1970s.

A fashion spread of October 15, 1967 in British *Vogue*, "Young Idea's Green Belt Girl" depicts the model Twiggy wearing a series of outfits in tweed within a rural, woodland setting. This feature appeared at a time that Whiteley has identified as a turning point between the pop emphasis on embracing technology and expendability and the focus within the emergent hippie counter-culture on "harmony with nature" and wearing natural, rather than synthetic fibers for ecological reasons.[149] Notably, the tweeds worn by Twiggy incorporate colorings and patterns long associated with masculine, sporting attire to be worn in the country. An outfit by Marrian-McDonnell, for example, is described as made from "Harris tweed, coloured green like misty moss" which has been made into a "three-piece suit new style, shaped jacket, waistcoat and shorts." This jacket also has "snakeskin patches on the shoulders, elbows and collar," which is a fashionable re-interpretation of

Figure 8.7 Twiggy wearing a Harris Tweed jacket, waistcoat and shorts by Marrian-McDonnell, October 15, 1967. Photograph by Jeanloup Sieff/ *Vogue* © The Condé Nast Publications Ltd.

Figure 8.8 Twiggy wearing a tweed trouser suit by Paul Babb and Pamela Proctor, October 15, 1967.
Photograph by Jeanloup Sieff/ *Vogue* © The Condé Nast Publications Ltd.

the leather detailing that featured on some nineteenth-century shooting jackets (Fig. 8.7). A "bark brown" tweed trouser suit by Paul Babb and Pamela Proctor for Twiggy, includes similar detailing on a "long, skinny jacket" that is worn with wide trousers with turn-ups (Fig. 8.8).[150]

These outfits of 1967 show the relevance of the statement by Matless that "neither nostalgia nor conservatism are simple phenomena."[151] They demonstrate, in particular, the enduring power of the man's tailored suit in tweed as a symbol of modernity and masculinity. Arnold argues that since the 1920s androgyny had been "associated with the search for greater independence for women, the merging of genders signifying a desire to inscribe masculine power upon the female body." As the Second Wave of feminism took on a concerted momentum in the late 1960s, these gender debates were vividly expressed through fashionable dress.[152]

Womenswear and Tweeds in the 1970s

The androgynous look was also important in the USA and internationally in the 1970s. Ralph Lauren's strong interest in menswear, for example, had a significant influence on his first womenswear collection of 1972, as an article in *The New York Times* stated, "With all the talk about classics, someone was bound to bring back the mannish tailored suit. Fortunately it was Ralph Lauren."[153] A fashionable look of the late 1970s, which involved women adopting men's Harris Tweed, tailored jackets was inspired by Ralph Lauren's clothes for Diane Keaton in the Woody Allen film, *Annie Hall*, of 1977. Lauren himself stated that Keaton's wardrobe included "Oversized jackets and vests, floppy men's hats and cowboy boots."[154] The journalist Joan Juliet Buck commented that this "truly new" androgynous way of dressing, which involved a man's Harris Tweed jacket "over everything" was highly influential at the time.[155] Significantly, Fred Davis questioned the potential of this look to challenge conventional gender roles and appearances. He stated:

> It is characteristic … for cross-gender clothing signals, even the more common and varie-gated women's borrowings from men, to be accompanied by some symbolic qualification … A striking case in point is the 1970s "Annie Hall look" with its comic undercutting of claims to masculinity through a gross oversizing of the men's clothes worn by the female.[156]

CONCLUSION

A significant shift of the post-war era was that tweeds began to have strong associations with notions of the past, while simultaneously being connected to the present and fashion innovation. These developments reflected wider cultural tensions and ambivalences related to notions of modernity and tradition. In the 1960s and 1970s, as the styling of men's and women's fashion became more pluralistic and influenced by nostalgia, the strong cultural and historical associations of tweeds became newly significant to their continued appeal. Significantly, the use of these textiles within historically inspired fashions of that era cannot simply be understood as associated with an imaginative escape to the past. As this chapter has shown, androgynous and rurally inspired tweed garments of the late 1960s were connected with emerging political debates related to ecology and feminism. It is notable that "mannish" tailoring in tweeds, this time with trousers, re-emerged as a contested symbol of female independence, nearly a century after the man's tweed suit first began to influence female dress.

9
TRADITION AND INNOVATION, 1981-2014

Tweeds currently retain their globally recognized cultural significance as a key element of Britain's fashion identity. That is despite the continued trend toward dramatic decline in tweed production in the UK from the 1980s onwards.[1] The chapter examines the changing scale and character of those sections of the British woolen industry that made tweeds between 1981 and 2014. That investigation primarily focuses on the two branches of woolen manufacturing that predominantly, or exclusively, made tweeds, namely those from the Outer Hebrides and the rest of Scotland. The distinctive features of and inter-connections between designing and making tweeds in different locations in the UK are also explored through contemporary case studies of the Lovat Mill, Linton Tweeds and Harris Tweed Hebrides. These examples reveal that British firms who are making tweeds today continue to be successful in fiercely competitive, international luxury markets, through selling cloths to leading fashion companies such as Chanel, J. Crew, Ralph Lauren and Dries van Noten.[2] A diverse range of interpretations of tweed within men's and women's global fashion between 1981 and 2014 are also examined. This includes a particular focus on the links of tweeds with notions of British style in the work of both UK and international fashion houses.

DECLINE, INNOVATION, AND LUXURY: MAKING AND SELLING BRITISH TWEEDS

Hardill's study shows that woolen manufacturing in Yorkshire, which was still by far the largest center of that industry in the UK had suffered major contraction by 1981.[3] Research for this book has identified that by 2014, the few firms trading from Yorkshire that made tweeds and other woolen cloths, included Abraham Moon, Marling & Evans Ltd, Marton Mills, and William Bliss & Son Ltd.[4] By the early 1980s, the West of England wool textiles industry was in an even worse condition than the Yorkshire trade, which amounted to a state of terminal decline. In 2014, the only manufacturer of tweeds and other wool cloths for apparel left in that region was Fox Brothers

& Co. Ltd of Somerset.[5] Key shifts within the global wool textiles industry will now be explored in order to place the subsequent discussion of Scottish and Hebridean tweed manufacturing in context.

Wool Textiles in UK and International Contexts, 1981–2014

Jenkins notes that a significant factor, which continued to affect the global consumption of wool textiles from the early 1980s onwards was the increased consumer preference for knitwear and casual clothing in cotton and synthetic fibers.[6] Furthermore, in the 1980s, the broad-shouldered, unstructured Armani suit came to be an icon of contemporary style. This new "Italian look" attained popular currency through copies at lower levels of the market. It prompted a major international trend for men's and women's tailored clothes to be increasingly made from lightweight, supple, wool or synthetic blends, many of which were made in Italy (Fig. 9.1). These fashion changes meant that the established products of British manufacturers of tweed had less appeal in UK and international markets.[7]

Many manufacturing industries in Britain continued to suffer severe decline from the beginning of the 1980s onwards, a scenario that Honeyman argues was particularly acute in textile and apparel production.[8] By the early 1980s, the British wool textiles industry had fallen substantially from its previous position as the largest producer in the world and its output of woven cloths was only about 25 percent of the 315 million square meters that were produced in 1950.[9] The continuing decline in that manufacturing sector was due to a complex mixture of major international changes in economic, industrial, cultural and social contexts and the British response to these shifts. Jenkins argues, for example, that the performance of the UK industry in that era was in marked contrast to the phenomenal success of Italy, which led world exports. The British wool industry consumption of wool dropped to 76 million kilograms by 1993, just under half of that used in 1972. Whereas, in a similar period Italian consumption of that fiber almost doubled to reach over 200 million kilograms in 1992.[10] In that period, Italy's stellar success continued to be a significant factor in Britain's declining share of UK and world markets for woven wool textiles for apparel, including tweeds.[11]

The emergence of new and increasing competition from India, Turkey and particularly from China, between 1970 and 1993 was noted by Ann Walker in a *Financial Times* report on the Western European wool industry. In 1970, China's consumption of raw wool for manufacturing was only 3.4 percent of world supply. However, figures prepared by the International Wool Textile Organisation show an exponential increase in the following four decades. By 2013, China consumed 48 percent of the total world imports of raw wool, as well as producing 14 percent of the global wool supply. In that year, India was the second largest consumer of imported wool at 12 percent, followed by Italy and the Czech Republic, which each accounted for 5 percent. Notably, these figures show a marked decline in the relative global position of Italy as an importer of raw wool for manufacturing.[12]

The major and ongoing shifts within global clothing and textile production encouraged the cyclical re-negotiation of the Multi-Fibre Arrangement and its continued existence up until 1994. Jenkins argued that this international trade agreement "perhaps" lessened the pressure on British textile manufacturers, while also accommodating economic expansion in "developing" countries.[13] The global trend toward clothing and textile production moving principally toward Asian countries

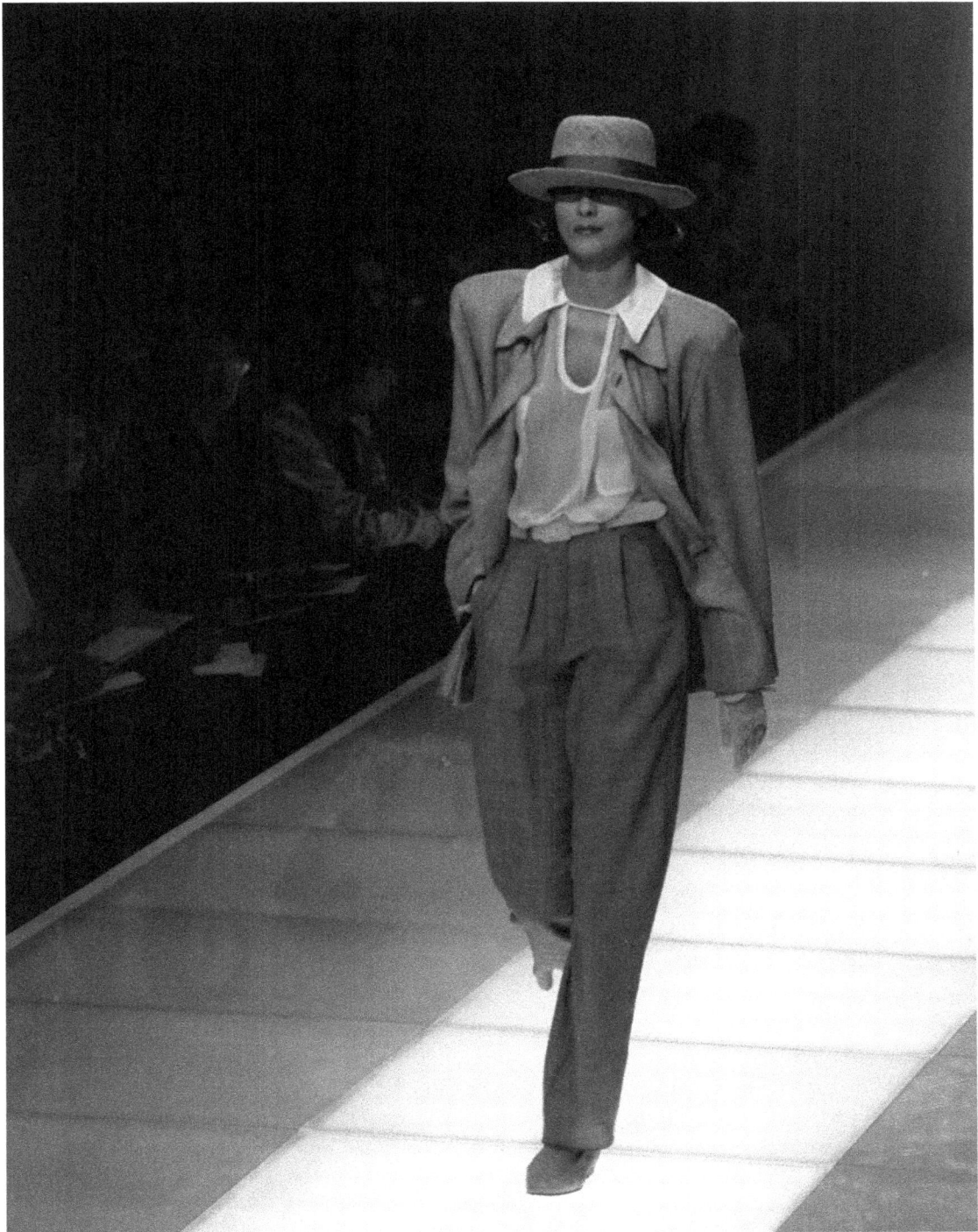

Figure 9.1 Woman's tailored jacket and trousers by Giorgio Armani, Milan, 1986. Photograph by Nino Leto, Mondadori Portfolio via Getty Images.

proved inexorable, however, as Honeyman noted in 2000. She stated that the "MFA may have created a relatively stable environment for international trade in clothing and textiles, but it was powerless to protect the domestic industry from real and growing competition."[14]

Jenkins argued in 2003 that poor standards of production control, planning, marketing and pricing in the British wool textiles industry contributed to its decline. He also noted that it had "been outshone by Italy in response to fashion and market changes. The Italian industry recognized early the importance of fashion and style, and showed itself inventive and willing to change. The British industry has been perceived as old-fashioned, uninventive and reluctant to change."[15] The chapter will now consider to what extent these comments related to the specific contexts of tweed design and manufacturing in Scotland and the Outer Hebrides.

Harris Tweed Industry, 1981–2012

The tweed industry in the Outer Hebrides fared considerably better in the first half of the 1980s than it had in the mid-to-late 1970s. Output reached 5.3 million yards in 1984, the highest figure attained since the late 1960s. In 1985, just shy of 5 million yards were woven, but this high figure disguises the fact that the industry was just beginning to enter an extended period of major contraction. By the late 1980s, Harris Tweed manufacturing was experiencing serious decline, which Hunter argues was largely due to the collapse of sales to North America.[16] The over-reliance of the industry on that market was encouraged by the preferential tariffs for single-width tweeds in the USA already discussed in Chapter 8. Ian A. Mackenzie was Secretary of the Weaver's Union during this period, which he described as follows:

> from the late seventies to 1985, the pound declined in value so Harris Tweed was getting cheaper all through these years and we were piling stuff into the States and people over-bought ... Then when the currency started turning against us, people starting cutting prices ... and that was just driving the cloth so much downmarket ... at the same time fashion was changing, and you know the gurus were saying Harris Tweed was out ... But I would say the main reason for the decline was the overbuying by the Americans, over-selling here, and over-concentration on that market because it was so easy ... you just piled the stuff out in the same styles and the other markets, the European markets, the Far Eastern markets were left and then when things turned really bad, the industry had to go to all these markets and virtually start again.[17]

By 1990, production of Harris Tweed had declined to 1,382,000 meters and apart from a brief period of improvement between 1993–1995, output has been consistently lower than that figure ever since.[18] The Chief Executive of the Harris Tweed Association commented in his review of 1990 that although its "impact on the island community was severe" the downturn in production was not as bad as that experienced by the rest of British textile manufacturing.[19] Nevertheless, the problems experienced by the Harris Tweed industry were extremely serious. The difficulties of the 1990s and the strategies taken to address them were summarized by Duncan Martin, Chairman of the Harris Tweed Authority in a report of 1998. He stated:

> It has to be recognised that the Harris Tweed industry was dying. Radical action had to be taken if the fate of so many other communities built round textiles was to be avoided. Many of the large scale customers of the glory years such as Hepworths, Burtons and

Dunns have gone or else changed beyond recognition. The world is no longer beating a path to our door to buy Harris Tweed. We have to change, adapt, evolve to satisfy the present day marketplace or pay the price.[20]

The key problems identified around 1990 included an "alarming" decline in the market for Harris Tweed, particularly in North America, and a reliance on antiquated weaving equipment. Furthermore, 85 percent of the weavers were over fifty and there was no recruitment of younger weavers, largely because of a lack of local, public confidence in the industry. In addition, new market research in Europe and the USA revealed that customers desired a wider, softer, lighter version of Harris Tweed, which was better suited to contemporary garment manufacturing methods and changes in consumer tastes. In response to these difficulties the Harris Tweed Association set up a working party, which included representatives from the Weaver's Union; Producers; Lews Castle College; *Comhairle nan Eilean Siar* (the local council); Highlands and Islands Enterprise and Western Isles Enterprise. This group agreed a radical program of modernization that focused on investment in new technologies, product development, marketing and re-training, while simultaneously preserving the key, defining characteristics of Harris Tweed. By 1993, a new pedal-driven double-width loom had been developed by Bonas Griffith Ltd.[21] Hunter argues that although this major change was unpopular with some of the weavers it reflected the commitment of the working party to retaining the existing definition, while addressing the needs of the contemporary market.[22] The ranges of the local mills also began to include relatively lighter and softer versions of Harris Tweed, which were having some success in the more fashion-driven ladies market. By 1998, all European Union applications to support investment in new technologies had been successful, 250 weavers had been re-trained and funding had also been secured for a major marketing campaign to promote the "new" Harris Tweed.[23]

The pivotal achievement of that transitional era was the passing of the Harris Tweed Act of 1993. The main purpose of this Act is to protect the benefits to the economy and people of the Outer Hebrides generated by this indigenous industry. This legislation contains the concise definition and detailed specifications already discussed in Chapter 2. The Act also established the Harris Tweed Authority (HTA), a statutory body, which replaced the non-statutory Harris Tweed Association, as the main organization representing the industry. Along with the famous Orb trademark, the Act has been crucial in helping prevent Harris Tweed from becoming just another generic product, which can be produced anywhere by anyone.[24]

Since 2006, the Harris Tweed industry has undergone a further period of significant restructuring. In that year, Brian Haggas, whose family firm had long been established in Yorkshire woolen manufacturing, bought the KM Group, which meant that he controlled the vast majority of the tweed industry in the Hebrides. The mills he bought were subsequently established under the name of Harris Tweed Scotland. Haggas had a new strategy to streamline the industry, which was to prove highly controversial on the Islands. His plan was to reduce the number of patterns woven from over a hundred to just four and to also drastically reduce the number of colors of yarn. The idea was to use all of the Harris Tweed woven to make just five types of men's tailored jackets under his own clothing label of Brook Taverner. At that time, the small mill at Carloway, Lewis, which was owned by Harris Tweed Textiles Manufacturing Ltd was the only other one in operation and Haggas's strategy therefore had a huge impact on the industry. It meant that there was limited cloth for well-established, international customers to buy and industry strategies to pursue new global

Figure 9.2 Nike, Harris Tweed trainers from Rif LA in downtown Los Angeles, 2010. Photograph by Bob Chamberlin/Los Angeles Times via Getty Images.

fashion markets were abandoned. Furthermore, many independent weavers were left without the yarns they needed to fulfill orders.[25] A document produced by the HTA stated that "By 2008 it was looking increasingly likely that the industry was on its last legs as Haggas announced his intention to cease production of the mill for the last six months of the year." A further low point was reached in 2009, when only 454,000 meters were stamped, the smallest output ever recorded in the industry.[26]

In retrospect, it is clear that these controversial developments had a positive and galvanizing effect on the industry. In 2007, they prompted the founding of a new Lewis-based firm, Harris Tweed Hebrides. Furthermore, the passionate debates about the future of the industry attracted substantial media coverage, which raised the profile of Harris Tweed in the UK and internationally. The brand was further boosted by Nike using the cloth to make trainers that were aimed at young consumers (Fig. 9.2). Since 2009, the industry has achieved a remarkable resurgence, with sales in 2012 reaching just over the 1,000,000 meters mark.[27] Recent developments will be discussed in detail later in the chapter through the case study of Harris Tweed Hebrides.

Tweed Production in Scotland, 1981–2014

After 1981, Scottish woven wool textile manufacturing, whose primary product continued to be tweeds, continued to contract. In 1984, the NASWM evolved into a new body called the Scottish Woollen Industry (SWI). The majority of firms in Scotland were members of that organization, therefore a survey of the SWI Annual Reports between 1985 and 1991 provides a revealing picture of key developments.[28] In 1985, the SWI had forty-seven members, including thirty-seven wool cloth manufacturers, five spinning firms, three dyers and two finishers. By 1991, it had only thirty-five members including twenty-seven cloth manufacturers, three spinning companies, three dyers and two finishers. By 1990, the total turnover of companies was £90 million and this represented a decrease of 13 percent since 1985.

The SWI reports also yield revealing information about UK and international sales. Between 1984 and 1985, the domestic market accounted for 36 percent of sales, but by 1991 it had continued to decline to constitute only 28 percent of woven cloth sold. The largest export market had changed from the USA to Japan, which accounted for 19 percent of sales in 1990, a figure that was virtually double that of 1984.[29] The SWI President, J. Alistair Buchanan, in his Report of 1991, stated that it was a year that "our industry will not remember with any affection." He discussed the reasons for this, as follows:

> Most of us no doubt felt that we had taken the necessary action in re-equipping and streamlining in the mid 1980's ready to take advantage of what promised to be a bright future for Scottish textiles, alas this was not to be. The unfortunate method our Government used to control inflation hit us in the home market, and also damaged our competitiveness overseas, whilst the Middle East Crisis, combined with what is hopefully a hiccup in the Japanese economy, has taken a vicious toll on our export sales. Sadly, we have also suffered from the continual decline of the United States economy causing massive re-structuring and cut backs for many of our major export customers.[30]

The decline in manufacturing continued in the late 1990s, as revealed by a *Briefing Paper on The Scottish Textile and Clothing Industry* of 2000. This paper reported: "Over the last 10–15 years, there has been substantial contraction in the number of weaving businesses in Scotland, with several well-known names going out of business." The firms cited were all renowned manufacturers of tweeds, namely J. & J. Crombie, G. & G. Kynochs of Keith, and Hunters of Brora. This report also indicated that employment in woven textiles in Scotland had declined from 5,900 in 1987, to 2,900 in 1997. The gross output of this industry was 202.1 (£million) in 1997 and the value of its exports was 103.0 (£million) in 1998.[31] Significantly, the author of this report ominously warned under the heading of "The Future," that it: "Is strong only for niche and quality players – producers cannot afford to be ordinary."[32]

In 2014, the Scottish manufacturers who design and weave tweeds as part of their ranges include long-established firms that have survived the challenges of recent decades and encouragingly some new firms. These companies cover a wide range of geographical areas. For example, in the Scottish Borders, the Lovat Mill and Robert Noble Ltd are the only firms of any size that design and weave these textiles as one of their primary products.[33] In the Highlands, tweeds are made by the major firm of Johnstons of Elgin and by the very small-scale, Knockando Woolmill Company Ltd. Johnstons of Elgin have enjoyed an illustrious history as designers and weavers of tweed from the mid-nineteenth century onwards and from the mid-1970s, they diversified successfully into knitwear.[34] Today, they make tweeds and other woven cloths, knitwear and accessories in cashmere and fine woolens for international luxury brands including Christopher Kane, Chanel and Hermes and for their own label. Johnstons are by far the largest firm in Scotland, which includes tweeds in their product range and in 2014 they employed around 800 people.[35]

Langholm in Dumfrieshire is the trading address of Neill Johnstone, who designs novelty tweeds for womenswear and Drove Weaving Ltd who weave tweeds and other wool fabrics to commission, including making some of the cloths that are designed by Dashing Tweeds.[36] Alexanders of Scotland are now the only firm in Aberdeenshire who design and weave tweeds and other woolen cloths. On the Scottish islands, firms that weave tweeds include Bute Fabrics Ltd, who make design-led furnishing fabrics and the very small-scale operations of Ardlanish, Isle of Mull Weavers and the Islay Woollen Mill.[37]

INNOVATION AND TRADITION IN CONTEMPORARY TWEED MANUFACTURE

The design, production and selling of tweeds within UK and international contexts will now be explored through three case studies of firms in the Outer Hebrides; the Scottish Borders and the North of England.

Harris Tweed Hebrides

This company was set up in 2007 and is based in the village of Shawbost on Lewis. It was the idea of Ian A. Mackenzie, then the Chief Executive of the Harris Tweed Authority, Ian Taylor, a leading oil company executive, and the current Non-Executive Chairman, Brian Wilson, a former UK Minister for Trade. This firm's main business is designing and manufacturing Harris Tweed to be used for menswear, womenswear, accessories and interiors. The setting up of Harris Tweed Hebrides (HTH) was a major boost to the industry as a whole because, once established, it provided a significant source of work for weavers and yarn for small, independent producers.[38] In 2013, I visited the mill and interviewed the Chief Executive Ian A. Mackenzie and the firm's Head Designer Ken Kennedy. These interviews form the primary focus of this case study.

Manufacturing processes employed at the Shawbost mill are characteristic of the unique structure of the Harris Tweed industry. They involve the dyeing, blending and spinning of Cheviot wool to make yarn, which is warped at the mill and then distributed to weavers to be handwoven at their home. The cloth is then sent back to the mill where it is inspected, darned as necessary, washed and finished. In 2013, HTH employed seventy-five staff at Shawbost and the firm was so busy that a night shift was being worked all year round.[39] At that time, the firm was using between 120 and 130 self-employed weavers, almost all of whom were working with double-width looms. In contrast, only about six single-width weavers were being used, which was mainly for the production of sample lengths. To put these figures into context, in 2013 there were only about 140 weavers working across the Harris Tweed industry as a whole.[40]

The success of HTH is demonstrated by the fact that between 2007 and 2013 its output increased five-fold. In the latter year the firm helped to nurture growth and sustainability in the local weaving force by purchasing seven double-width looms, which were leased to new entrants to the industry.[41] Mackenzie also noted their role in helping to "build confidence out there that weaving is a job worth having," by providing work all year round, rather than for just six months of the year, which they have achieved primarily by encouraging customers to place orders earlier. Owing to these efforts by HTH and others in the industry, Mackenzie argued that weaving capacity had "increased by maybe as much as 20 percent" between 2010 and 2013.[42]

Design and sampling are also carried out at the Shawbost mill. Between 2007 and early 2014, the Head Designer at HTH was Ken Kennedy, a Hebridean who had worked in the industry on and off since the 1950s and who trained by learning "on the job" from an experienced designer of Harris Tweed.[43] Every year, Kennedy puts together an autumn/winter range that consists of a mixture of new and existing designs and which is shown at the leading textile trade show, *Première Vision* in Paris. HTH are also asked by key customers to create "specials," meaning bespoke designs.[44] The firm receives many sample requests: for example, when I visited the mill Kennedy was preparing designs for a leading French fashion house. These sampling processes are very costly, because only a small proportion of requests turn into actual orders.[45] By early 2014, the firm had recruited a new Design Assistant, who stated that, "For me, it's about modernising traditional patterns and designs." Her main task was introducing "new technology into a business steeped in traditional design methods."[46]

Most of the cloth woven by HTH is exported around the world, but the company also experienced major growth in the British market between 2010 and 2013. In that period, they saw a "five or six fold" increase in sales, so that in 2013 the UK market accounted for about 22 percent of their output. Mackenzie considered that this expansion was primarily because Harris Tweed started to be used by brands such as Topman, which are aimed at younger, more fashion-conscious consumers. These developments helped the industry's efforts to change perceptions among British retailers that Harris Tweed was principally a cloth for mature men. The fact that, as Mackenzie noted, "It's a scarce fabric, you can only make so much of it," in addition to its strong associations with the Hebrides, also means that Harris Tweed still has connotations of exclusivity and authenticity. Most clothing companies who buy Harris Tweed, apart from the top designer brands, put the Orb label on their finished garments, which is highly unusual because most textiles are entirely anonymous as to their maker at the point of sale.[47] This fact indicates that the Harris Tweed brand itself is a unique selling point, which endorses the cloth's associations of authenticity, place and heritage within contemporary UK and global markets.

HTH exports to Japan, Germany, France, Italy, Canada, Korea, China and the USA, which includes selling to firms such as Ralph Lauren, J. Crew and Dries van Noten. Mackenzie posited that Japan was HTH's main export market between 2011 and 2013, as it accounted for at least 40 percent of the firm's sales.[48] In January 2014, Brian Wilson stated that "Japan is still our major market but the exchange rate has moved against us there. It is a reminder of why we always need to seek diversification of both markets and sectors."[49] Despite these shifting contexts, Harris Tweed remains extremely popular in Japan and it is worth exploring the reasons for that success. Mackenzie commented that Harris Tweed appeals to Japanese consumers because "we score on: the brand, the colour … I think Britishness more than Scottishness…. and, you know, the whole story, the heritage, they love that." He explained why associations of Britishness were seen as positive in the contemporary Japanese market for textiles, by stating that "tradition and quality are two things that they see as being British. Over the last five years probably all over the world there's been a lot of this British tradition."[50]

Mackenzie also emphasized the innovatory ways in which Harris Tweed has been used in Japan and other Asian countries. He noted that when HTH started up about 95 percent of what they produced was used to make men's tailored sports jackets. That scenario has, however, changed dramatically in recent years so that menswear jacketing represents less than 50 percent of their market. That shift has primarily been driven by the wide range of products that customers in countries such as Japan and Korea make for men and women from Harris Tweed. Mackenzie noted that he had seen these cloths made into coats, jackets, waistcoats, trousers, footwear, belts, all kinds of bags, purses, and iPad covers in Japan, and he commented that "they would use it in more ways than any other market." He also stated about the Japanese context that it "is a high-price market and it's almost exclusively a young person's market, which you know, people still say Harris Tweed is an old person's cloth. It's not, more than half of what we make is for young people."[51] The HTA archive includes several cuttings from Japanese magazines, which show Harris Tweed being used in these wide-ranging and contemporary ways within men's and women's fashion. An edition of *GLAMB* of Autumn, 2011, for example, featured a male model wearing a tartan Harris Tweed biker jacket.[52]

A key way that HTH staff keep up a personal dialogue with existing customers and meet new ones is by regularly attending *Première Vision*. Mackenzie also noted that they see their agents there and "get a good feel on what's happening in every market." He also discussed the positive impact on customer relationships of visits to the Outer Hebrides, which involve witnessing the highly distinctive mode of Harris Tweed weaving whereby "these guys are there sitting at their own homes, pedalling away." Furthermore, experiencing the remote beauty of the Hebridean landscape gives clients a more nuanced understanding of the specific sense of place and identity linked to Harris Tweed, which encourages perceptions that the cloth is distinctive from other British quality woolens.[53]

Lovat Mill

Hawick in the Scottish Borders is the home of this firm. The business was formerly known as Teviotex Ltd, which had its origins in Blenkhorn Richardson & Co. Ltd, a large woolen manufacturing firm that closed in 1975.[54] This case study is primarily based on an interview of 2013 with Stephen Rendle, the Managing Director, and Chairman and Alan Cumming, the Design Director. In 2013, the Lovat Mill had twenty full-time equivalent staff, which meant that the company had more than doubled in size since 1998, which is a considerable achievement in a period of global recession. The firm's design and sales activities are based in the mill, as well as the manufacturing processes of yarn twisting, warping, weaving, inspection and darning.[55]

Rendle summed up the core identity of the Lovat Mill by stating that since 1998, when he and Cumming became involved, they had "re-built the business on tweed."[56] The approaches taken have involved both radical modernization and a re-evaluation of long-established aspects of the business. Rendle and Cumming have replaced all of the old machinery and invested in the latest production technologies in order to increase efficiency, quality and design flexibility. These changes have included investing £500,000 in a computerized automatic warping machine and a computerized drawing machine. In addition, weaving is carried out on up-to-date, Dornier looms, the latest of which are computerized and operated via a touch screen. However, the production of Lovat's high quality tweeds still involves hand-crafted elements as well as new technologies. For example, after

Figure 9.3 Woman's coat, Bernhard Willhelm, autumn/winter 2004/5, fabric by Lovat Mill. © National Museums Scotland, Edinburgh.

the cloth comes from the loom and before finishing, every piece is inspected face and back for faults. This painstaking process involves looking and running the hands over the cloth at the same time and any minor imperfections found are mended by hand. A further 100 percent inspection is carried out after the textile returns from being finished.[57]

The firm's design activities have also drawn on the history of the mill in order to develop new cloths. Rendle and Cumming inherited several, designer notebooks, which were created by T. B. Redpath, an employee of Blenkhorn Richardson & Co. Ltd. These books date from the late nineteenth and early twentieth centuries and they contain a huge range of woolen samples, including tweeds, along with making particulars for each design. In the early days of their business these notebooks were "part of the inspiration" of what Rendle and Cumming wanted to do and in 2013 they still formed an important starting point for many of the Mill's new tweed designs.[58]

National Museums Scotland has in its collections a woman's "Kangoo" coat, which was created by the Belgian designer, Bernhard Willhelm for autumn/winter 2004/5. It has features that are based on a kangaroo including a hood with ears, a tail and two front pockets, which are pouch-like in shape (Fig.9.3). The coat is made from a black, blue and green birdseye weave fabric that was woven by the Lovat Mill and inspired by a menswear sample in one of the nineteenth-century designer notebooks. This womenswear garment confirms that many international fashion designers are inspired by tweeds that strongly connote the British tailoring tradition, even if these associations are subverted by the use of unusual styling.[59]

Cumming confirmed that although "85 percent of what we produce is tweed," they also make worsted suitings, which are particularly popular in Japan and Northern Europe. The Lovat Mill mostly sell medium-weight cloths of around 450g, but they also make a very wide range of weights from 250gms up to very heavy sporting tweeds at 1,200gms.[60] The majority of the textiles made by the Mill are used for menswear. However, Rendle noted that the "womenswear side is growing."[61] This prompted a discussion about how gender continues to play an important role in the design of tweeds. Cumming's view is that when designing for women, making lighter weights than for men is "not so important." Instead, customers are often looking for textiles that are finished differently from similar menswear cloths so that they are "softer" with "more supple finishes."[62]

In 2013, the Lovat Mill product range included estate tweeds, bunches of stock patterns, collection and accessories. Estate tweeds were described by Rendle as a "small but defining" part of the business. In other words, although these cloths usually involve orders for short lengths this prestigious trade is helpful in building the reputation of a firm that sells to the international market for country clothing. The Lovat Mill currently makes 190 estate tweeds for private customers such as the Dukes of Westminster, Buccleuch, and Roxburghe, as well as making several regimental tweeds. As discussed in Chapter 2, they also design new patterns for UK and international customers who own estates in Britain. Indeed, Rendle posits that they are the "leading estate tweed weaver."[63]

Significantly, the biggest part of Lovat Mill's trade is "collection," which is the most fashion-driven area of the business. The annual cycle of design, sales and production activities at the Mill are therefore closely linked to that of the international fashion industry. The Lovat Mill's design team create two main collections of samples each year, for autumn/winter and spring/summer. Cumming commented on how designing bi-annual collections relates to the fact that fashion companies are now producing several collections per year. He stated that these shifts have had a "big effect on their business" and now they are also designing "all the way through the year, including talking to customers and doing design developments. It's a very dynamic process."[64]

The majority of British firms that make tweeds today have several international agents who represent them and a website that they sell through. They also exhibit at trade shows such as *Première Vision*. However, Rendle and Cumming have chosen not to engage in these sales activities other than having an agent in Japan.[65] Instead, their successful design and sales approach is "all about direct contact" and they make regular international trips to see customers. Clients also sometimes come to the Lovat Mill to discuss design ideas.[66] These processes are very costly because they involve a substantial amount of staff time and travel, as well as production time spent creating numerous sample designs, of which only a small percentage will turn into actual orders. This focus on design innovation and personal dialogue is, however, an integral element of the business, as Rendle emphasized when he said that it is "very important to evolve" and to "dedicate a good deal of resources to developing collections."[67]

Rendle and Cumming's excellent connections in fashion circles were made evident when the Lovat Mill featured in an article about Stella Tennant titled "A Very British Allure," in *Harper's Bazaar* of July 2013. The article begins with the author, Laura Beatty, a friend from Tennant's childhood, visiting the famous Scottish model at her home, near Berwick-upon-Tweed.[68] The pair then meet Cumming and Rendle for a tour of the Lovat Mill, which prompts Beatty to comment that "I think I know what tweed is. It's that stuff that looks and feels like a hedge dead with winter. How horribly wrong I find I am." She then discusses that the range of what Lovat makes challenges her perceptions of tweed by stating that "Lovat produces tweed for Scottish estates, practical cloth for crawling through bogs and blending in with the hills, dead-hedge material, but they also supply Brooks Brothers, Ralph Lauren, Margaret Howell … and Chanel, among many others."[69]

About 50 percent of the Lovat Mill's business comes from export sales, which are "in quite a few markets, so not over-dependent on any one."[70] Japan is an important market for the firm and Rendle has extensive experience of direct contact with their agent and customers in that country, who are mostly young designers and tailors. He described the appeal of Lovat's tweeds in Japan by stating that their customers see them as having connotations of "authenticity and where it comes from." Rendle had also observed a recent trend in Japan toward "young people wanting to wear weight" because they believed that early tweeds were heavy cloths. These developments underline the importance of perceptions of authenticity and heritage in that market for British tweeds.[71]

Linton Tweeds

This firm remains based in Carlisle in the North of England, as discussed in Chapter 8. Leslie Walker is the current Chairman and his son, Keith, has been Managing Director since 1994. The involvement of the Lintons ceased in the 1980s, but it continues to be a family firm because the Walkers now hold the majority of the shares.[72] The main business of Linton Tweeds continues to be designing and manufacturing luxury, novelty womenswear fabrics that are sold all around the world. The author interviewed Keith Walker and was shown round Shaddon Mill by Leslie Walker in 2013 and that material forms the primary focus of this case study.

The company employs about fifty people who work directly for Linton Tweeds. This includes a three-person design team, which is headed up by the Design and Sales Director, Rob Irvine. Shaddon Mill is run on a fully integrated basis, in that they twist yarns, dye, weave, finish, inspect and mend on site. Lintons consistently work at maintaining high quality standards and Keith stated that "because we need to reach a high bar we have to keep up constant improvements of our working practices."[73] The need to balance a significant level of design flexibility with quality, costs and profits are met by a combination of automated machinery and craft skills. On the mill tour with Leslie Walker I saw how the firm twists white, standard yarns together to make novelty yarns such as loop or gimp. This gives a significant amount of design flexibility and control because Linton Tweeds can then dye these yarns to the exact shade desired by their in-house designers, or a client. The firm also sources novelty yarns externally, which is integrally connected to their design approach, as Keith Walker confirmed. He stated:

> We have a reputation for innovation so we scour the world looking for unusual yarns. If we find a cellophane yarn we will try to weave with it. If we find ribbons we will try to weave with them. The idea is to be as different as possible. Our staff are very experienced at problem solving and our fabrics reflect their capabilities.[74]

This design diversity was very evident when I toured the mill, because each loom I saw was producing a different fabric. Lintons have twenty-eight Dornier, rapier looms that are fast and efficient and which crucially can cope with the novelty yarns used. The firm also has two wooden hand looms that are used because staff find that this is the quickest way to produce samples for customers, which increases their chances of securing orders. After weaving, hand-craft techniques of inspection and darning are used to ensure that all fabrics meet the highest quality standards, as described in the study of the Lovat Mill.[75]

The design, manufacturing and sales activities of Linton Tweeds are, similarly to the Lovat Mill, integrally linked to the rapidly shifting calendar of the global fashion industry. Walker commented on the fact that fashion houses are producing far more than two collections per year, by stating that "In some ways it's helpful to us because as a manufacturer we don't like two massive peaks in the year. We still have them but it's been flattened out a little bit by, as you say, the bigger customers want a constant supply of new fabrics."[76] In addition to this continual cycle of design development, Lintons still design two collections each year for spring/summer and autumn/winter. Walker explained that this continued bi-annual focus is because *Première Vision* is structured around two shows per year and it is the primary trade show that the firm attends in order to make direct contact with their existing clients and prospective new ones. Lintons also sell through their international agents. In addition, Walker and Rob Irvine travel regularly to the USA, Europe and Asia to have direct dialogue with garment designers about design development. The considerable efforts made by Lintons to have personal contact with international customers reveals the continued importance of that dialogue to the firm's design and sales processes, as previously discussed in Chapter 8. Walker commented about the firm's contemporary design practices, as follows:

> The biggest and longest established customers, it's a two way process we basically show them what we have designed in the collection. Either they'll like it as it is ... or they'll then develop something that we've already designed in a way that suits them, or in a colour that suits them. So, we work very closely designer to designer, to get the right thing for them. So, we're always keen to say that with our bigger customers we don't miss the fashion, or the market because we're working together to produce what they want.[77]

This international design dialogue also sometimes involves customers visiting Shaddon Mills and being shown samples from the company archive, to help them think about ideas for development with Linton's design team. This use of past designs as a starting point for developing new fabrics reveals that Linton's innovative textiles are often informed by the company's design heritage, whether recent or decades old. The fact that Linton's *fantaisie* tweeds are all created for womenswear reveals that gender continues to play an important role in the design of tweeds. It is clear that these strong gender distinctions are mainly linked to the highly textured appearance and loose weave of these textiles, rather than color, as even the firm's primarily black and navy tweeds are not used for menswear.[78]

Linton Tweeds have a long-established relationship with Chanel, which is currently their main customer. This mill also sells to, among others, Burberry, J. Crew, Balenciaga, Celine, and Lanvin.[79] These examples from their customer list reveal the international focus of Linton's business and in 2013 Walker estimated that exports formed "about 78 percent" of their sales.[80] Similarly to HTH, the main country that Linton Tweeds exports to is Japan and it accounts for about a third of their current production. Walker noted that the firm is also "very strong in the States and in Germany and a little bit in Italy as well and after that we deal with probably another 30 countries but it's all relatively small business." He also commented that Linton's popularity in Japan is connected to the reputation of "Britain as providing quality fabrics" and more particularly to the efforts the firm has made to promote itself there. Notably, the concepts of tradition and heritage appear to be much less significant to the popularity of the firm's textiles in Japan, compared to HTH and the Lovat Mill, which aligns with the strong emphasis on innovation discussed by Walker.[81]

CONSUMING TWEED IN GLOBAL DRESS AND FASHION, 1981–2014

Tweeds have been widely used within international fashion since the early 1980s. The continued popularity of these textiles is linked to the fact that their colors, weaves and textures give substantial scope for designs to be endlessly reinvented. For example, the fashion journalist, Lisa Armstrong argued in her report on the Chanel autumn/winter 2013, couture show (Plate 20) that, "Of all the big French houses, Chanel is blessed with a set of codes that repeatedly prove their adaptability and timelessness. When tweed's good even the most technologically advanced thermo-synthetics can't beat it."[82] The strong cultural and historical associations of tweed also provide great inspiration for developing new fashions that reference past styles. In her seminal book about women's fashion of the 1990s and early noughties, Caroline Evans stated:

> It is a fact, now, that our sense of what it is to be modern is profoundly bound up in the past and the future, they are overlapped in our imaginations. We can no longer just live in the present and the fashion designers I have looked at make this evident. They excavate ideas and sensibilities from our cultural imagination and make them visible as images and solid as objects.[83]

This sense of oscillation or overlapping between the past and present has been a major feature of international fashion between 1981 and 2014, which has strongly encouraged the prevalence of tweeds in men's and women's clothing.[84] In order to explore in more depth the range of cultural, social and historical meanings associated with tweeds, the chapter will now focus on their links to notions of British style.

Tweed and "British Style" in UK and Global Contexts

Around the world, tweeds are still recognized as a symbol of Britishness and since the 1980s these strong cultural associations have been played with by UK and international fashion designers. These developments have included reinforcing, shaping and contesting notions of British identity through garments made from tweed.[85] British style since the early 1980s has not simply been about the diverse range of clothing that is designed, made or worn in the UK. The way that this term is used in this chapter encapsulates shifting global perceptions of British identities and how that has been expressed in fashion through the use of textiles and other stylistic elements.

In an article about British style in *Harpers Bazaar* of July 2013, Avril Mair stated: "Romance, tradition, subversion and terrible weather … If one were to try to sum up British style in all its eccentric, idiosyncratic glory, these would be the starting points. From extraordinary creativity to traditional expertise, from political statement to historical opulence, from the aristocracy to street culture, ours is a land of contradiction."[86] This article is primarily focused on aesthetic ideas, or cultural stereotypes that continue to have strong currency within international fashion. Although Mair is at pains to emphasize the diversity of British style, she also places a strong emphasis on lingering notions of British aristocratic lifestyles and country clothing as integral elements of it. For example, she states: "A love of dogs, horses and wellies seems to be a good place to begin… See also: tweeds, jodhpurs, duffel coats, trenches, kilts, cardigans, headscarves, twinsets and taffeta ballgowns."[87]

In 1996, Amy de la Haye argued that "designers such as Chanel, Kenzo and Ralph Lauren have highly successfully appropriated and transformed clothes associated with British aristocratic country life, giving them a heightened chic and gloss."[88] It is that appropriation and transformation, which explains the curious fact that, even today, notions of past British elite lifestyles and appearances retain mythologized connotations of glamor and exclusivity. Film and television have played a significant role in ensuring that now mythical ideas about British aristocratic appearances continue to resonate sufficiently with consumers that they form a core element of the design identities of leading brands such as Ralph Lauren.[89] However, it is simplistic and erroneous to view that resonance as merely a sign of conservative nostalgia. Arnold has argued that the preoccupation with androgyny in late twentieth-century fashion, which has continued into the present reflects "the attempt to reconcile the gender differences that had been thrown into such cold relief by contemporary debates" related to feminism.[90] Thus, tailored garments in tweed, which might be interpreted as epitomizing notions of British elite male style, have become transformed into androgynous American sportswear for women in the hands of Ralph Lauren (Plate 21). Furthermore, the continued centrality of the tweed suit to the brand Chanel is related to the simplicity and modernity of that clothing and its capacity to simultaneously encapsulate contradictory notions of "timelessness" historicism and contemporaneity, as discussed in Chapter 1.

Key elements of British style that relate strongly to how tweed has been used in international fashion are radical innovation and tradition, country clothing and tailoring. One of the most high-profile designers to use tweed since the 1980s has been Vivienne Westwood. Her autumn/winter 1987/88 collection was titled Harris Tweed and it epitomized the tendency for her work to, as Wilcox argues, "encapsulate a particular Britishness, a fearless unconformity combined with a sense of tradition."[91] An outfit in Harris Tweed from this collection includes a jacket that was inspired by the princess style coats worn by the Queen as a child and a mini-crini, which was Westwood's "flirtatiously" abbreviated take on the nineteenth-century crinoline (Plate 22). The royal references in this collection, which were partly about inspiration, part parody, also included crowns made from Harris Tweed (Fig. 9.4).[92]

Arnold has interpreted Westwood's use of that textile in her Harris Tweed collection, as evoking an "authentic English elitism" and being reminiscent of "generations of country living" by the upper classes.[93] That collection was undoubtedly inspired by a range of "traditional" fabrics and styles linked to the British establishment, which were used to make unconventional outfits.[94] The complex, cultural meanings linked to Harris Tweed, however, reach far beyond associations with upper class, English lifestyles and a generic Britishness. Researching these tweeds reveals that the ways in which textiles embody, local and national identities, varies according to people's perceptions and experiences. Westwood herself described the tweed crown as being "so English," although it is explicitly a symbol of the British monarchy, made from cloth woven in the Outer Hebrides.[95] The weaving of Harris Tweed is closely associated with the Gaelic-speaking crofting communities of the Outer Hebrides, which have historically been fiercely independent, but politically and economically marginalized by landowners. These textiles are therefore seen by many in those islands as symbolizing a distinctively, Hebridean cultural identity, rather than a generic Scottishness, or Britishness.[96] These perspectives transform the meanings associated with a Westwood Harris Tweed

Figure 9.4 Malcolm McLaren with Vivienne Westwood wearing a Harris Tweed crown, 1987. Photograph by Bernard Weill/Toronto Star via Getty Images.

crown from merely being a gentle parody of British royal symbols, into a more overtly political comment about contested power relationships in Britain. Westwood has repeatedly used Harris Tweed in men's and women's clothing ever since the influential collection that bears its name and this has encouraged others to view it as a textile for fashion.[97] For example, she stated in relation to her "Prince Charming" collection of autumn/winter 2010 that Harris Tweed was used "to evoke an element of tradition and history."[98]

Contemporary Tweeds, Country Clothing, and a "Sense of Place"

Tweed for sportswear has largely been replaced by more technical fabrics, but it is still used in the UK and internationally as a cloth for field sports and country wear. For example, the American brand Orvis, sells tweed hunting coats and "shooting breeks" and the Italian gun maker, Beretta offers a range of tweed garments for men and women that are designed to be worn for field sports. The design of these garments, which are aimed at upper levels of the market is closely inspired by British men's sporting attire of the late nineteenth century.[99]

Similar historical influences inspired the choice of a Johnstons of Elgin estate tweed for a woman's suit by Louis Vuitton of autumn/winter 2004/5 (Fig. 9.5). This outfit, held by National Museums Scotland includes a jacket of green wool tweed with brown and blue large overcheck and a skirt that is made from a slightly different pattern and colorway.[100] John Gillespie, who designed the tweeds, stated that they "do not pertain to any particular estate, but were design developed … in keeping with the ethos of estate tweeds." He also highlighted the direct influence of tweeds in Johnston's company archive on the design, by stating that "the exact number of warp and weft threads have been used as in the original cloth of 150 years ago."[101] The specific historical and geographical associations of these textiles reflect an important current within international fashion. Alison Goodrum argued in 2005 that "The disorientation and the rootlessness that are said to characterise global times have given rise to … the pursuit of a palpable 'sense of place' … the niche marketing of fashionable lifestyle brands is one mechanism that has tapped into this consumer longing."[102] Tweeds made in Britain by long-established firms eloquently meet these desires for fashion to encapsulate a sense of "placed identities for placeless times." The contemporary case studies along with other evidence show, however, that the majority of British tweeds are exported, with Japan being a key market for these textiles.[103] This reveals that the importance of a sense of place in relation to the consumption of UK-made tweeds is not primarily about British consumers seeking reassuring associations of home. Instead it is linked to more complex notions of the perceived cultural associations and value of British consumer goods in global markets. Goodrum stated in 2005:

> In the Japanese market, then, we see "ethnic" British clothing – Shetland jumpers and Fair Isle knits, Harris tweeds and Blackwatch tartan – assuming great importance, being valued for their realness, for their touristic quality and for fulfilling what has been described as a sartorial pilgrimage after authenticity. Encouraged to … collect the signs of many cultures, trophy-hunting consumers view such vernacular British styles as symbols through which to reflect their own cosmopolitanism and cultural capital.[104]

Underpinning these consumer perceptions of "realness" or "authenticity" is the fact that the origins and production of these textiles are seen as intimately connected to specific locations in Britain.

Figure 9.5 Woman's suit, Louis Vuitton, estate tweed by Johnstons of Elgin, autumn/winter 2004/5. © National Museums Scotland, Edinburgh.

This shows how the geographical and historical associations of a textile like Harris Tweed, become translated in the global marketplace into cultural and economic value, or distinction.

Tailoring and Tweed

Tweeds have historically had close links with tailoring, another key element of British style. Since the early nineteenth century, the area around Savile Row has been internationally renowned for bespoke tailoring. However, Italian tailoring, as exemplified by the Armani suit, had a much more significant influence internationally than styles and fabrics from Britain in the 1980s.[105] Nevertheless, from the mid-1980s and particularly from the 1990s, Savile Row has formed an important reference point for leading British and international designers such as Alexander McQueen, John Galliano, Tom Ford and Stella McCartney. In the early 1990s, London bespoke tailoring itself began a resurgence, largely through the efforts of a new, more fashion-conscious breed of Savile Row, or off-Savile Row tailor, including Ozwald Boateng, Richard James, Mark Powell and Timothy Everest. The importance of tailoring within international fashion has encouraged the continued prominence of tweeds and tweed patterns such as the Glenurquhart check in men's and women's clothing.[106]

The fact that tweed remains an integral part of the language of British tailoring has recently been reflected in UK and international menswear. In the September 2013 edition of *Esquire*, Jeremy Langmead reported on the autumn/winter London menswear collections as follows: "Tweeds … are still all the rage – gently interpreted on our shores by Richard James … more irreverently visited by E Tautz."[107] In addition, the September 2013 edition of *GQ* contained a Prada advert that featured a suit in a small, checked tweed with a velvet collar. That combination of cut and cloth related to a multiplicity of British sartorial references including late nineteenth-century menswear, Neo-Edwardian styling and mod suits of the 1960s.[108] This outfit encapsulates how contemporary designers often use tweed and tailoring together to both refer to the past and create something of the present, as Evans states: "against the myth of fashion as always striving for the new is a counter-tale of fashion looping back to earlier moments of modernity in the present."[109]

CONCLUSION

The contemporary case studies have shown the importance of creative dialogue between designers from British mills and their counterparts in the global fashion industry, a sector renowned for constant design innovation. These findings provide a revealing counterpoint to the focus within some fashion history books on the exclusive role of the individual fashion designer in design development. This publication has also shown, through the example of tweed, that the cycle of fashion change begins at a much earlier stage than is usually acknowledged within studies of fashionable dress. Today, international fashion designers continue to be inspired by the versatility of tweeds and their potential for design innovation. The powerful cultural and historical associations of tweed also provide great inspiration for creating new fashions that reference past styles. Furthermore, while some tweeds retain strong connotations of British rural environments, others have become explicitly part of the international language of urban tailoring. This book appropriately ends with a chapter that has considered how tweeds continue to express the powerful tensions and contradictions, which Arnold argues are inherent within fashion and contemporary culture.[110]

NOTES

Chapter 1: Introduction

1   Rebecca Arnold, "Vivienne Westwood's Anglomania," in Christopher Breward, Becky Conekin and Caroline Cox (eds), *The Englishness of English Dress* (Oxford: Berg, 2002), p. 166.

2   A non-exhaustive list of studies that have investigated the inter-relationships between fashion textiles and garments includes: Lou Taylor, "Wool Cloth and Gender: the use of woollen cloth in women's dress in Britain, 1865–85," in Amy de la Haye and Elizabeth Wilson (eds), *Defining Dress: Dress as Object, Meaning and Identity* (Manchester: Manchester University Press, 1999); Beverly Lemire, *Fashion's Favourite: The Cotton Trade and the Consumer in Britain 1660–1800* (Oxford: Oxford University Press, 1991); Lesley Ellis Miller, "Perfect Harmony: Textile Manufacturers and Haute Couture 1947–1957," in Claire Wilcox, *The Golden Age of Couture: Paris and London 1947–57* (London: V & A Publications, 2007); John Styles, *The Dress of the People: Everyday Fashion in Eighteenth Century England* (New Haven and London: Yale University Press, 2007); Jonathan Faiers, *Tartan* (Oxford: Berg Publishers, 2008); Christine Boydell, *Horrockses Fashions: Off-the-Peg Style in the 40s and 50s* (London: V & A Publications, 2010); Beverly Lemire, *Cotton* (Oxford: Berg Publishers, 2011).

3   Clifford Gulvin, *The Tweedmakers: A History of the Scottish Fancy Woollen Industry 1600–1914* (Newton Abbot: David & Charles, 1973).

4   Kenneth Ponting, "The Scottish Contribution to Wool Textile Design in the Nineteenth Century," in John Butt (ed.), *Scottish Textile History* (Aberdeen: Aberdeen University Press, 1987); Judith Hoad, *This is Donegal Tweed* (Inver, County Donegal: Shoestring Publications, 1987); E. P. Harrison, *Scottish Estate Tweeds* (Elgin: Johnstons of Elgin, 1995); Taylor, "Wool Cloth and Gender"; Lou Taylor, "'To attract the attention of fish as little as possible': An Object-Led Discussion of Three Garments, for Country Wear for Women, Made of Scottish Woollen Cloth Dating from 1883–1908," *Textile History* 38, No. 1 (2007): 92–105; Louise Crewe, "Tailoring and Tweed: Mapping the Spaces of Slow Fashion," in Stella Bruzzi and Pamela Church Gibson (eds), *Fashion Cultures Revisited* (Abingdon, Oxon: Routledge, 2013), pp. 200–14.

5   Janet Hunter, *The Islanders and the Orb: The History of the Harris Tweed Industry 1835–1995* (Stornoway, Lewis: Acair Ltd., 2001); Janice Helland, *British and Irish Home Arts and Industries 1880–1914: Marketing Craft, Making Fashion* (Dublin: Irish Academic Press, 2007), pp. 143–94.

6   Miles Lambert, "Drapers, tailors, salesmen and brokers: the retailing of woollen clothing in northern England, c.1660–c.1830," and Beverly Lemire, "Fashion and tradition: wearing wool in England during the Consumer Revolution, c.1660–1820," both in Giovanni Luigi Fontana and Gerard Gayot (eds), *Wool Products and Markets (13th–20th Century)* (Padova: CLEUP, 2004). I also refer the reader

to the extensive list of sources on the English wool textiles industry cited by Lemire in her essay on pp. 574–5.

7   Colin McDowell, *Ralph Lauren, The Man, the Vision, the Style* (London: Cassell Illustratec, 2002), p. 57; *Vogue*, September, 2012, inside front cover and p. 1; *Harper's Bazaar*, November, 2013, p. 220–3.

8   Some key studies include Christopher Breward, *The Hidden Consumer: Masculinities, Fashion and City Life 1860–1914* (Manchester: Manchester University Press, 1999); Laura Ugolini, *Men and Menswear: Sartorial Consumption in Britain 1880–1939* (Aldershot: Ashgate, 2007); Frank Mort, *Cultures of Consumption: Masculinities and Social Space in Late Twentieth-Century Britain* (London: Routledge, 1996); Paul Jobling, *Man Appeal: Advertising, Modernism and Menswear* (Oxford: Berg, 2005).

9   The limited list of relevant sources includes Faiers, *Tartan*; Laurie Anne Brewer, "The Material Education of the Dandy," in Kate Irvin and Laurie Anne Brewer (eds), *Artist, Rebel, Dandy* (New Haven: Yale University Press, 2013), pp. 105–29; Paul Jobling, *Advertising Menswear: Masculinity and Fashion in the British Media Since 1945* (London: Bloomsbury Academic, 2014), pp. 120–38.

10 Taylor, "Wool Cloth and Gender"; Fiona Anderson, "This Sporting Cloth: Tweed, Gender and Fashion 1860–1900," *Textile History* 37, No. 2 (2006); Helland, *British and Irish Home Arts*, pp. 143–94.

11 John Glendening, *The High Road: Romantic Tourism, Scotland and Literature, 1720–1820* (London: MacMillan, 1997), pp. 7–8; David Matless, *Landscape and Englishness* (London: Reaktion Books Ltd, 1998), pp. 16–17.

12 Glendening, *The High Road*, p. 7.

13 Fiona Anderson, "Spinning the Ephemeral with the Sublime," *Fashion Theory* 9 (2005).

14 Matless, *Landscape and Englishness*, pp. 16–17.

15 W. J. T. Mitchell, *Landscape and Power* (Chicago: University of Chicago Press, 1994), pp. 1–2; Kay Anderson, Mona Domosh, Steve Pile and Nigel Thrift, "A Rough Guide," in *Handbook of Cultural Geography* (London: Sage Publications Ltd, 2003), p. 7.

16 A. A. Gill, "Suits you sir: A man of the cloth," *Sunday Times Magazine*, March 13, 2011, p. 55.

17 T. M. Devine, *Clearance and Improvement: Land, Power and People in Scotland 1700–1900* (Edinburgh: John Donald, 2006), pp. 13–208.

18 *Twist*, February/March, 2013, Issue 49, p. 21.

19 The Outer Hebrides are also known as the Western Isles. The former term has been employed throughout this book because it has been more widely used within the Harris Tweed industry.

20 Hunter, *The Islanders and the Orb*, p. 14.

21 Lisa Armstrong, "Paris Haute Couture: Chanel autumn/winter 2013", *The Telegraph*, July 2, 2013. Available online: http://fashion.telegraph.co.uk/columns/lisa-armstrong/TMG10154874/Paris-Haute-Couture-autumnwinter-2013.html (accessed July 10, 2013).

Chapter 2: Tweed: Terms, Descriptions, and Characteristics

1   A recent promotional leaflet for the Lovat Mill of Hawick states that the firm is "Situated in Commercial Road where use of the name 'tweed' originated."

2   See, for example, Clifford Gulvin, *The Tweedmakers: A History of the Scottish Fancy Woollen Industry 1600–1914* (Newton Abbot: David & Charles, 1973); Michael James Denton and Paul N. Daniels, *Textile Terms and Definitions*, 11th edn (Manchester: The Textile Institute, 2002), p. 365; Marjory Taylor, *Technology of Textile Properties* (London, Forbes Publications Limited, 1981), p. 251; David Jenkins and Kenneth Ponting, *The British Wool Textile Industry 1770–1914* (Aldershot: Scolar Press, 1987), pp. 350–1; "Tweed," *Dictionary of the Scots Language*. Available online: http://www.dsl.ac.uk/entry/snd/tweed (accessed May 10, 2009).

3   *The Satirist*, September 2, 1838, front cover.

4   D. Watson, "The Early Manufactures of Hawick," *Transactions of the Hawick Archaeological Society* (1868): 14; Gulvin, *The Tweedmakers*, pp. 79–80; Ian Duncan, *Scott's Shadow: The Novel in Romantic Edinburgh* (Princeton: Princeton University Press, 2007), Preface, xi–xv.

5   James Locke, "A Few Facts on the Tweed Trade," *The Border Advertiser*, September 18, 1863, p. 3; Alexander Craig, "Reminiscences of the Tweed Trade (1829–1836) By a Pioneer," *The Border Advertiser*, December 9, 1874, p. 2; "Tweel," *Dictionary of the Scots Language*. Available online: http://www.dsl. ac.uk/entry/snd/tweel.n_v, DSL-SND1, entry for Tweel (accessed May 10, 2009).

6   Gulvin, *The Tweedmakers*, p. 35; Kenneth Ponting, "The Scottish Contribution to Wool Textile Design in the Nineteenth Century," in John Butt (ed.), *Scottish Textile History* (Aberdeen: Aberdeen University Press, 1987), pp. 78–9.

7   E. S. Harrison, *Scottish Woollens* (Edinburgh: The National Association of Scottish Woollen Manufacturers, 1956), p. 3; Taylor, *Technology of Textile Properties,* pp. 68–70.

8   Harrison, *Scottish Woollens*, p. 4; T. A. Stillie, "The Evolution of Pattern Design in the Scottish Woollen Textile Industry in the Nineteenth Century," *Textile History* 3 (1970): 311; Gulvin, *The Tweedmakers*, pp. 72–3; Ponting, "The Scottish Contribution," p. 83; E. P Harrison, *Scottish Estate Tweeds* (Elgin: Johnstons of Elgin, 1995), p. 49; Janet Hunter, *The Islanders and the Orb: The History of the Harris Tweed Industry 1835–1995* (Stornoway, Lewis: Acair Ltd, 2001), p. 22.

9   David Bremner, *The Industries of Scotland: Their Rise, Progress and Present Condition* (Edinburgh: Adam and Charles Black, 1869), p. 155.

10   "Tweed," *Dictionary of the Scots Language*.

11   Locke, "A Few Facts," p. 3; James Locke, *Tweed and Don; or, Recollections and Reflections of an Angler for the Last Fifty Years* (London: Simpkin, Marshall and Co., 1860), p. 37; "Tweedle," *Dictionary of the Scots Language*. Available online: http://www.dsl.ac.uk/entry/snd/tweedle_v1_n1, DSL-SND1, entry for Tweedle (accessed May 10, 2009).

12   Locke, "A Few Facts," p. 3.

13   Harrison, *Scottish Woollens,* p. 4; Stillie, "The Evolution of Pattern Design," p. 311; Gulvin, *The Tweedmakers*, pp. 72–3; Ponting, "The Scottish Contribution," p. 83; Harrison, *Scottish Estate Tweeds*, p. 49; Hunter, *The Islanders and the Orb*, p. 22.

14   Locke, "A Few Facts," p. 3; Craig, "Reminiscences of the Tweed Trade," p. 2.

15   Locke, "A Few Facts," p. 3.

16   Locke, *Tweed and Don*, p. 37.

17   Locke, *Tweed and Don*, p. 37; Locke, "A Few Facts," p. 3.

18   Letter from Mr Irvine, "Origin of the Term 'Tweed,'" *Hawick Advertiser*, October 27, 1855, front page. This version of the story was repeated in a further account by Watson, "The Early Manufactures of Hawick," p. 14.

19   Bremner, *The Industries of Scotland*, pp. 155–6; Locke, *Tweed and Don,* p. 37; Locke, "A Few Facts," p. 3; "Tweed," *Dictionary of the Scots Language*.

20   Locke, "A Few Facts," p. 3; Gulvin, *The Tweedmakers*, p. 205.

21   *The Satirist*, September 2, 1838, front cover.

22   *Punch,* February 24, 1844, p. 88; August 10, 1844, p. 65; November 16, 1844, p. 206; April 19, 1845, p. 178; August 23, 1845, p. 81.

23   Letter from Thomas Carlyle to Charles Redwood, July 4, 1843, MS: NLS Acc. 9294.

24   Letter from Thomas Carlyle to John A. Carlyle, July 18, 1843, MS: NLS 524.47.

25   Hunter, *The Islanders and the Orb*, pp. 14–68.

26   *The New Statistical Account of Scotland, Vol. XII* (Edinburgh and London: William Blackwood and Sons, 1845), p. 171; Locke, "A Few Facts," p. 3; Craig, "Reminiscences of the Tweed Trade," p. 2.

27   Harrison, *Scottish Woollens*, p. 148–50; *British Wool Cloth Sample Book* (London: The International Wool Secretariat, undated), p. 6c, Tweeds; Gulvin, *The Tweedmakers*, p. 75; Denton and Daniels, *Textile Terms and Definitions*, p. 365.

28   David Christie, *The Manufacture of Scotch Tweeds,* unpublished promotional booklet for Peter Anderson, Ltd, undated.

29   Craig, "Reminiscences of the Tweed Trade," p. 2; Gulvin, *The Tweedmakers*, pp. 76–7; Ian Angus

Mackenzie, interview with the author, Harris Tweed Hebrides, Shawbost, September 28, 2010; Alan Cumming, interview with the author, Lovat Mill, Hawick, November 14, 2013.

30 Jenkins and Ponting, *The British Wool Textile Industry*, p. 174; Ponting, "The Scottish Contribution," p. 93; Harrison, *Scottish Estate Tweeds*, pp. 48–56.

31 Kenneth Ponting, *The Wool Trade: Past and Present* (Manchester: Columbine Press, 1961), p. 185; Denton and Daniels, *Textile Terms and Definitions*, p. 365.

32 Valerie Mendes and Frances Hinchcliffe, *Ascher: Fabric, Art, Fashion* (London: V & A Museum, 1987), pp. 121–76.

33 Escada outfit, object number, K. 2005.338.1–2, National Museums Scotland.

34 Harrison, *Scottish Woollens*, pp. 148–50; Gulvin, *The Tweedmakers*, p. 75; Taylor, *Technology of Textile Properties*, p. 53.

35 Christie, *The Manufacture of Scotch Tweeds*, p. 7; E. Ostick, *Textiles for Tailors* (London: The Tailor and Cutter Limited, undated), p. 37; Harrison, *Scottish Woollens*, p. 3; Ponting, "The Scottish Contribution," pp. 79–84; Judith Hoad, *This is Donegal Tweed* (Inver, County Donegal: Shoestring publications, 1987), p. 75.

36 Ponting, "The Scottish Contribution," p. 84.

37 Harrison, *Scottish Estate Tweeds*, p. 65.

38 Harrison, *Scottish Woollens*, p. 150.

39 Ostick, *Textiles for Tailors*, p. 36.

40 *British Wool Cloth Sample Book*, p. 6c, Tweeds.

41 K.2013.7.12, Bunch, 1934, 113/3, Otterburn Mill Collection, National Museums Scotland; "Scotch Tweeds for Germany," *The Wool Record and Textile World*, 1934, in Miscellaneous Cuttings Book (1934–37), NC2/1, Archive of Historical Records and Business Archives, Heriot-Watt University, Galashiels.

42 Amy de la Haye, *Chanel* (London: V & A Publishing, 2011), pp. 82–5; *The Guardian*, "Supermodel sweep 'Riot' breaks out at Chanel's shopping-aisle show," March 5, 2014, p. 9.

43 *Twist*, February/March 2013, p. 26; "Tissus Tweeds – Boutique de Tissus," Vente de Tissus Au Metre. Available online: http://www.ventedetissusaumetre.com/fr/15-tweed?p=2 (accessed February 28, 2014).

44 K.2013.7.12, Bunch, 1934, 113/3, Otterburn Mill Collection, National Museums Scotland; "Scotch Tweeds for Germany," *The Wool Record and Textile World*, 1934 in Miscellaneous Cuttings Book (1934–37), NC2/1, Archive of Historical Records and Business Archives, Heriot-Watt University, Galashiels; Harrison, *Scottish Woollens*, p. 170; Carolyn A. Farnfield and P. J. Alvey, *Textile Terms and Definitions*, 7th edn (Manchester: The Textile Institute, 1975), pp. 71–4.

45 Klein, *Eye for Colour*, pp. 116–19; Bernat Klein and Lesley Jackson, *Bernat Klein: Textile Designer, Artist, Colourist* (Gattonside, Roxburghshire: Bernat Klein Trust, 2005), p. 59.

46 T.90&A-1974, Victoria and Albert Museum.

47 Harrison, *Scottish Woollens*, p. 150.

48 Craig, "Reminiscences of the Tweed Trade," p. 2; T.140-1981, T.158-1963, T.159-1963, Victoria and Albert Museum.

49 Ostick, *Textiles for Tailors*, p. 3; Taylor, *Technology of Textile Properties*, p. 251.

50 Henry Poole and Co. private archive, Savile Row, London, sales ledgers O and Q, 1861, entries for Earl Dunmore and sales ledgers C-D 8, 1900, entries for Drayton J. Coleman; R.& A. Sanderson archives. RAS 6/1/31 Spring and Winter Trials 1901, 2 and 4, Archive of Historical Records and Business Archives, Heriot-Watt University, Galashiels.

51 *Henry Ballantyne and Sons Ltd*, London: Biographical Publishing Company, 1929, p. 75.

52 Locke, "A Few Facts," p. 3; Craig, "Reminiscences of the Tweed Trade," p. 2; Gulvin, *The Tweedmakers*, p. 193.

53 *Henry Ballantyne and Sons Ltd*, p. 77.

54 Locke, "A Few Facts," p. 3; Alan Cumming, November 14, 2013.

55   Gulvin, *The Tweedmakers*, pp. 48–51.

56   Robert Johnston, *Tweed Designer's Handbook* (Galashiels: Scottish Borders Record Office, 5th Edition, 1888), p. 3; Ponting, "The Scottish Contribution," p. 90.

57   Denton and Daniels, *Textile Terms and Definitions*, p. 63.

58   "Fibre Fineness," New Zealand Wool Testing Authority Ltd. Available online: http://www.nzwta.co.nz/assets/Docs/technical-details/fibre-diameter.pdf (accessed November 10, 2013).

59   *Henry Ballantyne and Sons Ltd*, p. 77.

60   Harrison, *Scottish Woollens*, p. 152.

61   *The Tailor and Cutter*, August 27, 1870; *Henry Ballantyne and Sons Ltd*, p. 77; "Hobson of Copenhagen," *The Ambassador*, No. 10, 1962, p. 96; "In-stock," Alexanders of Scotland. Available online: http://www.alexandersofscotland.com/in-stock/ (accessed February 11, 2014).

62   *Henry Ballantyne and Sons Ltd*, pp. 77–9.

63   Hunter, *The Islanders and the Orb*, pp. 27–45; Hoad, *This is Donegal Tweed*, pp. 95–100.

64   *Henry Ballantyne and Sons Ltd*, p. 77; Hunter, *The Islanders and the Orb*, pp. 45–55.

65   Hunter, *The Islanders and the Orb*, pp. 115–32.

66   Ostick, *Textiles for Tailors*, pp. 36–7.

67   Farnfield and Alvey, *Textile Terms and Definitions*.

68   Harris Tweed Act, 1993 (c.xi) (London: HMSO, 1993), p. 6.

69   Taylor, *Technology of Textile Properties*, p. 251; Ian Angus Mackenzie, September 28, 2010.

70   Ian Angus Mackenzie, interview with the author, Harris Tweed Hebrides, Shawbost, October 31, 2013; "Why Harris Tweed," Harris Tweed Authority. Available online: http://www.harristweed.org/harris-tweed/why-harris-tweed.php (accessed November 15, 2013).

71   David Jenkins, "The Western Wool Textile Industry in the Nineteenth Century," in David Jenkins, *The Cambridge History of Western Textiles, II* (Cambridge: Cambridge University Press, 2003), p. 785.

72   Hoad, *This is Donegal Tweed*, p. 75; Range book, 1960s, Magee of Donegal private archive; Range book, 1960s, Convoy, private archive.

73   Hoad, *This is Donegal Tweed*, pp. 107–26.

74   "Donegal Tweed Trousers," Austin Reed. Available online: http://www.austinreed.co.uk/fcp/product/austinreed/Trousers (accessed May 30, 2012); "Tweed Jacket," Hobbs. Available online: http://www.hobbs.co.uk/search (accessed May 30, 2012).

75   On a research trip to County Donegal in July 2012 the author visited Magee of Donegal; Molloy & Sons Weaving Ltd and Studio Donegal.

76   *Henry Ballantyne and Sons Ltd*, p. 79.

77   *Henry Ballantyne and Sons Ltd*, pp. 77–9; Ponting, "The Scottish Contribution," pp. 86–90.

78   Harrison, *Scottish Woollens*, p. 55.

79   *Shetland Textile Sector Review* (Shetland Islands Council, 2012), p. 32; 'Highest protection for organic "Native Shetland Wool," Soil Association. Available online: http://www.soilassociation.org/news/newsstory/articleid/2794 (accessed November 24, 2013); "Shetland," Abraham Moon & Sons Ltd. Available online: http://www.moons.co.uk/apparel/heritage-collection/shetland (accessed February 4, 2014); "About Us," Jamieson's of Shetland. Available online: www.jamiesonsofshetland.co.uk (accessed February 4, 2014).

80   *British Wool Cloth Sample Book*, p. 6c, Tweeds.

81   Jenkins and Ponting, *The British Wool Textile Industry*, pp. 86–174.

82   Jenkins and Ponting, *The British Wool Textile Industry*, pp. 174.

83   Ponting, "The Scottish Contribution," notes, pp. 172–3.

84   *Twist*, Issue 26, November 2010, pp. 46–7; "Makers Of The World's Finest Flannel," Fox Brothers & Co. Ltd. Available online: http://www.foxflannel.com/index.php (accessed February 10, 2014).

85   Gulvin, *The Tweedmakers*, pp. 76–81.

86   *The Textile Manufacturer*, January 15, 1878, pp. 19–20.

87   Jenkins, "The Western Wool Textile Industry," pp. 767–8; Jenkins and Ponting, *The British Wool Textile Industry*, p. 170 and p. 289; Ponting, "The Scottish Contribution," p. 88.

88   *British Wool Cloth Sample Book,* p. 6c, Tweeds.

89   Chris Holland, "Weaving wool back into Bradford's industrial future," *The Telegraph and Angus*, July 12, 2011. Available online: http://www.thetelegraphandargus.co.uk/business/9134180.Weaving_ wool_back_into_Bradford_s_industrial_future/ (accessed November 5, 2013).

90   "Survey of UKFT List," in *Twist*; Gareth Wyn Davies, 'Abraham Moon: the name on everyone's lips – and labels', *The Telegraph*, November 21, 2011. Available online: http://fashion.telegraph. co.uk/news-features/TMG8904041/Abraham-Moon-the-name-on-everyones-lips-and-labels-html (accessed February 26, 2014); "About Us," Marton Mills. Available online: http://www.martonmills. com/aboutus.htm (accessed February 26, 2014); "View Our Latest Collections," Marling & Evans Ltd. Available online: http://www.marlingandevansltd.co.uk (accessed February 26, 2014); "Our Heritage," William Bliss & Son Ltd. Available online: http://www.williamblisstextiles.co.uk/ our-heritage (accessed February 26, 2014). William Bliss & Son Ltd were previously based in Oxfordshire and owned by Fox Brothers & Co. Ltd. Marling & Evans was originally a West of England woolen manufacturer.

91   John Geraint Jenkins, *The Welsh Woollen Industry* (Cardiff: National Museum of Wales, 1969), Introduction, xvii- xviii; John Geraint Jenkins, *The Flannel Makers: A Brief History of the Welsh Woollen Industry* (Conwy, Wales: Gwasg Carreg Gwalch, 2005), p. 31.

92   Jenkins, *The Welsh Woollen Industry*, pp. 80–1.

93   Ponting, "The Scottish Contribution," pp. 79–81; Harrison, *Scottish Estate Tweeds*, p. 173; Tom Devine, *Clearance and Improvement: Land, Power and People in Scotland 1700–1900* (Edinburgh: John Donald, 2006), pp. 201–10.

94   Stillie, "The Evolution of Pattern Design," p. 328.

95   E. S. Harrison, *Our Scottish District Checks* (Edinburgh: The National Association of Scottish Woollen Manufacturers, 1968); Harrison, *Scottish Estate Tweeds*, 1995.

96   Harrison, *Scottish Estate Tweeds,* p. 139.

97   Gulvin, *The Tweedmakers*, p. 75; Stephen Rendle, interview with the author, Lovat Mill, Hawick, November 14, 2013.

98   Angus Blackburn, "The Home of Tweed," *The Scottish Sporting Gazette & International Traveller*, Issue 32, 2013, p. 76.

99   Locke, *Tweed and Don*, p. 37; Locke, "A Few Facts," p. 3.

Chapter 3: Origins and Early Development of Tweed to 1850

1   James Locke, "A Few Facts on the Tweed Trade," *The Border Advertiser*, September 18, 1863, p. 3; Adam Cochrane, "Notes on the Scotch Tweed Trade," *Transactions of the National Association for the Promotion of Social Science* (London: Longman, Roberts and Green, 1864); Alexander Craig, "Reminiscences of the Tweed Trade (1829–1836) By a Pioneer," *The Border Advertiser*, December 9, 1874, p. 2; J. & A. Ogilvie pattern book, Textile Archive, Heriot-Watt University, GH.6.1.1; John Glendening, *The High Road: Romantic Tourism, Scotland and Literature, 1720–1820* (London: MacMillan, 1997); T. M. Devine, *Clearance and Improvement: Land, Power and People in Scotland 1700–1900* (Edinburgh: John Donald, 2006); Elizabeth Wilson, *Adorned in Dreams: Fashion and Modernity* (London: I. B. Tauris, 2nd edn, 2003), p. 61.

2   Anne Hollander, *Sex and Suits* (New York: Kodansha America Ltd, 1995), pp. 92–3; Laurie Anne Brewer, "The Material Education of the Dandy," in Kate Irvin and Laurie Anne Brewer (eds), *Artist, Rebel, Dandy* (New Haven: Yale University Press, 2013), pp. 105–9.

3   Clifford Gulvin, *The Tweedmakers: A History of the Scottish Fancy Woollen Industry 1600–1914* (Newton Abbot: David & Charles, 1973), pp. 19–39; David Jenkins and Kenneth Ponting, *The British Wool Textile Industry 1770–1914* (Aldershot: Scolar Press, 1987), pp. 58–71.

4   Kenneth Ponting, "The Scottish Contribution to Wool Textile Design in the Nineteenth Century," in John Butt (ed.), *Scottish Textile History* (Aberdeen: Aberdeen University Press, 1987), p. 78.

5   Gulvin, *The Tweedmakers,* pp. 19–59. The private archive of Johnston's of Elgin includes a daybook that covers the period 1813 to 1822. It shows that although they sold a range of woolen cloths the majority of their orders were for "blue plain" cloth (Daybook 2, 1813–22).

6   Gulvin, *The Tweedmakers,* pp. 63–4.

7   Gulvin, *The Tweedmakers,* pp. 64–9; Christopher Whatley, *The Industrial Revolution in Scotland* (Cambridge: Press Syndicate of the University of Cambridge, 1997), p. 32.

8   Gulvin, *The Tweedmakers,* p. 78.

9   Locke, "A Few Facts," p. 3; Craig, "Reminiscences of the Tweed Trade," p. 2; *A Guide to Weaves and Designs in Thistle Cloths* (Edinburgh: George Harrison & Co, undated), pp. 28–9; Hugh Cheape, *Tartan* (Edinburgh: National Museums Scotland, 2006), pp. 7–9; X.FR 483, woolen fragment, National Museums Scotland.

10   Alexander Craig, "The Early Stages of the Tweed Trade," *The Border Advertiser*, October 20, 1875, p. 2.

11   Craig, "Reminiscences of the Tweed Trade," p. 2; Craig, "The Early Stages of the Tweed Trade," p. 2. Craig does not mention the name of the company he worked for in either of these published letters.

12   Letter from Mr Irvine, "Origin of the Term 'Tweed,'" *Hawick Advertiser*, October 27, 1855, front page; Craig, "The Early Stages of the Tweed Trade," p. 2.

13   Craig, "The Early Stages of the Tweed Trade," p. 2.

14   Craig, "Reminiscences of the Tweed Trade," p. 2.

15   Craig, "Reminiscences of the Tweed Trade," p. 2; Craig, "The Early Stages of the Tweed Trade," p. 2.

16   Locke, "A Few Facts," p. 3.

17   Cochrane, "Notes on the Scotch Tweed Trade," p. 793; Gulvin, *The Tweedmakers,* p. 72.

18   Locke, "A Few Facts," p. 3.

19   Ponting, "The Scottish Contribution," p. 84.

20   Locke, "A Few Facts," p. 3.

21   Alistair Durie, "'Unconscious Benefactors': Grouse-shooting in Scotland, 1780–1914," *The International Journal of the History of Sport* 15, No. 3 (1998): 58–9.

22   *The Satirist*, September 2, 1838, front cover.

23   Locke, "A Few Facts," p. 3.

24   Locke, "A Few Facts," p. 3; Craig, "Reminiscences of the Tweed Trade," p. 2.

25   J. & A. Ogilvie pattern book, Textile Archive, Heriot-Watt University, GH.6.1.1; *Harrisons of Edinburgh 1863–1963* (Edinburgh: George Harrison & Co, undated), pp. 5–6 . This cloth merchant bought the firm, J. & A. Ogilvie in 1863.

26   Craig, "The Early Stages of the Tweed Trade," p. 2.

27   Cochrane, "Notes on the Scotch Tweed Trade," p. 793; Craig, "Reminiscences of the Tweed Trade," p. 2.

28   Gulvin, *The Tweedmakers,* pp. 191–4; T. A. Stillie, "The Evolution of Pattern Design in the Scottish Woollen Textile Industry in the Nineteenth Century," *Textile History* 3 (1970): Ponting, "The Scottish Contribution."

29   James Locke, *Tweed and Don; or, Recollections and Reflections of an Angler for the Last Fifty Years* (London: Simpkin, Marshall and Co., 1860), p. 27; Locke, "A Few Facts," p. 3; Craig, "Reminiscences of the Tweed Trade," p. 2.

30   E. S. Harrison, *Scottish Woollens* (Edinburgh: The National Association of Scottish Woollen Manufacturers, 1956), p. 150.

31   Locke, "A Few Facts," p. 3; Craig, "The Early Stages of the Tweed Trade," p. 2.

32   Gulvin, *The Tweedmakers,* p. 76; *The Tailor and Cutter*, August 27, 1870, p. 464.

33   Locke, "A Few Facts," p. 3.

34   Cochrane, "Notes on the Scotch Tweed Trade," p. 798.

35   Locke, "A Few Facts," p. 3.

36   *The New Statistical Account of Scotland, Vol. III* (Edinburgh and London: William Blackwood and Sons, 1845), p. 21.

37   Jenkins and Ponting, *The British Wool Textile Industry*, pp. 80–1; Whatley, *The Industrial Revolution in Scotland*, p. 28.

38   Gulvin, *The Tweedmakers*, pp. 104–5.

39   Cochrane, "Notes on the Scotch Tweed Trade," p. 794; John Allan, *Crombies of Grandholm and Cothal 1805–1960* (Aberdeen: The Central Press, 1960), p. 54; Jenkins and Ponting, *The British Wool Textile Industry*, pp. 81–2; E. P Harrison, *Scottish Estate Tweeds* (Elgin: Johnstons of Elgin, 1995), p. 88.

40   Assistant Commissioner's Report from South of Scotland, P.P., 1839 (195), XLII, p. 41.

41   David Jenkins, "The Western Wool Textile Industry in the Nineteenth Century," in David Jenkins (ed.), *The Cambridge History of Western Textiles, Vol. II* (Cambridge: Cambridge University Press, 2003), p. 763.

42   Gulvin, *The Tweedmakers*, p. 103.

43   Jenkins, "The Western Wool," p. 763.

44   Gulvin, *The Tweedmakers*, p. 103.

45   Gulvin, *The Tweedmakers*, p. 85.

46   Devine, *Clearance and Improvement*, pp. ix-15.

47   Devine, *Clearance and Improvement*, p. 13.

48   Devine, *Clearance and Improvement*, pp. 16–207; Eric Richards, *The Highland Clearances* (Edinburgh: Birlinn, 2013), pp. 369–71.

49   Devine, *Clearance and Improvement*, p. 17.

50   Devine, *Clearance and Improvement*, p. 220; Richards, *The Highland Clearances*, pp. 243–9.

51   Janet Hunter, *The Islanders and the Orb: The History of the Harris Tweed Industry 1835–1995* (Stornoway, Lewis: Acair Ltd., 2001), pp. 27–45.

52   Mrs MacDonald, "Harris Home Industries: Lady Dunmore's Work," in *Scottish Home Industries* (Dingwall: Lewis Munro, 1895), pp. 69–70; Hunter, *The Islanders*, pp. 30–41.

53   Gulvin, *The Tweedmakers*, pp. 79–80; Ian Duncan, *Scott's Shadow: The Novel in Romantic Edinburgh* (Princeton: Princeton University Press, 2007), Preface, xi.

54   Gulvin, *The Tweedmakers*, pp. 79–80; Cheape, *Tartan*, p. 65; Jonathan Faiers, *Tartan* (Oxford: Berg Publishers, 2008), pp. 64–6.

55   Elizabeth Wilson, *Adorned in Dreams*, p. 61.

56   Hollander, *Sex and Suits*, pp. 83–91; Joanne Entwhistle, *The Fashioned Body: Fashion, Dress and Modern Social Theory* (Cambridge: Polity Press, 2000), pp. 121–2.

57   Hollander, *Sex and Suits*, p. 81.

58   Hollander, *Sex and Suits*, pp. 81–93.

59   Locke, "A Few Facts," p. 3.

60   Craig, "Reminiscences of the Tweed Trade," p. 2.

61   Locke, "A Few Facts," p. 3.

62   Gulvin, *The Tweedmakers*, pp. 71; Stillie, "The Evolution of Pattern Design," pp. 310–11; Ponting, "The Scottish Contribution," p. 80; Allan, *Crombies of Grandholm and Cothal*, p. 52.

63   Locke, "A Few Facts," p. 3; Craig, "The Early Stages of the Tweed Trade," p. 2; Duncan, *Scott's Shadow*, Preface, xi.

64   John Gibson Lockhart, *Memoirs of the Life of Sir Walter Scott, Vol. IV* (Paris: Baudry's European Library, 1838), p. 289; Locke, "A Few Facts," p. 3; Craig, "Reminiscences of the Tweed Trade," p. 2. A survey of the major portraits and engravings in the Walter Scott Digital Archive and those in the National Portrait Gallery collections reveals that none of them show Scott wearing shepherd's check trousers. "Portraits," Walter Scott Digital Archive. Available online: http://www.walterscott.lib.ed.ac.

uk/portraits.html (accessed October 23, 2010); "Search the Collection," National Portrait Gallery. Available online: http://www.npg.org.uk/collections/search/portrait/mw40349/Sir-Walter-Scott-1st-Bt (accessed December 23, 2010).

65   Walter Scott, *Waverley* (London: Simpkin and Marshall, 1829 edition), p. 324; Cochrane, "Notes on the Scotch Tweed Trade," p. 793.

66   *Punch*, August 10, 1844, p. 65; Locke, "A Few Facts," p. 3; Michael Lobban, "Brougham, Henry Peter, first Baron Brougham and Vaux (1778–1868)," *Oxford Dictionary of National Biography*. Available online: http://www.oxforddnb.com/view/article/3581 (accessed October 16, 2013).

67   Norman McCord and Bill Purdue, *British History 1815–1914* (Oxford: Oxford University Press, 2007), pp. 145–6; Lobban, "Brougham, Henry Peter."

68   *Punch*, August 10, 1844, p. 65.

69   McCord and Purdue, *British History*, pp. 145–59.

70   *The Morning Chronicle*, December 8, 1843, p. 3; *Punch*, November 16, 1844, p. 206;

71   Edwina Ehrman, "Clothing a World City: 1830–60," in Christopher Breward, Edwina Ehrman and Caroline Evans (eds), *The London Look: Fashion from Street to Catwalk* (London and New Haven, Yale University Press, 2004), pp. 32–5.

72   Durie, "Unconscious Benefactors," pp. 58–61.

73   Glendening, *The High Road*, pp. 7–8.

74   Devine, *Clearance and Improvement*, pp. 204–10; Glendening, *The High Road*, p. 7.

75   Leonore Davidoff, *The Best Circles: Society, Etiquette and the Season* (London: Croom Helm, 1973), pp. 14–28.

76   Davidoff, *The Best Circles*, p. 15.

77   Davidoff, *The Best Circles*, pp. 21–31; David Cannadine, *The Decline and Fall of the British Aristocracy* (London: Papermac, 1996), pp. 341–2.

78   Fiona Anderson, "Fashioning the Gentleman: A Study of Henry Poole and Co., Savile Row Tailors 1861–1900," *Fashion Theory* 4, Issue 4 (2000): 411–12.

79   William Scrope, *The Art of Deer-stalking; Illustrated By A Narrative Of A Few Day's Sport In The Forest Of Atholl* (London: John Murray, 1838), pp. 122–3.

80   Locke, "A Few Facts," p. 3; Penelope Byrde, *Nineteenth Century Fashion* (London: B. T. Batsford Limited, 1992), pp. 93–5; Ponting, "The Scottish Contribution," p. 78.

81   Scrope, *The Art of Deer-stalking*, p. 122.

82   John Tosh, *Manliness and Masculinities in Nineteenth-Century Britain* (Harlow: Pearson Education Ltd, 2005), p. 87.

83   Louisa M. Connor Bulman, "Titian in Connemara," *Apollo* 159, No. 506 (2004): 45.

84   Stephen Jackson, "Recent Fieldwork in Argyll," *Furniture and Fittings in the Traditional Scottish Home, Vernacular Building* 30 (2006): 65–6.

85   Byrde, *Nineteenth Century Fashion*, pp. 95–8; Scrope, *The Art of Deer-stalking*, p. 124. I refer to the garments worn by Cattermole and Evans as jackets rather than coats, because Scrope uses the term shooting jacket to describe very similar attire.

86   Previous research by the author has placed the adoption of tweeds for men's shooting jackets as primarily happening from the 1850s onwards. Fiona Anderson, "Spinning the Ephemeral with the Sublime," *Fashion Theory* 9 (2005): 287.

87   Scrope, *The Art of Deer-stalking*, pp. 124–30.

88   Locke, "A Few Facts," p. 3; Durie, "Unconscious Benefactors," p. 60.

89   Stuart Maxwell, *Scottish Costume, 1550–1850* (London: A&C Black, 1958), p. 132.

90   Jackson, "Recent Fieldwork in Argyll," p. 65.

91   Cochrane, "Notes on the Scotch Tweed Trade," p. 793.

92   Della Clason Sperling, "Cattermole, George (1800–1868)," *Oxford Dictionary of National Biography*. Available online: http://www.oxforddnb.com/view/article/4899 (accessed December 23, 2009).

93   Christopher Breward, *The Hidden Consumer: Masculinities, Fashion and City Life 1860–1914* (Manchester: Manchester University Press, 1999), p. 29.

94   Sperling, "Cattermole, George (1800–1868)."

95   Louisa M. Connor Bulman, "Evans, William (1798–1877)," *Oxford Dictionary of National Biography*. Available online: http://www.oxforddnb.com/view/article/8990 (accessed December 23, 2009).

96   Locke, *Tweed and Don*, p. 37; Locke, "A Few Facts," p. 3; Craig, "Reminiscences of the Tweed Trade," p. 2; Craig, "The Early Stages of the Tweed Trade," p. 2.

97   Raymond Williams, *Keywords: A Vocabulary of Culture and Society* (London: Fontana Press, 1988), p. 319.

98   Glendening, *The High Road*, p. 7.

99   *The Morning Chronicle*, December 8, 1843, p. 3; *Punch*, November 16, 1844, p. 206; Locke, "A Few Facts," p. 3; Ehrman, "Clothing a World City," pp. 32–5.

Chapter 4: Tweed, Male Fashion, and Modern Masculinities, 1851–1918

1   E. Cheadle, *Manners of Modern Society* (London: Cassell, 1872), pp. 87–8; Fiona Anderson, "Henry Poole and Co. Savile Row Tailors, 1861–1900," unpublished RCA/V & A Museum MA dissertation.

2   Fiona Anderson, "Spinning the Ephemeral with the Sublime," *Fashion Theory* 9, No. 3 (2005).

3   W. J. T. Mitchell, *Landscape and Power* (Chicago: University of Chicago Press, 1994); David Cannadine, *The Decline and Fall of the British Aristocracy* (London: Papermac, 1996); Christopher Breward, *The Hidden Consumer: Masculinities, Fashion and City Life 1860–1914* (Manchester: Manchester University Press, 1999); John Tosh, *Manliness and Masculinities in Nineteenth-Century Britain* (Harlow: Pearson Education Ltd, 2005); Peter Brooker, *Bohemia in London: The Social Scene of Early Modernism* (Basingstoke and New York: Palgrave MacMillan, 2007).

4   James Locke, "A Few Facts on the Tweed Trade," *The Border Advertiser*, September 18, 1863, p. 3; Clifford Gulvin, *The Tweedmakers: A History of the Scottish Fancy Woollen Industry 1600–1914* (Newton Abbot: David & Charles, 1973), p. 80; Farid Chenoune, *A History of Men's Fashion* (Paris: Flammarion, 1993), pp. 84–5.

5   Juror's Report on Woollen Goods in the International Exhibition of 1862, in Adam Cochrane, "Notes on the Scotch Tweed Trade," *Transactions of the National Association for the Promotion of Social Science* (London: Longman, Roberts and Green, 1864): 799.

6   Locke, "A Few Facts," p. 3.

7   R. & A. Sanderson & Co. Ltd, archive, Heriot-Watt University, RAS.6.2.1.

8   *Gazette of Fashion*, November 1, 1858, pp. 40–1.

9   *Gazette of Fashion*, editions from January 1, 1857 to November 1, 1858 were surveyed.

10   Gulvin, *The Tweedmakers*, p. 159.

11   Letter from Mr Irvine, "Origin of the Term 'Tweed'," *Hawick Advertiser*, October 27, 1855, front page.

12   Gulvin, *The Tweedmakers*, p. 146.

13   Gulvin, *The Tweedmakers*, pp. 156–7.

14   David Christie, *The Manufacture of Scotch Tweeds* (promotional booklet for Peter Anderson Ltd, undated), pp. 4–5.

15   A.1996.279, National Museums Scotland.

16   Gulvin, *The Tweedmakers*, pp. 74–5.

17   Gulvin, *The Tweedmakers*, pp. 120–49; Katrina Honeyman, *Well Suited: A History of the Leeds Clothing Industry 1850–1990* (Oxford: Oxford University Press, 2000), pp. 20–1.

18   Gulvin, *The Tweedmakers*, pp. 125–41; E. P Harrison, *Scottish Estate Tweeds* (Elgin: Johnstons of Elgin, 1995), pp. 57–62.

19   Gulvin, *The Tweedmakers*, p. 143.

20   "Tweeds and the Tariff," *Glasgow Herald*, August 24, 1909, p. 6.

21   Gulvin, *The Tweedmakers,* pp. 123–4.

22   Locke, "A Few Facts," p. 3.

23   Gulvin, *The Tweedmakers*, pp. 73–4.

24   Alexander Craig, "Reminiscences of the Tweed Trade (1829–1836) By a Pioneer," *The Border Advertiser*, December 9, 1874, p. 2.

25   Cochrane, "Notes on the Scotch Tweed Trade," p. 794; Gulvin, *The Tweedmakers,* pp. 73–105; Tom Devine, *The Scottish Nation 1700–2000* (London: Penguin Books, 2000), p. 253.

26   David Jenkins and Kenneth Ponting, *The British Wool Textile Industry 1770–1914* (Aldershot: Scolar Press, 1987), p. 73.

27   Gulvin, *The Tweedmakers,* p. 137.

28   Gulvin, *The Tweedmakers,* pp. 139–45.

29   Gulvin, *The Tweedmakers,* p. 145.

30   "Dear Wool and Hostile Tariffs," *The Times*, June 24, 1907, p. 195.

31   Gulvin, *The Tweedmakers,* p. 147.

32   Gulvin, *The Tweedmakers,* pp. 146–8; Jenkins and Ponting, *The British Wool Textile Industry*, p. 168.

33   Gulvin, *The Tweedmakers,* pp. 147–8.

34   Jenkins and Ponting, *The British Wool Textile Industry*, pp. 142–70.

35   Jenkins and Ponting, *The British Wool Textile Industry*, p. 112.

36   David Jenkins, "The Western Wool Textile Industry in the Nineteenth Century," in David Jenkins (ed.), *The Cambridge History of Western Textiles, II* (Cambridge: Cambridge University Press, 2003), p. 763.

37   Jenkins and Ponting, *The British Wool Textile Industry*, pp. 111–17.

38   Scottish Home Industries Association*, Scottish Home Industries* (Dingwall: Scottish Home Industries Association, 1895), pp. 75–6; Gulvin, *The Tweedmakers,* p. 159; Jenkins and Ponting, *The British Wool Textile Industry*, p. 115.

39   David Jenkins, "Wool Textiles In The Twentieth Century," in David Jenkins (ed.), *The Cambridge History of Western Textiles, II* (Cambridge: Cambridge University Press, 2003), p. 995.

40   *Henry Ballantyne and Sons Ltd* (London: Biographical Publishing Company, 1929), p. 31.

41   Janet Hunter, *The Islanders and the Orb: The History of the Harris Tweed Industry 1835–1995* (Stornoway, Lewis: Acair Ltd., 2001), pp. 27–45.

42   Mrs MacDonald, "Harris Home Industries: Lady Dunmore's Work," in Scottish Home Industries Association*, Scottish Home Industries*, p. 70.

43   Alice Leslie, "Harris Home Industries: Mrs Thomas's Work," in Scottish Home Industries Association*, Scottish Home Industries*, p. 73.

44   Leslie, "Harris Home Industries: Mrs Thomas's Work," pp. 74–6; Hunter, *The Islanders,* p. 30.

45   *Report To The Board of Agriculture For Scotland On Home Industries In The Highlands and Islands*, 1914, p. 34.

46   Scottish Home Industries Association*, Scottish Home Industries*, pp. 80–173.

47   Hunter, *The Islanders,* p. 47.

48   Hunter, *The Islanders,* pp. 47–9.

49   Hunter, *The Islanders,* p. 48.

50   Janice Helland, *British and Irish Home Arts and Industries 1880–1914: Marketing Craft, Making Fashion* (Dublin: Irish Academic Press, 2007), pp. 181–4.

51   *Report To The Board of Agriculture For Scotland On Home Industries In The Highlands and Islands*, p. 35; Hunter, *The Islanders,* p. 48.

52   MacDonald, "Harris Home Industries: Lady Dunmore's Work," pp. 70–1.

53   *Report of the Commissioners of Inquiry into the Conditions of the Crofters and Cottars in the Highlands and Islands of Scotland*, 1883, pp. 1183–4.

54   Frank Ormerod, *Wool* (London: Constable and Company Ltd, 1918), p. 145.

55   Tom Devine, *Clearance and Improvement: Land, Power and People in Scotland 1700–1900* (Edinburgh: John Donald, 2006), p. 17.

56   Devine, *Clearance and Improvement*, pp. 24.

57   Helland, *British and Irish Home Arts*, p. 144.

58   Hunter, *The Islanders*, p. 49; Helland, *British and Irish Home Arts*, pp. 144–54.

59   Helland, *British and Irish Home Arts*, p. 149.

60   *Report To The Board of Agriculture For Scotland On Home Industries In The Highlands and Islands*, 1914, p. 43.

61   Gillian Naylor, *The Arts and Crafts Movement* (London: Studio Vista, 1980), p. 27.

62   Ormerod, *Wool*, p. 148.

63   Scottish Home Industries Association, *Scottish Home Industries*, p. 173.

64   Hunter, *The Islanders*, pp. 12–64.

65   Hunter, *The Islanders*, pp. 64–5.

66   Penelope Byrde, *Nineteenth Century Fashion* (London: B. T. Batsford Limited, 1992), pp. 101–2; Breward, *The Hidden Consumer*, p. 46; Anderson, "Henry Poole and Co. Savile Row Tailors, 1861–1900."

67   *Gazette of Fashion*, Fashion Plate, May 1, 1857.

68   Fiona Anderson, "Fashioning the Gentleman: A Study of Henry Poole and Co., Savile Row Tailors 1861–1900," *Fashion Theory* 4, No. 4 (2000): pp. 411–14.

69   Locke, "A Few Facts," p. 3.

70   *The Tailor and Cutter*, January 2, 1869, p. 54.

71   "Materials for Winter 1869–70," *The Tailor and Cutter*, October 2, 1869, p. 67.

72   Locke, "A Few Facts," p. 3; *Textile Manufacturer*, January 15, 1878, pp. 2–19; Gulvin, *The Tweedmakers*, p. 147.

73   *Gazette of Fashion*, December 1, 1861, p. 47; Byrde, *Nineteenth Century Fashion*, p. 102.

74   Locke, "A Few Facts," p. 3.

75   *The Tailor and Cutter*, October, 1896, p. 23; *The London Tailor*, Fashion Plate, July 1897.

76   Breward, *The Hidden Consumer*, pp. 39–48; Laura Ugolini, *Men and Menswear: Sartorial Consumption in Britain 1880–1939* (Aldershot: Ashgate, 2007), pp. 28–31.

77   Catherine Horwood, *Keeping Up Appearances: Fashion and Class Between the Wars* (Stroud: Sutton, 2005), p. 140.

78   Brooker, *Bohemia in London*, p. 3.

79   Brooker, *Bohemia in London*, Preface, p. viii.

80   Brooker, *Bohemia in London*, p. 55.

81   Katrina Rolley and Caroline Aish, *Fashion in Photographs 1900–1920* (London: B. T. Batsford, 1992), pp. 103; Ormerod, *Wool*, p. 184.

82   Phillis Cunnington and Alan Mansfield, *English Costume for Sports and Outdoor Recreation* (London: A. and C. Black, 1969), pp. 197–223.

83   Alistair J. Durie, *Scotland for the Holidays: Tourism in Scotland c. 1780–1939* (East Linton: Tuckwell Press, 2003), pp. 111–12.

84   Cannadine, *The Decline and Fall*, p. 2.

85   Cannadine, *The Decline and Fall*, p. 21.

86   Cannadine, *The Decline and Fall*, p. 11; Devine, *Clearance and Improvement*, pp. 207–9.

87   Leonore Davidoff, *The Best Circles: Society, Etiquette and the Season* (London: Croom Helm, 1973), pp. 28–9; Mike Huggins, *The Victorians and Sport* (London: Hambledon and London, 2004), p. 19.

88   Henry Hope Crealock, *Deer-Stalking in the Highlands of Scotland* (London: Longmans, Green, 1892), p. 2.

89 Cannadine, *The Decline and Fall*, pp. 341–2.

90 Cunnington and Mansfield, *English Costume for Sports,* pp. 73–334; Byrde, *Nineteenth Century Fashion,* p. 104; Durie, *Scotland for the Holidays,* pp. 109–28.

91 Kay Anderson, Mona Domosh, Steve Pile and Nigel Thrift, "A Rough Guide," in *Handbook of Cultural Geography* (London: Sage Publications Ltd, 2003), p. 7.

92 Mitchell, *Landscape and Power*, pp. 1–2.

93 This extract is from Fiona Anderson, "Spinning the Ephemeral with the Sublime," *Fashion Theory: The Journal of Dress, Body & Culture,* 9, Issue 3 (2005): 295. Taylor & Francis Ltd, http://www.tandfonline.com/ reprinted by permission of the publisher.

94 *Mountain, Moor and Loch: On The Route of the West Highland Railway* (Colonsay: House of Lochar, 2002), Synopsis; W. J. T. Mitchell, *Landscape and Power*, p. 15; Devine, *Clearance and Improvement,* p. 207.

95 Devine, *Clearance and Improvement*, pp. 201–7.

96 Durie, *Scotland for the Holidays,* pp. 112.

97 This extract is from Fiona Anderson, "Spinning the Ephemeral with the Sublime," *Fashion Theory: The Journal of Dress, Body & Culture* 9, Issue 3 (2005): 296. Taylor & Francis Ltd, http://www.tandfonline.com/ reprinted by permission of the publisher.

98 John Mackenzie, *The Empire of Nature* (Manchester: Manchester University Press, 1988), p. 50.

99 Delabere P. Blaine, *An Encyclopaedia of Rural Sports* (London: Longman, Brown, Green and Longmans, 1852), p. 115.

100 Tosh, *Manliness and Masculinities*, p. 88.

101 Tosh, *Manliness and Masculinities,* pp. 86–97.

102 Tosh, *Manliness and Masculinities,* p. 98.

103 Tosh, *Manliness and Masculinities,* pp. 192–3.

104 Patrick F. McDevitt, *May The Best Man Win: Sport, Masculinity and Nationalism in Great Britain and the Empire, 1880–1935* (New York: Palgrave MacMillan, 2004), p. 2.

105 Blaine, *An Encyclopaedia of Rural Sports*, p. 115.

106 Mitchell, *Landscape and Power*, p. 17.

107 This extract is from: Fiona Anderson, "Spinning the Ephemeral with the Sublime," *Fashion Theory: The Journal of Dress, Body & Culture* 9, Issue 3 (2005): 300. Taylor & Francis Ltd, http://www.tandfonline.com/ reprinted by permission of the publisher.

108 Breward, *The Hidden Consumer,* pp. 39–40.

109 Cannadine, *The Decline and Fall*, pp. 2–21; Breward, *The Hidden Consumer,* pp. 77–8; Durie, *Scotland for the Holidays,* pp. 111–12.

Chapter 5: Tweed, Femininity, and Fashion, 1851–1918

1 Lou Taylor, "Wool Cloth and Gender: the use of woollen cloth in women's dress in Britain, 1865–85," in Amy de la Haye and Elizabeth Wilson (eds), *Defining Dress: Dress as Object, Meaning and Identity* (Manchester: Manchester University Press, 1999); Regina Lee Blaszczyk, *The Color Revolution* (Cambridge, MA: MIT Press, 2012).

2 Antoinette Burton, *Burdens of History: British Feminists, Indian Women and Imperial Culture 1865–1915* (North Carolina: University of North Carolina Press, 1994); Clare Midgley, *Gender and Imperialism* (Manchester, Manchester University Press, 1998); John Tosh, *Manliness and Masculinities in Nineteenth-Century Britain* (Harlow: Pearson Education Ltd, 2005), pp. 192–214.

3 James Locke, "A Few Facts on the Tweed Trade," *The Border Advertiser*, September 18, 1863, p. 3.

4 *The Englishwoman's Domestic Magazine*, October 1, 1868, pp. 194–5.

5 *The Englishwoman's Domestic Magazine*, October 1, 1868, p. 194.

6 *The Englishwoman's Domestic Magazine*, October 1, 1868, p. 194.

7 Locke, "A Few Facts," p. 3; Adam Cochrane, "Notes on the Scotch Tweed Trade," *Transactions of the*

National Association for the Promotion of Social Science (London: Longman, Roberts and Green, 1864), p. 798.

8   Locke, "A Few Facts," p. 3; *The Englishwoman's Domestic Magazine*, October 1, 1868, p. 194.

9   *The Englishwoman's Domestic Magazine*, October 1, 1868, p. 195.

10   Kenneth Ponting, "The Scottish Contribution to Wool Textile Design in the Nineteenth Century," in John Butt (ed.), *Scottish Textile History* (Aberdeen: Aberdeen University Press, 1987), p. 85.

11   T. A. Stillie, "The Evolution of Pattern Design in the Scottish Woollen Textile Industry in the Nineteenth Century," *Textile History* 3 (1970): 330–1.

12   Ponting, "The Scottish Contribution to Wool Textile Design," p. 85.

13   E. S. Harrison, *Scottish Woollens* (Edinburgh: The National Association of Scottish Woollen Manufacturers, 1956), pp. 169–70; E. P. Harrison, *Scottish Estate Tweeds* (Elgin: Johnstons of Elgin, 1995), p. 65.

14   "Dear Wool and Hostile Tariffs," *The Times*, June 24, 1907, p. 195.

15   Clifford Gulvin, *The Tweedmakers: A History of the Scottish Fancy Woollen Industry 1600–1914* (Newton Abbot: David & Charles, 1973), p. 147.

16   Taylor, "Wool Cloth and Gender," p. 43.

17   Frank Ormerod, *Wool* (London: Constable and Company Ltd, 1918), p. 156.

18   David Jenkins and Kenneth Ponting, *The British Wool Textile Industry 1770–1914* (Aldershot: Scolar Press, 1987), p. 232.

19   Gulvin, *The Tweedmakers,* p. 146.

20   *Myra's Journal of Dress and Fashion*, October 1889, p. 532.

21   *Myra's Journal of Dress and Fashion*, October 1889, p. 493.

22   *Textile Manufacturer*, January 15, 1878, pp. 2–19; Fiona Anderson, "Fashioning the Gentleman: A Study of Henry Poole and Co., Savile Row Tailors 1861–1900," *Fashion Theory* 4, Issue 4 (2000): 407–9.

23   Taylor, "Wool Cloth and Gender," pp. 35–41; Edwina Ehrman, "Glamorous Modernity: 1914–30," in Christopher Breward, Edwina Ehrman and Caroline Evans (eds), *The London Look: Fashion from Street to Catwalk* (London and New Haven, Yale University Press, 2004), p. 79.

24   Jenkins and Ponting, *The British Wool Textile Industry*, p. 354.

25   Lou Taylor came to a similar conclusion in her essay "Wool Cloth and Gender," p. 42.

26   David Jenkins, "The Western Wool Textile Industry in the Nineteenth Century," in David Jenkins, *The Cambridge History of Western Textiles, II* (Cambridge: Cambridge University Press, 2003), p. 769.

27   *Myra's Journal of Dress and Fashion*, July 1876, p. 49, October 1, 1886, p. 482.

28   Taylor, "Wool Cloth and Gender," p. 38.

29   *The Englishwoman's Domestic Magazine*, October 1, 1868, p. 195; *The Englishwoman's Domestic Magazine*, June, 1870, p. 366; H.NAB.93, cloak, H.TO 59, cape, National Museums Scotland.

30   Taylor, "Wool Cloth and Gender," pp. 40–1.

31   Blaszczyk, *The Color Revolution,* p. 39.

32   Taylor, "Wool Cloth and Gender," p. 40.

33   *The Queen*, March 28, 1891, p. 499.

34   Susan North, "John Redfern and Sons, 1847–1892," *Costume*, Number 42 (2008): 152.

35   *The Tailor and Cutter,* January 26, 1911, p. 65.

36   Scottish Home Industries Association, *Scottish Home Industries* (Dingwall: Scottish Home Industries Association, 1895), p. 173.

37   Janice Helland, *British and Irish Home Arts and Industries 1880–1914: Marketing Craft, Making Fashion* (Dublin: Irish Academic Press, 2007), pp. 169–71.

38   *The Tailor and Cutter,* February 16, 1911, p. 116.

39   Letter from Thomas Carlyle to Charles Redwood, July 4, 1843, MS: NLS Acc. 9294.

40   Archival reference, ALB-6-49-4, University of St Andrews.

41   Penelope Byrde, *Nineteenth Century Fashion* (London: B. T. Batsford Limited, 1992), pp. 60–1.

42   Phillis Cunnington and Alan Mansfield, *English Costume for Sports and Outdoor Recreation* (London: A. and C. Black, 1969), pp. 118–19; Janet Arnold, "Dashing Amazons: the development of women's riding dress, c. 1500–1900," in Amy de la Haye and Elizabeth Wilson (eds), *Defining Dress: Dress as Object, Meaning and Identity* (Manchester: Manchester University Press, 1999), pp. 22–3.

43   Arnold, "Dashing Amazons," p. 22; Taylor, "Wool Cloth and Gender," p. 31.

44   Taylor, "Wool Cloth and Gender," p. 31.

45   *The Englishwoman's Domestic Magazine*, June 1870, p. 366.

46   Byrde, *Nineteenth Century Fashion*, pp. 53–74.

47   *Myra's Journal of Dress and Fashion*, October 1886, pp. 482–93; Taylor, "Wool Cloth and Gender," p. 36.

48   *Myra's Journal of Dress and Fashion*, October 1886, p. 482.

49   Byrde, *Nineteenth Century Fashion*, pp. 69–71.

50   Taylor, "Wool Cloth and Gender," pp. 34–5; North, "John Redfern and Sons," pp. 146–53.

51   Object description of overcoat with detachable cape, 1888, 1987.471.1a-b, Chicago History Museum. Available online: http://digitalcollection.chicagohistory.org/cdm/compoundobject/collection/p16029 coll3/id/933/rec/1 (accessed December 7, 2013).

52   North, "John Redfern and Sons," p. 147.

53   *The Lady*, February 19, 1885, p. 45.

54   *Myra's Journal of Dress and Fashion*, January 1, 1889, p. 14; *Myra's Journal of Dress and Fashion*, February 1, 1889, p. 69; Byrde, *Nineteenth Century Fashion*, pp. 69–81; Anne Hollander, *Sex and Suits* (New York: Kodansha America Ltd, 1995), p. 143; North, "John Redfern and Sons," p. 156.

55   *Myra's Journal of Dress and Fashion*, January 1, 1900, p. 6.

56   Valerie Steele, *Paris Fashion: A Cultural History* (New York: Oxford University Press, Inc., 1988), pp. 219–23.

57   Steele, *Paris Fashion,* p. 237.

58   *The Tailor and Cutter*, August 9, 1917, pp. 575–83; *The Tailor and Cutter*, September 20, 1917, colored fashion plate; Steele, *Paris Fashion,* p. 238.

59   Tranter, *Sport, Economy and Society,* p. 84; Mike Huggins, *The Victorians and Sport* (London: Hambledon and London, 2004), p. 19.

60   Tranter, *Sport, Economy and Society,* pp. 13–83.

61   Tranter, *Sport, Economy and Society,* p. 85.

62   Jennifer Hargreaves, *Sporting Females: Critical Issues in the History and Sociology of Women's Sports* (London: Routledge, 1993), pp. 44–66; Tranter, *Sport, Economy and Society,* pp. 81–7; Midgley, *Gender and Imperialism*, p. 162.

63   Tranter, *Sport, Economy and Society,* p. 88.

64   John Hargreaves, "The Body, Sport and Power Relations," *Sociological Review* 33 (May 1985): 140.

65   Taylor, "Wool Cloth and Gender," p. 40.

66   Alistair Durie, "Unconscious Benefactors": Grouse-shooting in Scotland, 1780–1914," *The International Journal of the History of Sport* 15, No. 3 (1998): 66.

67   Ronald Eden, *Going to the Moors* (London: John Murray (Publishers) Ltd, 1979), p. 137.

68   Eden, *Going to the Moors,* pp. 137–8.

69   Charles St. John, *Sportsman's and Naturalist's Tour in Sutherlandshire* (London: Simpkin, Marshall and Co., 1891), pp. 300–1.

70   The Major, *Clothes and the Man: Hints on the Wearing and Caring of Clothes* (London: Grant Richards, 1900), pp. 19–21; Anderson, "Fashioning the Gentleman," pp. 412–17.

71   *The Queen*, January 17, 1891, p. 106; *The Queen*, May 23, 1891, p. 829.

72   Eden, *Going to the Moors,* pp. 137–8.

73   *The Queen,* January 25, 1896, p. 169; *The Tailor and Cutter,* February 16, 1911, p. 116.

74   Neil Tranter, *Sport, Economy and Society in Britain 1750–1914* (Cambridge: Cambridge University Press, 1998), p. 84.

75   *The Queen,* January 25, 1896, p. 158.

76   *The Queen,* January 25, 1896, p. 169.

77   *Punch,* January 12, 1895, p. 23.

78   Tranter, *Sport, Economy and Society,* p. 84.

79   T.20 to D-1960, Victoria and Albert Museum.

80   Greensmith Downes catalogs, 1914, HAKMG: 08.0150 and 1916, HAKMG: 08.0152, Scottish Borders Council Museum Service; Harrison, *Scottish Woollens,* p. 170; British *Vogue,* September 15, 1964, p. 20; Judith Clark and Amy de la Haye, *Jaeger 125* (London: Jaeger, 2009), p. 32.

81   Diana Crane, *Fashion and Its Social Agendas: Class, Gender and Identity in Clothing* (Chicago: University of Chicago Press, 2000), p. 101.

82   Taylor, "Wool Cloth and Gender," p. 44.

83   Burton, *Burdens of History*; Midgley, *Gender and Imperialism*; Tosh, *Manliness and Masculinities,* pp. 192–214; Philippa Levine, *The British Empire: Sunrise to Sunset* (Abingdon,Oxon: Routledge, 2013), pp. 155–79.

84   Burton, *Burdens of History,* p. 207.

85   James A. Mangan, "Duty Unto Death: English Masculinity and Militarism in the Age of the New Imperialism," in James A. Mangan, *Tribal Identities: Nationalism, Europe, Sport* (London: Frank Cass & Co. Ltd., 1996), p. 12.

86   *The Queen,* January 25, 1896, p. 169.

87   Tranter, *Sport, Economy and Society,* pp. 81–7; Midgley, *Gender and Imperialism,* p. 162.

88   Tosh, *Manliness and Masculinities,* p. 194.

89   Hollander, *Sex and Suits,* p. 143; Hargreaves, *Sporting Females,* pp. 49–51.

Chapter 6: Suits You: Men and Tweed, 1919–1952

1   *Garment News,* January 16, 1922, in Scottish Woollen Trade Mark Association, Cuttings Book 1921–1947, NC1/1/2, Archive of Historical Records and Business Archives, School of Textiles, Heriot-Watt University, Galashiels.

2   David Cannadine, *The Decline and Fall of the British Aristocracy* (London: Papermac, 1996); Catherine Horwood, *Keeping Up Appearances: Fashion and Class Between the Wars* (Stroud: Sutton, 2005); Laura Ugolini, *Men and Menswear: Sartorial Consumption in Britain 1880–1939* (Aldershot: Ashgate, 2007); Peter Brooker, *Bohemia in London: The Social Scene of Early Modernism* (Basingstoke and New York: Palgrave MacMillan, 2007).

3   David Jenkins, "Wool Textiles in the Twentieth Century," in David Jenkins, *The Cambridge History of Western Textiles, II* (Cambridge: Cambridge University Press, 2003), p. 995.

4   John Allan, *Crombies of Grandholm and Cothal 1805–1960* (Aberdeen: The Central Press, 1960), p. 120.

5   Jenkins, "Wool textiles in the twentieth century," pp. 995–6.

6   Jean S. Pattison, "The Tweed Section of the Scottish Woollen Industry," in H. A. Silverman (ed.), *Studies In Industrial Organisation* (London: Methuen & Co. Ltd, 1946), p. 152.

7   *The Clothier and Furnisher,* December 1921 and Press Release, December 20, 1921, both in Scottish Woollen Trade Mark Association, Cuttings Book 1921–47.

8   Press Release, December 30, 1921, in Scottish Woollen Trade Mark Association, Cuttings Book 1921–47.

9   Scottish Woollen Trade Mark Association, Cuttings Book 1921–47.

10   *The Clothier and Furnisher,* December 1921.

11   *Daily News Record,* December 1, 1922, in Scottish Woollen Trade Mark Association, Cuttings Book 1921–1947.

12   E. P Harrison, *Scottish Estate Tweeds* (Elgin: Johnstons of Elgin, 1995), p. 68.

13   Pattison, "The Tweed Section," pp. 119–20.

14   Pattison, "The Tweed Section," p. 122.

15   Pattison, "The Tweed Section," p. 111.

16   K.1997.1139.1, Order Book, 1933, National Museums Scotland.

17   Kenneth Ponting, "The Scottish Contribution to Wool Textile Design in the Nineteenth Century," in John Butt (ed.), *Scottish Textile History* (Aberdeen: Aberdeen University Press, 1987), p. 83.

18   Frank Ormerod, *Wool* (London: Constable and Company Ltd, 1918), p. 148.

19   Janet Hunter, *The Islanders and the Orb: The History of the Harris Tweed Industry 1835–1995* (Stornoway, Lewis: Acair Ltd., 2001), p. 94.

20   *Report of The Committee on the Crofter Woollen Industry, 1946*, p. 14.

21   Hunter, *The Islanders*, pp. 96–132.

22   Hunter, *The Islanders*, pp. 85–9.

23   Hunter, *The Islanders*, pp. 119–32.

24   Hunter, *The Islanders*, p. 132.

25   *Report of The Committee on the Crofter Woollen Industry*, 1946, pp. 16–17.

26   Pattison, "The Tweed Section," p. 112.

27   Ugolini, *Men and Menswear*, pp. 21–104.

28   Horwood, *Keeping Up Appearances*, pp. 34–9; Ugolini, *Men and Menswear*, p. 102.

29   R. H. Mottram, *Another Window Seat or Life Observed: Vol. 2 1919–1953* (London: Hutchinson, 1957), p. 15.

30   Elizabeth Owen, *Fashion in Photographs 1920–1940* (London: B. T. Batsford in association with The National Portrait Gallery, 1993), pp. 106–7; Ugolini, *Men and Menswear*, pp. 102–3.

31   Owen, *Fashion in Photographs*, pp. 106–7; Horwood, *Keeping Up Appearances*, p. 34.

32   Horwood, *Keeping Up Appearances*, pp. 69–71.

33   Scottish Woollen Trade Mark Association Advertisement, NC 1/2/2, Archive of Historical Records and Business Archives, School of Textiles, Heriot-Watt University, Galashiels.

34   Horwood, *Keeping Up Appearances*, pp. 29–31.

35   *Empire*, April 1933 in press cutting album, February 1932–August 1933, Victor Steibel Archive, Victoria and Albert Museum, AAD/1994/1/1.

36   Martin Pugh, *We Danced All Night: A Social History of Britain Between the Wars* (London: Vintage, 2009) p. 283.

37   Josephine Ross, *Society in Vogue: The International Set Between the Wars* (London: Condé Nast Publications Ltd., 1992), p. 10.

38   R. Longrigg, *The English Squire and His Sport* (London: Joseph, 1977), p. 289.

39   Cannadine, *The Decline and Fall*, p. 392.

40   Cannadine, *The Decline and Fall*, pp. 392–3.

41   Cannadine, *The Decline and Fall*, p. 342.

42   Cannadine, *The Decline and Fall*, p. 359.

43   J. M. Lee, *Social Leaders and Public Persons: A Study of County Government in Cheshire since 1888* (Oxford: Clarendon Press, 1963), p. 42.

44   Cannadine, *The Decline and Fall*, pp. 343, 370.

45   Ross, *Society in Vogue*, pp. 68–9.

46   Ross, *Society in Vogue*, p. 99.

47   Ross, *Society in Vogue*, pp. 68–105; K.2006.246, men's tweed ski trousers, National Museums Scotland.

48   Horwood, *Keeping Up Appearances*, pp. 80–8.

49   Owen, *Fashion in Photographs*, p. 35; Horwood, *Keeping Up Appearances*, p. 80.

50   "The Truth About Sport," *Vogue*, October 15, 1930, p. 40.

51   Farid Chenoune, *A History of Men's Fashion* (Paris: Flammarion, 1993), p. 165; Horwood, *Keeping Up Appearances,* p. 86.

52   *Henry Ballantyne and Sons Ltd* (London: Biographical Publishing Company, 1929), p. 32.

53   The Duke of Windsor, *A Family Album* (London: Cassell, 1960), p. 125.

54   Horwood, *Keeping Up Appearances,* p. 74.

55   Owen, *Fashion in Photographs,* p. 35.

56   Men in golf attire appear in numerous Wodehouse novels, including P. G. Wodehouse, *Doctor Sally* (Harmondsworth: Penguin Books Ltd, 1959).

57   Owen, *Fashion in Photographs,* p. 43.

58   *Garment News,* January 16, 1922.

59   Horwood, *Keeping Up Appearances,* p. 73.

60   Horwood, *Keeping Up Appearances,* pp. 40–72.

61   Horwood, *Keeping Up Appearances,* p. 73.

62   Horwood, *Keeping Up Appearances,* pp. 8–9.

63   Owen, *Fashion in Photographs,* p. 35; Horwood, *Keeping Up Appearances,* pp. 73–4.

64   Chenoune, *A History of Men's Fashion,* p. 160.

65   Curzio Malaparte, *Journal d'un étranger à Paris* (Paris: Editions Denoel, 1967), pp. 105–6.

66   William Dettloff, "The first Hispanic world boxing champion," ESPN, September 15, 2008. Available online: http://sports.espn.go.com/espn/hispanicheritage2008/news/story?id+3588817 (accessed October 10, 2013).

67   Harrison, *Scottish Estate Tweeds,* p. 139; Chenoune, *A History of Men's Fashion,* pp. 176–80.

68   A survey of images of several male film stars of the 1930s on www.getty.co.uk revealed that tweed garments often featured in film stills and publicity shots.

69   Patricia Mears, *Ivy Style* (New Haven and London: Yale University Press, 2012), pp. 19–24.

70   A survey of images of several male film stars of the 1930s on www.getty.co.uk revealed that patterned tweed garments often featured in film stills and publicity shots.

71   Jane Gaines, "Costume and narrative; how dress tells the woman's story," in Jane Gaines and Charlotte Herzog (eds), *Fabrications: Costume and the Female Body* (London: Routledge, 1990), p. 184.

72   *The Tailor and Cutter,* May 15, 1931 in Owen, *Fashion in Photographs,* p. 66.

73   Brooker, *Bohemia in London,* Preface, p. viii.

74   Owen, *Fashion in Photographs,* p. 66.

75   Sybille Bedford, *Aldous Huxley, A Biography, Vol. 1, 1894–1939* (London: Chatto & Windus, 1973), p. 127.

76   Owen, *Fashion in Photographs,* p. 72.

77   Bedford, *Aldous Huxley,* p. 127.

78   Louise Baring, *Norman Parkinson: A Very British Glamour* (New York: Rizzoli, 2009), p. 80.

79   Jane Ashelford, "Utility Fashion," in *CC41 Utility Furniture and Fashion 1941–1951* (London: Geffrye Museum Trust, 1995), pp. 33–5; Jenkins, "Wool Textiles in the Twentieth Century," p. 1002.

80   Edward. S. Harrison, "A Scottish Woollen Mill in War Time," in *Scottish Woollens* (Edinburgh: The National Association of Scottish Woollen Manufacturers, 1956), p. 106.

81   Harrison, *Scottish Woollens,* p. 116.

82   *Memorandum and Articles of Association of the National Wool Textile Export Corporation* (London: Jordan & Sons Limited, 1940), pp. 1–4; HC Deb July 25, 1950, vol 478, cc 385–7.

83   *International Textiles,* No. 3, 1946, p. 59.

84   *The Ambassador,* no. 1, 1951, pp. 72–89.

85   Ashelford, "Utility Fashion," p. 35; Amy de la Haye, *The Cutting Edge: 50 Years of British Fashion 1947–1997* (London: V & A Museum, 1996), p. 40.

86   *Garment News,* January 16, 1922.

1   Catherine Horwood, Keeping Up Appearances: Fashion and Class Between the Wars (Stroud: Sutton, 2005); Fiona Skillen, "It's possible to play the game marvellously and at the same time look pretty and be perfectly fit: Sport, Women and Fashion in Inter-war Britain," *Costume* 46, Number 2 (2012).

2   *Garment News*, January 16, 1922, in The Scottish Woollen Trade Mark Association, Cuttings Book 1921–1947, NC 1/1/2, Archive of Historical Records and Business Archives, School of Textiles, Heriot-Watt University, Galashiels.

3   E. S. Harrison, *Scottish Woollens* (Edinburgh: The National Association of Scottish Woollen Manufacturers, 1956), p. 170.

4   Jean S. Pattison, "The Tweed Section of the Scottish Woollen Industry," in H. A. Silverman (ed.) *Studies In Industrial Organisation* (London: Methuen & Co. Ltd, 1946), p. 120.

5   Harrison, *Scottish Woollen*s, pp. 168–9.

6   Harrison, *Scottish Woollens*, p. 169.

7   American *Vogue*, October 1927, p. 10.

8   American *Vogue*, October 1927, p. 10.

9   Harrison, *Scottish Woollens*, pp. 168–9.

10 Pattison, "The Tweed Section," p. 122; Leslie Walker, interview with the author, Linton Tweeds, Carlisle, November 22, 2013.

11 *Women's Wear*, January 14, 1922, in The Scottish Woollen Trade Mark Association, Cuttings Book 1921–1947.

12 American *Vogue*, October 1927, p. 10.

13 Harrison, *Scottish Woollens*, p. 169.

14 Harrison, *Scottish Woollens*, p. 169.

15 Hardy Amies, *Just So Far* (London: Collins, 1954), p. 50.

16 Patricia Hitchon, *Chanel and the Tweedmaker: Weavers of Dreams* (Carlisle: P3 Publications, 2012).

17 That specialization in womenswear is made evident by artifacts in the Otterburn Mill Collection.

18 Mary Delane, "A Story of Private Enterprise," *Sunday Times*, July 14, 1946, p. 6; D. J. W. Mawson, "Langthwaite Cotton Mill," *Transactions Cumberland & Westmorland Antiquarian Archaeological Society* XXXVI (1976): 159–83.

19 Hitchon, *Chanel and the Tweedmaker*, pp. 8–14; "New Local Company: Waddell's Ltd," *Carlisle Journal*, November 22, 1912, p. 4; "Waddell's Ltd," *Carlisle Journal*, December 20, 1912, p. 4.

20 "Sale of Property: Warwick Bridge Woollen Mill," *Carlisle Journal*, October 14, 1919, p. 5; Hitchon, *Chanel and the Tweedmaker*, pp. 39–60.

21 K.2013.7.10, Order Book, 1926, Otterburn Mill Collection, National Museums Scotland.

22 Katrina Honeyman, *Well Suited: A History of the Leeds Clothing Industry* 1850–1990 (Oxford: Oxford University Press, 2000), p. 281; "Bradley (/Label Resource)," Vintage Fashion Guild. Available online: http://vintagefashionguild.org/labels/6/ (accessed November 7, 2013).

23 "History – Dormeuil," Dormeuil. Available online: http://www.dormeuil.com/en/about-us/history/ (accessed November 10, 2013).

24 K.2013.7.11, Bunch, 1934, 113/1, National Museums Scotland.

25 K.2013.7.12, Bunch, 1934, 113/3, National Museums Scotland.

26 An example of an object from the Otterburn Mill Collection that demonstrates these developments is K.2013.7.12, Bunch, 1934, 113/3.

27 Elizabeth Owen, *Fashion in Photographs 1920–1940* (London: B. T. Batsford in association with The National Portrait Gallery, 1993), p. 94.

28 "Scotch Tweeds for Germany," *The Wool Record and Textile World*, 1934, in Miscellaneous Cuttings Book (1934–37), NC 2/1, Archive of Historical Records and Business Archives, School of Textiles, Heriot-Watt University, Galashiels.

29 Harrison, *Scottish Woollens*, p. 170

30   Edwina Ehrman, "Glamorous Modernity: 1914–30," in Christopher Breward, Edwina Ehrman and Caroline Evans (eds) *The London Look: Fashion from Street to Catwalk* (London and New Haven: Yale University Press, 2004), p. 79.

31   Ehrman, "Glamorous Modernity: 1914–30," p. 81.

32   Ehrman, "Glamorous Modernity: 1914–30," pp. 79–81.

33   Christopher Price, "Depression and Recovery," in Francesca Carnevali and Julie-Marie Strange (eds) *20th Century Britain: Economic, Cultural and Social Change* (Harlow: Pearson Education Limited, 2007), p. 152.

34   Price, "Depression and Recovery," p. 152.

35   Edwina Ehrman, "Broken Traditions: 1930–55," in Christopher Breward, Edwina Ehrman and Caroline Evans (eds) *The London Look: Fashion from Street to Catwalk* (London and New Haven, Yale University Press, 2004), p. 97.

36   British *Vogue*, April, 1930, p. 47.

37   J. M. Lee, *Social Leaders and Public Persons: A Study of County Government in Cheshire since 1888* (Oxford: Clarendon Press, 1963), p. 42; David Cannadine, *The Decline and Fall of the British Aristocracy* (London: Papermac, 1996), p. 392.

38   Cannadine, *The Decline and Fall*, pp. 392–3; Ehrman, "Glamorous Modernity: 1914–30," p. 85.

39   "Tweeds Acquire a New Significance," *Harper's Bazaar*, October 1929, p. 67.

40   British *Vogue*, February 3, 1932, p. 55.

41   This information is courtesy of Alex Anthony at the Norman Parkinson Archive.

42   Ehrman, "Broken Traditions: 1930–55," p. 107.

43   Hardy Amies, *Still Here: an autobiography* (London: Weidenfeld & Nicholson, 1984), pp. 20–1; Linda Watson, *Vogue Twentieth Century Fashion: 100 Years of Style by Decade and Designer* (London: Carlton, 1999), p. 172.

44   Amies, *Still Here*, p. 21.

45   Martin Pugh, *We Danced All Night: A Social History of Britain Between the Wars* (London: Vintage, 2009), p. 297.

46   *S.M.T. Magazine and Scottish Country Life,* Vol. XIX, No. 5, November, 1937, p. 18.

47   Josephine Ross, *Society in Vogue: The International Set Between the Wars* (London: Condé Nast Publications Ltd., 1992), p. 113.

48   Amies, *Still Here*, p. 21.

49   Watson, *Vogue Twentieth Century Fashion*, p. 195

50   Amies, *Still Here*, p. 21.

51   Amies, *Still Here*, p. 143.

52   Amies, *Still Here*, p. 25.

53   Harrison, *Scottish Woollens*, p. 170.

54   David Jenkins and Kenneth Ponting, *The British Wool Textile Industry 1770–1914* (Aldershot: Scolar Press, 1987), p. 170; David Jenkins, "Wool textiles in the twentieth century," in David Jenkins, *The Cambridge History of Western Textiles, II* (Cambridge: Cambridge University Press, 2003), p. 999.

55   Sarah Tomalin Lee, *American Fashion* (London,: Andre Deutsch, 1975), p. 218.

56   Elizabeth Wilson, *Adorned in Dreams: Fashion and Modernity* (London: I. B. Tauris, 2nd edn, 2003), p. 40.

57   Skillen, "It's Possible to Play the Game," p. 165.

58   Skillen, "It's Possible to Play the Game," pp. 166–7.

59   Skillen, "It's Possible to Play the Game," p. 167.

60   Anne Hollander, *Seeing Through Clothes* (New York: Avon Books, 1980), p. 152; Skillen, "It's Possible to Play the Game," p. 168.

61   Skillen, "It's Possible to Play the Game," p. 169.

62   Skillen, "It's Possible to Play the Game," pp. 165–75.

63   Horwood, *Keeping Up Appearances*, p. 90.
64   Mrs R. J. McNair, "Should Women Wear Plus Fours?" *Golf Illustrated*, January 23, 1925, p. 84.
65   *Golf Illustrated*, November 9, 1934, p. 86.
66   Horwood, *Keeping Up Appearances,* p. 91.
67   Amies, *Still Here,* p. 143.
68   Pugh, *We Danced All Night*, pp. 276–7.
69   David Matless, *Landscape and Englishness* (London: Reaktion Books Ltd, 1998), p. 14.
70   Pugh, *We Danced All Night*, p. 276.
71   Pugh, *We Danced All Night*, p. 276.
72   This information is courtesy of Alex Anthony at the Norman Parkinson Archive.
73   Valerie Steele, "Chanel in Context," in Juliet Ash and Elizabeth Wilson (eds) *Chic Thrills: A Fashion Reader* (London: Harper Collins Publishers, 1992), p. 119.
74   Bonnie English, *A Cultural History of Fashion in the 20th and 21st Centuries: From Catwalk to Sidewalk* (London: Bloomsbury, 2013), p. 38.
75   American *Vogue*, October 1927, p. 10.
76   American *Vogue*, November 1, 1926, p. 82.
77   *Harper's Bazaar*, October 1929, p. 66.
78   Amy de la Haye, *Chanel: Couture and Industry* (London: V & A Publishing, 2011), pp. 19–33.
79   de la Haye, *Chanel*, p. 41.
80   de la Haye, *Chanel*, p. 41.
81   Phillis Cunnington and Alan Mansfield, *English Costume for Sports and Outdoor Recreation* (London: Adam & Charles Black, 1969).
82   Steele, "Chanel in Context," p. 119; Wilson, *Adorned in Dreams*, pp. 40–1; English, *A Cultural History of Fashion*, pp. 32–41.
83   Jane Ashelford, "Utility Fashion," in *CC41 Utility Furniture and Fashion 1941–1951* (London: Geffrye Museum Trust, 1995), pp. 33–5; Georgina Howell, *Wartime Fashion: From Haute Couture to Homemade 1939–1945* (London: Bloomsbury Academic, 2012), pp. 99–108.
84   Ashelford, "Utility Fashion," p. 33; Howell, *Wartime Fashion*, pp. 168–70. Examples of Utility tweed suits in the Victoria and Albert Museum collection are: T.43&A-1942 and T.48&A-1942.
85   British *Vogue*, July 1941, p. 24.
86   Christian Dior, *Dior by Dior* (London: Weidenfeld & Nicolson, 1957), p. 21.
87   Claire Wilcox, "The New Look," in Claire Wilcox *The Golden Age of Couture: Paris and London 1947–57* (London: V & A Publishing, 2007), p. 60.
88   British *Vogue*, February, 1950; Amy de la Haye, *The Cutting Edge: 50 Years of British Fashion 1947–1997* (London: V & A Publications, 1996), pp. 40–1.
89   INCSOC Annual Report, 1950, Victoria and Albert Museum Archives.
90   *The Ambassador* (3) 1951, p. 13.
91   American *Vogue*, October 1927, p. 10; Harrison, *Scottish Woollens*, p. 170.
92   Skillen, "It's possible to play the game," pp. 165–8.
93   Hollander, *Seeing Through Clothes*, p. 152.
94   British *Vogue*, July 1941, p. 24; Howell, *Wartime Fashion*, p. 170.

Chapter 8: Couture to Pop and Nostalgic Fashion, 1953–1980
1   Alexandra Palmer, *Couture & Commerce: The Transatlantic Fashion Trade in the 1950s* (Vancouver: University of British Columbia Press, 2001), pp. 161–8.
2   G. F. Rainnie, *The Woollen and Worsted Industry: An Economic Analysis* (Oxford: Clarendon Press, 1965), pp. 29–31.
3   Alan Brearley and John A. Iredale, *The Woollen Industry* (Leeds: WIRA, 1977, 2nd edn), pp. 12–14.
4   Jim Tomlinson, "Managing the economy, managing the people," in Francesca Carnevali and Julie-Marie

Strange (eds), *20th Century Britain: Economic, Cultural and Social Change* (Harlow: Pearson Education Limited, 2007), p. 233.

5   Rainnie, *The Woollen and Worsted Industry*, pp. 44–5.

6   Scottish Development Agency in association with Research Associates and the Shirley Institute, *Opportunities for The Scottish Wool Textile and Knitwear Industries* (Glasgow: Scottish Development Agency, 1981), p. 12; David Jenkins, "Wool Textiles in the Twentieth Century," in David Jenkins (ed.), *The Cambridge History of Western Textiles, II* (Cambridge: Cambridge University Press, 2003), p. 1012.

7   Jenkins, "Wool Textiles," p. 1014.

8   Lou Taylor and Fiona Anderson, "Fashion for Women and Men in the Twentieth Century," in Jenkins (ed.), *The Cambridge History*, pp. 1067–8; Jenkins, "Wool Textiles," p. 1017.

9   Rodney Bennett-England, *Dress Optional: the Revolution in Menswear* (London: Peter Owen Limited, 1967), p. 185; Paul Jobling, *Advertising Menswear: Masculinity and Fashion in the British Media Since 1945* (London: Bloomsbury Academic, 2014), pp. 6–7.

10   *Man About Town*, Spring, 1953, p. 62.

11   Nik Cohn, *Today There Are No Gentlemen* (London: Weidenfeld & Nicolson, 1971), p. 44.

12   Jenkins, "Wool Textiles," p. 1017.

13   Irene Hardill, *The Regional Implications of Restructuring in the Wool Textile Industry* (Aldershot: Gower, 1987), p. 199.

14   Tomlinson, "Managing the economy," p. 239.

15   Anthony Moreton, "Textiles: the struggle at Lake Geneva: Multi-Fibre Arrangement," *Financial Times*, October 29, 1984, p. 15.

16   Market Studies International, "A Market Data Report on Wool, Vol. 2: Fabric" (London: Inter Company Comparisons, 1982), p. 5; Moreton, "Textiles," p. 15.

17   E. S. Harrison, *Scottish Woollens* (Edinburgh: The National Association of Scottish Woollen Manufacturers, 1956), pp. xi–xiv; The National Association of Scottish Woollen Manufacturers, *The Scottish Woollen Industry* (Edinburgh: The National Association of Scottish Woollen Manufacturers, 1970), pp. 4–5; Scottish Woollen Publicity Council, *Scottish Wool Cloth Sample Book* (London: International Wool Secretariat for the Scottish Woollen Publicity Council, undated), p. 2; Scottish Development Agency, *Opportunities*, p. 12.

18   Harrison, *Scottish Woollens*, pp. xi–xiv; NASWM, *The Scottish Woollen Industry*, p. 6.

19   Rainnie, *The Woollen and Worsted Industry*, p. 50; NASWM, *The Scottish Woollen Industry*, p. 4.

20   NASWM, *The Scottish Woollen Industry*, pp. 4–25; SWPC, *Scottish Wool Cloth Sample Book*, p. 2.

21   Harrison, *Scottish Woollens*, pp. xi–xiv; NASWM, *The Scottish Woollen Industry*, pp. 6–7.

22   SWPC, *Scottish Wool Cloth Sample Book*, p. 9.

23   NASWM, *The Scottish Woollen Industry*, p. 4.

24   SWPC, *Scottish Wool Cloth Sample Book*, p. 9.

25   SWPC, *Scottish Wool Cloth Sample Book*, p. 9; "Timeline", Robert Noble. Available online: http://robert-noble.co.uk/about/timeline (accessed May 5, 2013).

26   Scottish Development Agency, *Opportunities*, p. 37.

27   NASWM, *The Scottish Woollen Industry*, p. 5.

28   SWPC, *Scottish Wool Cloth Sample Book*, p. 4.

29   NASWM, *The Scottish Woollen Industry*, p. 5.

30   SWPC, *Scottish Wool Cloth Sample Book*, p. 5.

31   Scottish Development Agency, *Opportunities*, pp. 5–7.

32   NASWM, *The Scottish Woollen Industry*, pp. 6–7; Scottish Development Agency, *Opportunities*, pp. 5–12.

33   Scottish Development Agency, *Opportunities*, p. 7.

34   Scottish Development Agency, *Opportunities*, pp. 13–14.

35   Scottish Development Agency, *Opportunities*, p. 13.

36 Scottish Development Agency, *Opportunities*, p. 5.

37 Janet Hunter, *The Islanders and the Orb: The History of the Harris Tweed Industry 1835–1995* (Stornoway, Lewis: Acair Ltd, 2001), pp. 196–267.

38 Hunter, *The Islanders,* pp. 198–204.

39 Hunter, *The Islanders,* pp. 196–265.

40 Hunter, *The Islanders,* p. 264.

41 Hunter, *The Islanders,* p. 16 and p. 279.

42 Hunter, *The Islanders,* pp. 284–7.

43 "Shortage of Weavers Tweed Deliveries Overdue," *The Stornoway Gazette*, June 1, 1974, cutting in Harris Tweed Association (HTA) archive.

44 "Weavers To Decide Future," *The Daily Telegraph*, March 10, 1976, HTA archive.

45 "Weavers Reject Move," *The Daily Telegraph*, April 17, 1976; "Hebrides weavers reject proposal to make Harris tweed by machine," *The Times*, April 17, 1976, HTA archive.

46 "Moves To Redefine Tweed Orb," *West Highland Free Press*, February 28, 1975, HTA archive.

47 "Tweed guild oppose change in Orb mark," *The Scotsman*, March 6, 1975, HTA archive.

48 "The power of Harris Tweed," *Draper's Record,* February 15, 1975, HTA archive.

49 "Hebrides weavers reject proposal to make Harris tweed by machine," *The Times,* April 17, 1976, HTA archive.

50 "Tangled threads," *The Glasgow Herald*, April 19, 1976, HTA archive.

51 Hunter, *The Islanders,* p. 16.

52 Hunter, *The Islanders,* pp. 321–2.

53 Tomlinson, "Managing the economy," p. 241.

54 Ian Angus Mackenzie, interview with the author, Harris Tweed Hebrides, Shawbost, October 31, 2013.

55 *The Ambassador* (4), 1966, pp. 4–7.

56 W. G. Lucas, "Harris Tweed industry's new production record," *The Scotsman*, June 23, 1967, p. 9.

57 Hunter, *The Islanders,* p. 339.

58 Patricia Mears, *Ivy Style* (New Haven and London: Yale University Press, 2012), pp. 97–8.

59 Mears, *Ivy Style,* pp. 147–8.

60 *The Ambassador,* (8) 1958, p. 72 and (8) 1962, pp. 60–1.

61 *The Ambassador,* (8) 1962, p. 62.

62 Lucas, "Harris Tweed," p. 8.

63 Francis Thompson, *Harris Tweed: The Story of a Hebridean Industry* (New York: Augustus M. Kelley, 1969), p. 154.

64 Claire Wilcox, "Introduction," in Claire Wilcox, *The Golden Age of Couture: Paris and London 1947–57* (London: V & A Publishing, 2007), pp. 12–15.

65 Lesley Ellis Miller, "Perfect Harmony: Textile Manufacturers and Haute Couture 1947–1957," in Wilcox, *The Golden Age*, p. 130.

66 *"Face A L'Hiver,"* in *L'art et La Mode*, No. 4, 1959, pp. 250–1.

67 Jeannette A. Jarnow and Beatrice Judelle, *Inside the Fashion Business: Text and Readings* (New York: John Wiley and Sons Inc., 1965), p. 95.

68 Miller, "Perfect Harmony" p. 119.

69 Miller, "Perfect Harmony" p. 122.

70 List of *Fournisseurs*, Un Livre de Collection, Summer, 1964; Un Livre de Collection, Winter, 1964; Un Livre de Collection, Summer, 1966; Un Livre de Collection, Winter, 1967; Un Livre de Collection, c. 1967; Un Livre de Collection, Summer, 1968; all in Balenciaga private archive.

71 Ladies Tweed Suit, "Chantecler," Christian Dior, Haute Couture Collection, Autumn/Winter, 1954–55, the fabric is by Linton Tweeds; Collections Charts of the CD London Collections, Winter, 1961; Spring; 1962 ; Summer, 1962; Autumn, 1962; Winter, 1962; Spring, 1963; Summer, 1963; Autumn, 1964; all in Dior private archive.

72 *"Le Tweed Chez Chanel,"* unpublished document, Chanel private archive, pp. 6–7; Amy de la Haye, *Chanel: Couture and Industry* (London: V & A Publishing, 2011), pp. 76–81.

73 Mahlia Kent, *La Pharaonne* (Paris: Editions Acropole, 1980), pp. 74–76; *"Le Tweed Chez Chanel,"* pp. 23–6.

74 Bernat Klein and Lesley Jackson, *Bernat Klein: Textile Designer, Artist, Colourist* (Gattonside, Roxburghshire: Bernat Klein Trust, 2005), p. 13.

75 Mary Brogan, "Haute Couture for Survival," *Sunday Telegraph*, December 6, 1964, cutting from Press Book, K.2010.94.10, Bernat Klein Collection, National Museums Scotland.

76 Klein and Jackson, *Bernat Klein,* pp. 13–17.

77 Leslie Walker, interview with the author, Linton Tweeds, Carlisle, November 22, 2013.

78 Patricia Hitchon, *Chanel and the Tweedmaker: Weavers of Dreams* (Carlisle: P3 Publications, 2012), pp. 120–40.

79 Agnes Linton, "Notes on Linton Tweeds, 1950s," Tullie House Art Gallery and Museum, Carlisle.

80 Hardy Amies, *Just So Far* (London: Collins, 1954), p. 50; Leslie Walker, November 22, 2013.

81 Leslie Walker, November 22, 2013.

82 Leslie Walker, November 22, 2013.

83 Order Book, early 1950s, Linton Tweeds private archive.

84 Leslie Walker, November 22, 2013.

85 Order Book, 1956–1957, Linton Tweeds private archive; Caroline Rennolds Milbank, *New York Fashion: The Evolution of American Style* (New York: Harry N. Abrams, Inc., 1989), pp. 124–94.

86 Leslie Walker, November 22, 2013.

87 Miller, "Perfect Harmony," p. 118.

88 Leslie Walker, November 22, 2013.

89 Palmer, *Couture & Commerce*, pp. 161–8.

90 Leslie Walker, November 22, 2013.

91 Milbank, *New York Fashion*, p. 125.

92 Leslie Walker, November 22, 2013.

93 Geoffrey Aquilina Ross, *The Day of the Peacock: Style for Men 1963–1973* (London: V & A Publishing, 2011), pp. 25–6.

94 Christopher Breward, *Fashioning London: Clothing and the Modern Metropolis* (Oxford: Berg, 2004), p. 126; Jobling, *Advertising Menswear*, pp. 70–1.

95 *Man About Town*, Spring, 1953, pp. 43–7.

96 Breward, *Fashioning London,* p. 144.

97 *Man About Town*, Spring, 1953, pp. 109–13.

98 *Man About Town*, Spring, 1953, pp. 109.

99 *Man About Town*, Spring, 1953, pp. 111.

100 *Man About Town*, Spring, 1953, pp. 113.

101 Breward, *Fashioning London,* p. 144.

102 *Man About Town*, Spring, 1953, pp. 122.

103 *Man About Town*, Autumn/Winter, 1959, pp. 115–31; James Sherwood, *Savile Row: The Master Tailors of British Bespoke* (London: Thames and Hudson, 2010), p. 208.

104 Cohn, *Today There Are No Gentlemen*; Taylor and Anderson, "Fashion for Women and Men," p. 1068.

105 Frank Mort, *Cultures of Consumption: Masculinities and Social Space in Late Twentieth-Century Britain* (London: Routledge, 1996), pp. 132–3.

106 Taylor and Anderson, "Fashion for Women and Men," p. 1068.

107 Cohn, *Today There Are No Gentlemen,* pp. 60–71; Ross, *The Day of the Peacock*, pp. 37–45.

108 Cohn, *Today There Are No Gentlemen,* pp. 64–9.

109 Cohn, *Today There Are No Gentlemen,* p. 70; Ross, *The Day of the Peacock*, p. 43.

110 Ross, *The Day of the Peacock*, p. 43.

111 Cohn, *Today There Are No Gentlemen,* pp. 78–84.
112 Cohn, *Today There Are No Gentlemen,* p. 79.
113 Francis Megahy and Fred Burnley, *An Easter with Rod* (London: Rediffusion, 1965). British Film Institute Reference Number, N-40270.
114 David Cannadine, *Ornamentalism: How The British Saw Their Empire* (London: Penguin Books Ltd, 2002), pp. 172–3.
115 Mort, *Cultures of Consumption*, pp. 131–2.
116 Christopher Breward, "Foreword," in Ross, *The Day of the Peacock*, p. 13.
117 Breward, "Foreword," p. 13.
118 Nigel Whiteley, *Pop Design: Modernism to Mod* (London: The Design Council, 1987), p. 209.
119 Cannadine, *Ornamentalism*, p. 172.
120 Stuart Ward, *British Culture and the End of Empire* (Manchester: Manchester University Press, 2001), p. 15.
121 Whiteley, *Pop Design*, p. 208.
122 Ward, *British Culture*, pp. 11–12.
123 Cover of "Dance to the Music," Sly & the Family Stone, CD, 2010, Sony Music Entertainment.
124 Christopher Breward, "Boutiques and Beyond: The Rise of British Fashion," in Christopher Breward and Ghislaine Wood (eds), *British Design from 1948: Innovation in the Modern Age* (London: V & A Publishing, 2012), pp. 209–11.
125 Kelly Boyd and Rohan McWilliam, *The Victorian Studies Reader* (Abingdon, Oxon: Routledge, 2007), pp. 13–14.
126 Boyd and McWilliam, *The Victorian*, p. 14.
127 *Men in Vogue,* November, 1965, pp. 90–1; Whiteley, *Pop Design*, pp. 210–16.
128 Ross, *The Day of the Peacock*, pp. 129–33; Sherwood, *Savile Row*, pp. 208–11.
129 Miller, "Perfect Harmony," p. 128.
130 Miller, "Perfect Harmony," p. 128.
131 Wilcox, "Introduction," p. 12.
132 Christian Dior, *The Little Dictionary of Fashion: A guide to dress sense* for every woman (London: V & A Publishing, 2008), p. 111.
133 Dior, *The Little Dictionary of Fashion*, p. 58.
134 Dior, *The Little Dictionary of Fashion*, p. 111.
135 Palmer, *Couture & Commerce,* p. 90; "Les Tissus Masculins," unpublished folder, Dior private archive.
136 GAL1988.70.18, Palais Galliera; "Favoris de la mode nouvelle. Au dîner: une robe de tweed," *Vogue* (France), October 1953, p. 81.
137 American *Vogue*, October 1, 1953, p. 148.
138 American *Vogue*, September 1, 1963, p. 126.
139 *Mary Quant's London* (London: London Museum, 1973), pp. 14–31.
140 *Mary Quant's London*, p. 14.
141 *Man About Town*, Autumn/Winter 1959, p. 117.
142 Catherine Join-Diéterle, "Dior and Balenciaga: A Different Approach to the Body," in Wilcox, *The Golden Age*, pp. 138–45.
143 Whiteley, *Pop Design*, p. 96.
144 "Brash New Breed of British Designers," in *Life*, October 18 1963, p. 82; K.2013.7.11, Otterburn Mill Collection, National Museums Scotland.
145 Breward, "Boutiques," p. 211.
146 Mary Brogan, "Haute Couture for Survival," Press Book cutting, K.2010.94.10, Bernat Klein Collection, National Museums Scotland.
147 British *Vogue*, September 15, 1964, p. 95.
148 British *Vogue*, September 15, 1964, p. 98.

149 Whiteley, *Pop Design*, p. 178.
150 British *Vogue*, "Young Idea's Green Belt Girl," October 15, 1967, pp. 120–1.
151 David Matless, *Landscape and Englishness* (London: Reaktion Books Ltd, 1998), p. 17.
152 Rebecca Arnold, *Fashion, Desire and Anxiety: Image and Morality in the 20th Century* (London: I. B. Tauris & Co. Ltd, 2001), p. 122.
153 Colin MacDowell, *Ralph Lauren: The Man, the Vision, the Style* (London: Cassell Illustrated, 2002), p. 40.
154 Kathleen Baird-Murray, *Vogue On Ralph Lauren* (London: Quadrille Publishing, 2013), pp. 42–3.
155 Joan Juliet Buck, in Baird-Murray, *Vogue On Ralph Lauren*, p. 44.
156 Fred Davis, *Fashion, Culture and Identity* (Chicago: The University of Chicago Press, 1992), pp. 42–4.

Chapter 9: Tradition and Innovation, 1981–2014

1   Janet Hunter, *The Islanders and the Orb: The History of the Harris Tweed Industry 1835–1995* (Stornoway, Lewis: Acair Ltd, 2001), p. 324; Lara Platman, *Harris Tweed: From Land to Street* (London: Frances Lincoln Limited Publishers, 2011), pp. 123–7; *Harper's Bazaar*, July 2013, p. 46; Ian Angus Mackenzie, interview with the author, Harris Tweed Hebrides, Shawbost, October 31, 2013.
2   Ian Angus Mackenzie, October 31, 2013; Keith Walker, interview with the author, Linton Tweeds, Carlisle, November 22, 2013.
3   Irene Hardill, *The Regional Implications of Restructuring* (Aldershot: Gower Publishing Company Limited, 1987), pp. 193–4.
4   "Survey of UKFT List," in *Twist*, Issue 49, February/March 2013, pp. 24–7; Gareth Wyn Davies, "Abraham Moon: the name on everyone's lips – and labels," *The Telegraph*, November 21, 2011. Available online: http://fashion.telegraph.co.uk/news-features/TMG8904041/Abraham-Moon-the-name-on-everyones-lips-and-labels.html (accessed November 7, 2013); "About Us," Marton Mills. Available online: http://www.martonmills.com/aboutus.htm (accessed February 26, 2014); "View Our Latest Collections," Marling and Evans Ltd. Available online: http://www.marlingandevansltd.co.uk (accessed February 26, 2014); "Our Heritage," William Bliss & Son Ltd. Available online: http://www.williamblisstextiles.co.uk/our-heritage (accessed February 26, 2014). Marling & Evans was originally a West of England woolen manufacturer. William Bliss & Son Ltd were previously based in Oxfordshire and owned by Fox Brothers & Co. Ltd.
5   *Twist*, Issue 26, November 2010, pp. 46–7; Royston Berrett, notes from conversation with the author, Trowbridge, July 5, 2013; "Finishes and Weights," Fox Brothers & Co. Ltd. Available online: http://www.foxflannel.com/finishes.php (accessed February 26, 2014).
6   David Jenkins, "Wool Textiles in the Twentieth Century," in David Jenkins (ed.), *The Cambridge History of Western Textiles, Vol. II* (Cambridge: Cambridge University Press, 2003), p. 1017.
7   Farid Chenoune, *A History of Men's Fashion* (Paris: Flammarion, 1993), pp. 294–6; Lou Taylor and Fiona Anderson, "Fashion for Women and Men in the Twentieth Century," in Jenkins (ed.), *The Cambridge History*, p. 1071; Ann Walker, *The Structure of the West European Wool Industry: Prospects and Strategies for a Changing Market* (London: Pearson Professional Ltd, 1995), p. 98.
8   Katrina Honeyman, *Well Suited: A History of the Leeds Clothing Industry 1850–1990* (Oxford: Oxford University Press, 2000), p. 248; Martin Pugh, *State and Society: a Social and Political History of Britain Since 1870* (London: Bloomsbury Academic, 2012), pp. 344–6.
9   Walker, *The Structure*, p. 34; Jenkins, "Wool Textiles," p. 1015.
10 Walker, *The Structure*, pp. 2–34; Jenkins, "Wool Textiles," pp. 1015–20.
11 Jenkins, "Wool Textiles," pp. 1014–15.
12 Walker, *The Structure*, pp. 38–9; *IWTO Market Information 2014 – Statistics for the Global Wool Production and Textile Industry* (Brussels: International Wool Textile Organisation, 2014), pp. 31–81.
13 Jenkins, "Wool Textiles," p. 1018; "Textiles Monitoring Body (TMB): The Agreement on Textiles and

Clothing," World Trade Organisation, 2013. Available online: https://www.wto.org/english/tratop_e/texti_e/texintro_e.htm (accessed November 8, 2013).

14 Honeyman, *Well Suited,* p. 240.

15 Jenkins, "Wool Textiles," p. 1018.

16 Hunter, *The Islanders*, p. 324.

17 Ian Angus Mackenzie, October 31, 2013.

18 Harris Tweed Authority, "HTA Information Pack," unpublished, 2012, p. 42.

19 Harris Tweed Association Minutes, July 12, 1991, in Hunter, *The Islanders*, p. 339.

20 Duncan Martin, "Report to 'The Western Isles: An Economy In Crisis A Challenge For The Millennium' conference," 1998, p. 3.

21 Martin, "Report," pp. 1–2.

22 Hunter, *The Islanders*, pp. 344–6.

23 Martin, "Report," p. 2.

24 Hunter, *The Islanders*, pp. 14–15; Harris Tweed Act, 1993 (c.xi) (London: HMSO, 1993).

25 *Spectrum*, February 20, 2011, p. 16; Donald John Mackay, interview with the author, Luskentyre, Harris, September 24, 2011; Harris Tweed Authority, "An Overview of the Harris Tweed Industry," unpublished, 2012, p. 6.

26 Harris Tweed Authority, "An Overview," p. 6.

27 *Spectrum*, February 20, 2011, p. 17; Harris Tweed Authority, "HTA Information Pack," p. 42.

28 Scottish Woollen Industry, Annual Report, 1985, pp. 2–3.

29 Scottish Woollen Industry, Annual Report, 1985, pp. 12–18; Scottish Woollen Industry, Annual Report, 1991, pp. 10–16.

30 Scottish Woollen Industry, Annual Report, 1991, p. 3.

31 DTZ Pieda Consulting, *Briefing Paper on The Scottish Textile and Clothing Industry* (Edinburgh: Scottish Executive Enterprise and Lifelong Learning Department and Scottish Textiles Network, 2000), p. 10. Available online: http://www.gov.scot/Resource/Doc/158182/0042809.pdf (accessed September 5, 2013).

32 DTZ Pieda Consulting, *Briefing Paper*, p. 11.

33 Alan Cumming, interview with the author, Lovat Mill, Hawick, November 14, 2013; "Collections," Robert Noble Ltd. Available online: http://robert-noble.co.uk/collections (accessed December 5, 2013).

34 E. P Harrison, *Scottish Estate Tweeds* (Elgin: Johnstons of Elgin, 1995); "Our Range," Knockando Woolmill Company Ltd. Available online: http://www.knockandowoolmill.org.uk/collections/our-range (accessed February 26, 2014).

35 *Harper's Bazaar*, July 2013, p. 47 and p. 120; *Drapers,* October 7, 2011, p. 41; "Our Most Valuable Assets," Johnstons of Elgin. Available online: http://www.johnstonscashmere.com/index.php/retail/about-johnstons-of-elgin/careers (accessed January 15 2014).

36 Alan Cumming, November 14, 2013; "Creativity Captured in Cloth," Neill Johnstone. Available online: http://www.neilljohnstone.com/ (accessed February 26, 2014).

37 "Organic Suppliers," *Selvedge,* Issue 31 (November/December 2009): 11; "About Bute," Bute Fabrics Ltd. Available online: http://www.butefabrics.com/about-us (accessed December 7, 2013); Alexanders of Scotland. Available online: http://www.alexandersofscotland.com/home/ (accessed December 7, 2013); "About Us," Islay Woollen Mill. Available online: http://www.islaywoollenmill.co.uk/about-us/ (accessed December 7, 2013).

38 Donald John Mackay, September 24, 2011; Harris Tweed Authority, "HTA Information Pack," pp. 17–43; Ian Angus Mackenzie, October 31, 2013.

39 Ian Angus Mackenzie, October 31, 2013.

40 Ian Angus Mackenzie, October 31, 2013.

41 Ian Angus Mackenzie, October 31, 2013.

42   Ian Angus Mackenzie, October 31, 2013; *Press and Journal*, January 7, 2014, p. 32.

43   Ken Kennedy, interview with the author, Harris Tweed Hebrides, Shawbost, October 31, 2013.

44   Ken Kennedy, October 31, 2013.

45   Ian Angus Mackenzie, October 31, 2013; Ken Kennedy, October 31, 2013.

46   Katie Laing, "Secret of Sweet Tweed? It's All In The Eye," April 17, 2014. Available online: http://www.harristweedhebrides.com/blogs/news (accessed April 20, 2014).

47   Ian Angus Mackenzie, October 31, 2013.

48   Ian Angus Mackenzie, October 31, 2013.

49   *Press and Journal*, January 7, 2014, p. 32.

50   Ian Angus Mackenzie, October 31, 2013.

51   Ian Angus Mackenzie, October 31, 2013.

52   GLAMB, Autumn, 2011, cutting in Harris Tweed Authority Archive.

53   Ian Angus Mackenzie, October 31, 2013.

54   Stephen Rendle, interview with the author, Lovat Mill, Hawick, November 14, 2013; "Blenkhorn Richardson & Co. Ltd, Woollen Manufacturers Hawick," Heriot-Watt University Archive, Records Management and Museum Service. Available online: http://archiveshub.ac.uk/features/textiles-blenkhornrichardson.html (accessed November 18, 2013).

55   Alan Cumming, November 14, 2013; Stephen Rendle, November 14, 2013.

56   Stephen Rendle, November 14, 2013.

57   Alan Cumming, November 14, 2013; Stephen Rendle, November 14, 2013.

58   Alan Cumming, November 14, 2013; Blenkhorn Richardson & Co. Ltd designer notebooks, Lovat Mill private archive.

59   K.2005.330, National Museums Scotland.

60   Alan Cumming, November 14, 2013.

61   Stephen Rendle, November 14, 2013.

62   Alan Cumming, November 14, 2013.

63   Stephen Rendle, November 14, 2013.

64   Alan Cumming, November 14, 2013.

65   Stephen Rendle, November 14, 2013.

66   Alan Cumming, November 14, 2013.

67   Stephen Rendle, November 14, 2013.

68   *Harper's Bazaar*, July 2013, p. 115.

69   *Harper's Bazaar*, July 2013, p. 117.

70   Stephen Rendle, November 14, 2013.

71   Stephen Rendle, November 14, 2013.

72   Patricia Hitchon, *Chanel and the Tweedmaker: Weavers of Dreams* (Carlisle: P3 Publications, 2012), pp. 210–11; Keith Walker, November 22, 2013.

73   Keith Walker, November 22, 2013.

74   Keith Walker, November 22, 2013.

75   Leslie Walker, notes from conversation with the author, Linton Tweeds, Carlisle, November 22, 2013; Keith Walker, November 22, 2013.

76   Keith Walker, November 22, 2013.

77   Keith Walker, November 22, 2013.

78   Keith Walker, November 22, 2013.

79   Lisa Armstrong, "British Tweed: A brilliant yarn," *The Telegraph*, February 15, 2013. Available online: http://fashion.telegraph.co.uk/news-features/TMG987141/British-tweed-A-brilliant-yarn.html (accessed November 20, 2013); Keith Walker, November 22, 2013.

80   Keith Walker, November 22, 2013.

81   Keith Walker, November 22, 2013.

82   Lisa Armstrong, "Paris Haute Couture: Chanel autumn/winter 2013," *The Telegraph*, July 2, 2013. Available online: http://fashion.telegraph.co.uk/Article/TMG10154874/844/Paris-Haute-Couture-Chanel-autumnwinter-2013.html (accessed November 20, 2013).

83   Caroline Evans, *Fashion at the Edge: Spectacle, Modernity and Deathliness* (New Haven and London: Yale University Press, 2003), pp. 299–300.

84   Elizabeth Wilson, "Fashion and the Postmodern Body," in Juliet Ash and Elizabeth Wilson (eds), *Chic Thrills: A Fashion Reader* (London: Pandora, 1992), p. 6; Evans, *Fashion at the Edge*, pp. 299–300.

85   Amy de la Haye, *The Cutting Edge: 50 Years of British Fashion 1947–1997* (London: V & A Publications, 1996), p. 133; Lara Platman, *Harris Tweed*, pp. 123–7; Claire Wilcox, *Vivienne Westwood* (London: V & A Publications, 2004), p. 21; Alison Goodrum, *The National Fabric: Fashion, Britishness, Globalization* (Oxford: Berg, 2005), pp. 93–128.

86   *Harper's Bazaar*, July 2013, p. 46.

87   *Harper's Bazaar*, July 2013, pp. 46–7.

88   de la Haye, *The Cutting Edge*, p. 133.

89   Colin McDowell, *Ralph Lauren, The Man, the Vision, the Style* (London: Cassell Illustrated, 2002), p. 57; *Vogue*, September, 2012, inside front cover and p. 1; *Harper's Bazaar*, November, 2013, p. 220–3.

90   Rebecca Arnold, *Fashion, Desire and Anxiety: Image and Morality in the 20th Century* (London: I. B. Tauris & Co. Ltd, 2001), p. 122.

91   Wilcox, *Vivienne Westwood*, p. 9.

92   Wilcox, *Vivienne Westwood*, pp. 20–82.

93   Rebecca Arnold, "Vivienne Westwood's Anglomania," in Christopher Breward, Becky Conekin and Caroline Cox (eds), *The Englishness of English Dress* (Oxford: Berg, 2002), p. 166.

94   Wilcox, *Vivienne Westwood*, pp. 20–1.

95   Wilcox, *Vivienne Westwood*, p. 21.

96   The author spoke at a study day, "Harris Tweed: Past, Present and Future," held at Shawbost, Lewis in 2011. Attending this event made it clear that Harris Tweed is closely linked to the local community and culture.

97   Wilcox, *Vivienne Westwood*, p. 21–153; Platman, *Harris Tweed*, p. 125.

98   Platman, *Harris Tweed*, p. 125.

99   An example of these garments is the "Beretta St James Woman's Coat." Available online: http://www.beretta.com/en/st-james-woman-s-coat/gd186211/ (accessed February17, 2014); Orvis United Kingdom. Available online: http://www.orvis.co.uk/store/product_search_tnail.aspx?keyword=tweed (accessed December 2, 2013).

100   K.2006.225.1-2, National Museums Scotland.

101   John Gillespie, email to the author, May 3, 2005.

102   Goodrum, *The National Fabric*, p. 32.

103   "Manufacturing Focus," *Twist*, Issue 55, October, 2013, p. 15.

104   Goodrum, *The National Fabric*, p. 104.

105   Chenoune, *A History of Men's Fashion*, pp. 294–6; Fiona Anderson, "Fashioning the Gentleman: A Study of Henry Poole and Co., Savile Row Tailors 1861–1900," *Fashion Theory*, Vol. 4, No. 4 (2000): 407–10.

106   de la Haye, *The Cutting Edge*, pp. 60–1; James Sherwood, *Savile Row: the Master Tailors of British Bespoke* (London: Thames & Hudson, 2010), pp. 176–236; Christopher Breward, "Su{i}ture: Tailoring and the Fashion Metropolis," in Claire Wilcox (ed.), *Alexander McQueen* (London: V & A Publishing, 2015), pp. 37–40.

107   *Esquire*, September 2013, p. 87.

108   *GQ*, September 2013, p. 3.

109   Evans, *Fashion at the Edge*, p. 307.

110   Arnold, *Fashion, Desire and Anxiety*, p. 125.

BIBLIOGRAPHY

Allan, John. *Crombies of Grandholm and Cothal 1805–1960*. Aberdeen: The Central Press, 1960.

Amies, Hardy. *Just So Far*. London: Collins, 1954.

Amies, Hardy. *Still Here: An Autobiography*. London: Weidenfield & Nicholson, 1984.

Anderson, Fiona. "Henry Poole and Co. Savile Row Tailors, 1861–1900." MA diss., Royal College of Art/ Victoria and Albert Museum, London, 1998.

Anderson, Fiona. "Fashioning the Gentleman: A Study of Henry Poole and Co., Savile Row Tailors 1861–1900." *Fashion Theory: The Journal of Dress, Body & Culture* 4 (4) (2000): 405–26.

Anderson, Fiona. "Spinning the Ephemeral with the Sublime: Modernity and Landscape in Men's Fashion Textiles 1860–1900." *Fashion Theory: The Journal of Dress, Body & Culture* 9 (3) (2005): 283–304.

Anderson, Fiona. "This Sporting Cloth: Tweed, Gender and Fashion 1860–1900." *Textile History* 37 (2) (2006): 166–86.

Anderson, Kay, Mona Domosh, Steve Pile and Nigel Thrift. *Handbook of Cultural Geography*. London: Sage Publications Ltd, 2003.

Arnold, Janet. "Dashing Amazons: The Development of Women's Riding Dress, c. 1500–1900." In *Defining Dress: Dress as Object, Meaning and Identity*, edited by Amy de la Haye and Elizabeth Wilson, 10–29. Manchester: Manchester University Press, 1999.

Arnold, Rebecca. *Fashion, Desire and Anxiety: Image and Morality in the 20th Century*. London: I. B. Tauris & Co. Ltd, 2001.

Arnold, Rebecca. "Vivienne Westwood's Anglomania." In *The Englishness of English Dress,* edited by Christopher Breward, Becky Conekin and Caroline Cox, 161–70. Oxford: Berg, 2002.

Arnold, Rebecca. "Modern Fashions for Modern Women: The Evolution of New York Sportswear in the 1930s." *Costume* 41 (2007): 111–25.

Ashelford, Jane. "Utility Fashion." In *CC41 Utility Furniture and Fashion 1941–1951*, 33–6. London: Geffrye Museum Trust, 1995.

Baird-Murray, Kathleen. *Vogue On Ralph Lauren*. London: Quadrille Publishing, 2013.

Baring, Louise. *Norman Parkinson: A Very British Glamour*. New York: Rizzoli, 2009.

Bedford, Sybille. *Aldous Huxley, A Biography, Vol. 1, 1894–1939*. London: Chatto & Windus, 1973.

Benjamin, Walter. "Theses on the Philosophy of History." In *Illuminations,* edited by Hannah Arendt, 245–55. London: Pimlico, 1999.

Blaine, Delabere P. *An Encyclopedia of Rural Sports*. London: Longman, Brown, Green and Longmans, 1852.

Blaszczyk, Regina Lee. *The Color Revolution*. Cambridge, MA: MIT Press, 2012.

Brearley, Alan. *The Woollen Industry*. London: Sir Isaac Pitman & Sons Ltd, 1965.

Brearley, Alan and John A. Iredale. *The Woollen Industry.* 2nd edn. Leeds: WIRA, 1977.

Bremner, David. *The Industries of Scotland: Their Rise, Progress and Present Condition*. Edinburgh: Adam and Charles Black, 1869.

Breward, Christopher. *The Hidden Consumer: Masculinities, Fashion and City Life 1860–1914*. Manchester: Manchester University Press, 1999.

Breward, Christopher. Edwina Ehrman and Caroline Evans. *The London Look: Fashion from Street to Catwalk*. London and New Haven: Yale University Press, 2004.

Breward, Christopher. *Fashioning London: Clothing and the Modern Metropolis*. Oxford: Berg, 2004.

Breward, Christopher, David Gilbert and Jenny Lister. *Swinging Sixties: Fashion in London and Beyond 1955–1970*. London: V & A Publications, 2006.

Breward, Christopher and Ghislaine Wood. "Introduction." In *British Design from 1948: Innovation in the Modern Age*, edited by Christopher Breward and Ghislaine Wood, 12–27. London: V & A Publishing, 2012.

Brewer, Laurie Anne. "The Material Education of the Dandy." In *Artist, Rebel, Dandy: Men of Fashion*, edited by Kate Irvin and Laurie Anne Brewer, 105–29. New Haven: Yale University Press, 2013.

Brooker, Peter. *Bohemia in London: The Social Scene of Early Modernism*. Basingstoke and New York: Palgrave MacMillan, 2007.

Brown, Ian. *From Tartan to Tartanry: Scottish Culture, History and Myth*. Edinburgh: Edinburgh University Press, 2012.

Bulman, Louisa M. Connor. "Titian in Connemara." *Apollo* 159 (506) (2004): 45–53.

Burton, Antoinette. *Burdens of History: British Feminists, Indian Women and Imperial Culture 1865–1915*. North Carolina: University of North Carolina Press, 1994.

Byrde, Penelope. *Nineteenth Century Fashion*. London: B. T. Batsford Limited, 1992.

Cannadine, David. *The Decline and Fall of the British Aristocracy*. London: Papermac, 1996.

Cheadle, E. *Manners of Modern Society*. London: Cassell, 1872.

Cheape, Hugh. "A Song On The Lowland Shepherds: Popular Reaction To The Highland Clearances." *Scottish Economic and Social History* 15 (1995): 85–100.

Cheape, Hugh. *Tartan*. Edinburgh: National Museums of Scotland, 2006.

Chenoune, Farid. *A History of Men's Fashion*. Paris: Flammarion, 1993.

Clark, Judith and Amy de la Haye. *Jaeger 125*. London: Jaeger, 2009.

Cochrane, Adam. "Notes on the Scotch Tweed Trade." *Transactions of the National Association for the Promotion of Social Science* (1864): 792–9.

Cohn, Nik. *Today There Are No Gentlemen*. London: Weidenfeld & Nicolson, 1971.

Crane, Diana. *Fashion and Its Social Agendas: Class, Gender and Identity in Clothing*. Chicago: University of Chicago Press, 2000.

Creed, Charles. *Maid to Measure*. London: Jarrolds Publishers, 1961.

Crewe, Louise. "Tailoring and Tweed: Mapping the Spaces of Slow Fashion." In *Fashion Cultures Revisited*, edited by Stella Bruzzi and Pamela Church Gibson, 200–14. Abingdon, Oxon: Routledge, 2013.

Cunnington Phillis and Alan Mansfield. *English Costume for Sports and Outdoor Recreation*. London: A & C Black, 1969.

Davidoff, Leonore. *The Best Circles: Society, Etiquette and the Season*. London: Croom Helm, 1973.

Denton, Michael J. and Paul N. Daniels. *Textile Terms and Definitions*. 11th edn. Manchester: The Textile Institute, 2002.

Devine, Tom. *The Scottish Nation 1700–2000*. London: Penguin Books, 2000.

Devine, Tom. *Clearance and Improvement: Land, Power and People in Scotland 1700–1900*. Edinburgh: John Donald, 2006.

Dior, Christian. *Dior by Dior*. London: Weidenfeld & Nicolson, 1957.

Dior, Christian. *The Little Dictionary of Fashion: A guide to dress sense for every woman*. 1954. Republished London: V & A Publishing, 2008.

Dossena, Marina. "The Voice of Witnesses in Nineteenth-Century Accounts of the Highland Clearances." *Review of Scottish Culture* 13 (2000): 40–50.

Duke of Windsor. *A Family Album*. London: Cassell, 1960.

Duncan, Ian. *Scott's Shadow: The Novel in Romantic Edinburgh*. Princeton: Princeton University Press, 2007.

Durie, Alistair. "'Unconscious Benefactors': Grouse-shooting in Scotland, 1780–1914." *The International Journal of the History of Sport* 15 (3) (1998): 57–73.

Durie, Alistair *Scotland for the Holidays: Tourism in Scotland c. 1780–1939*. East Linton: Tuckwell Press, 2003.

Eden, Ronald. *Going to the Moors*. London: John Murray (Publishers) Ltd, 1979.

Edwards, Tim. *Men in the Mirror: Men's Fashion, Masculinity and Consumer Society*. London: Cassell, 1997.

English, Bonnie. *A Cultural History of Fashion in the 20th and 21st Centuries: From Catwalk to Sidewalk*. London: Bloomsbury Academic, 2013.

Entwhistle, Joanne. *The Fashioned Body: Fashion, Dress and Modern Social Theory*. Cambridge: Polity Press, 2000.

Evans, Caroline. *Fashion at the Edge: Spectacle, Modernity and Deathliness*. New Haven and London: Yale University Press, 2003.

Faiers, Jonathan. *Tartan*. Oxford: Berg Publishers, 2008.

Farnfield, Carolyn A. and P. J. Alvey. *Textile Terms and Definitions*. 7th edn. Manchester: The Textile Institute, 1975.

Field, Jacqueline. "Bernat Klein's Couture Tweeds: Color and Fabric Innovation, 1960–1980." *Dress* 33 (2006): 41–55.

Flugel, J. C. *The Psychology of Clothes*. London: Hogarth Press, 1930.

Gaines, Jane. "Costume and Narrative; How Dress Tells the Woman's Story." In *Fabrications: Costume and the Female Body*, edited by Jane Gaines and Charlotte Herzog, 180–211. London: Routledge, 1990.

Glendening, John. *The High Road: Romantic Tourism, Scotland and Literature, 1720–1820*. London: Macmillan, 1997.

Goodrum, Alison. *The National Fabric: Fashion, Britishness, Globalization*. Oxford: Berg, 2005.

Gordon, Eleanor and Gwyneth Nair. *Public Lives: Women, Family and Society in Victorian Britain*. New Haven and London: Yale University Press, 2003.

Grant, Elizabeth. *Memoirs of a Highland Lady*, Vol. 2. 1898. 2nd edn. Edinburgh: Canongate Publishing Ltd. 1988.

Gulvin, Clifford. *The Tweedmakers: A History of the Scottish Fancy Woollen Industry 1600–1914*. Newton Abbot: David & Charles, 1973.

Hall, Robert. *History of Galashiels*. Galashiels: Alexander Walker & Son Publishers, 1898.

Hardill, Irene. *The Regional Implications of Restructuring in the Wool Textile Industry*. Aldershot: Gower, 1987.

Hargreaves, Jennifer. *Sporting females: Critical Issues in the History and Sociology of Women's Sports*. London: Routledge, 1993.

Hargreaves, John. "The Body, Sport and Power Relations." *Sociological Review* 33 (May 1985): 139–59.

Harrison, E. S. *Scottish Woollens*. Edinburgh: The National Association of Scottish Woollen Manufacturers, 1956.

Harrison, E. S. *Our Scottish District Checks*. Edinburgh: The National Association of Scottish Woollen Manufacturers, 1968.

Harrison, E. P. *Scottish Estate Tweeds*. Elgin: Johnstons of Elgin, 1995.

Haye, Amy de la. *The Cutting Edge: 50 Years of British Fashion 1947–1997*. London: V & A Publications, 1996.

Haye, Amy de la. *Chanel: Couture and Industry*. London: V & A Publishing, 2011.

Helland, Janice. *British and Irish Home Arts and Industries 1880–1914: Marketing Craft, Making Fashion*. Dublin: Irish Academic Press, 2007.

Henry Ballantyne and Sons Ltd. London: Biographical Publishing Company, 1929.

Hitchon, Patricia. *Chanel and the Tweedmaker: Weavers of Dreams*. Carlisle: P3 Publications, 2012.

Hoad, Judith. *This is Donegal Tweed*. Inver, County Donegal: Shoestring Publications, 1987.

Hollander, Anne. *Sex and Suits*. New York: Kodansha America Ltd, 1995.

Hollander, Anne. *Fabric of Vision: Dress and Drapery in Painting*. London: National Gallery Company, 2002.

Honeyman, Katrina. *Well Suited: A History of the Leeds Clothing Industry 1850–1990*. Oxford: Oxford University Press, 2000.

Hopkins, Harry. *The New Look: A Social History of the Forties and Fifties*. London: Secker & Warburg, 1964.

Horwood, Catherine. *Keeping Up Appearances: Fashion and Class Between the Wars*. Stroud: Sutton, 2005.

Howell, Georgina. *Wartime Fashion: From Haute Couture to Homemade 1939–1945*. London: Bloomsbury Academic, 2012.

Huggins, Mike. *The Victorians and Sport*. London: Hambledon and London, 2004.

Hunter, Janet. *The Islanders and the Orb: The History of the Harris Tweed Industry 1835–1995*. Stornoway, Lewis: Acair Ltd, 2001.

Hutchison, I. G. C. *A Political History of Scotland, 1832–1924: Parties, Elections and Issues*. Edinburgh: Donald, 1986.

Jackson, Stephen. "Recent Fieldwork in Argyll." *Furniture and Fittings in the Traditional Scottish Home, Vernacular Building* 30 (2006): 63–77.

Jenkins, David. "The Western Wool Textile Industry in the Nineteenth Century." In *The Cambridge History of Western Textiles, II*, edited by David Jenkins, 761–89. Cambridge: Cambridge University Press, 2003.

Jenkins, David. "Wool Textiles In The Twentieth Century." In *The Cambridge History of Western Textiles, II*, edited by David Jenkins, 993–1022. Cambridge: Cambridge University Press, 2003.

Jenkins, David and Kenneth Ponting. *The British Wool Textile Industry 1770–1914*. Aldershot: Scolar Press, 1987.

Jenkins, John Geraint. *The Welsh Woollen Industry*. Cardiff: National Museum of Wales, 1969.

Jenkins, John Geraint. *The Flannel Makers: A Brief History of the Welsh Woollen Industry*. Conwy, Wales: Gwasg Carreg Gwalch, 2005.

Jobling, Paul. *Man Appeal: Advertising, Modernism and Menswear*. Oxford: Berg, 2005.

Jobling, Paul. *Advertising Menswear: Masculinity and Fashion in the British Media Since 1945*. London: Bloomsbury Academic, 2014.

Johnston, Robert. *Tweed Designer's Handbook*. 5th edn. Galashiels: Scottish Borders Record Office, 1888.

Kestner, Joseph A. *Masculinities in Victorian Painting*. London: Scolar Press, 1994.

Klein, Bernat. *Eye for Colour*. London: Bernat Klein Scotland with Collins, 1965.

Klein, Bernat and Lesley Jackson. *Bernat Klein: Textile Designer, Artist, Colourist*. Gattonside, Roxburghshire: Bernat Klein Trust, 2005.

Krebs, Paula. *Gender, Race and the Writing of Empire: Public Discourse and the Boer War*. Cambridge: Cambridge University Press, 1999.

Lambert, Miles. *Fashion in Photographs 1860–1880*. London: B. T. Batsford, 1991.

Lambert, Miles. "Drapers, Tailors, Salesmen and Brokers: The Retailing of Woollen Clothing in Northern England, c.1660–c.1830." In *Wool Products and Markets (13th–20th Century)*, edited by Giovanni Luigi Fontana and Gerard Gayot, 1083–101. Padova: CLEUP, 2004.

Lee, J. M. *Social Leaders and Public Persons: A Study of County Government in Cheshire since 1888*. Oxford: Clarendon Press, 1963.

Lee, Sarah Tomalin. *American Fashion*. London: Andre Deutsch, 1975.

Lemire, Beverly. "Fashion and tradition: wearing wool in England during the Consumer Revolution, c. 1660–1820." In *Wool Products and Markets (13th–20th Century)*, edited by Giovanni Luigi Fontana and Gerard Gayot, 573–94. Padova: CLEUP, 2004.

Lemire, Beverly. *Cotton*. Oxford: Berg Publishers, 2011.

Leslie, Alice. "Harris Home Industries: Mrs Thomas's Work." In *Scottish Home Industries*, Scottish Home Industries Association, 73–6. Dingwall: Lewis Munro, 1895.

Locke, James. *Tweed and Don; or, Recollections and Reflections of an Angler for the Last Fifty Years*. London: Simpkin, Marshall and Co., 1860.

Lockhart, John Gibson. *Memoirs of the Life of Sir Walter Scott, Vol. IV*. Paris: Baudry's European Library, 1838.

Longrigg, Roger. *The English Squire and His Sport*. London: Joseph, 1977.

MacDonald, Mrs. "Harris Home Industries: Lady Dunmore's Work." In *Scottish Home Industries,* Scottish Home Industries Association, 68–72. Dingwall: Lewis Munro, 1895.

Mackenzie, John. *The Empire of Nature*. Manchester: Manchester University Press, 1988.

Mangan, James A. "Duty Unto Death: English Masculinity and Militarism in the Age of the New Imperialism." In *Tribal Identities: Nationalism, Europe, Sport*, edited by James A. Mangan, 10–38. London: Frank Cass & Co. Ltd., 1996.

Mary Quant's London. London: London Museum, 1973.

Matless, David. *Landscape and Englishness*. London: Reaktion Books Ltd, 1998.

Maxwell, Stuart. *Scottish Costume, 1550–1850*. London: A & C Black, 1958.

McCord, Norman and Bill Purdue. *British History 1815–1914*. Oxford: Oxford University Press, 2007.

McDevitt, Patrick F. *May The Best Man Win: Sport, Masculinity and Nationalism in Great Britain and the Empire, 1880–1935*. New York: Palgrave Macmillan, 2004.

McDowell, Colin. *Ralph Lauren, The Man, the Vision, the Style*. London: Cassell Illustrated, 2002.

Mendes, Valerie and Frances Hinchcliffe. *Ascher: Fabric, Art, Fashion*. London: Victoria and Albert Museum, 1987.

Midgley, Clare. *Gender and Imperialism*. Manchester, Manchester University Press, 1998.

Miller, Lesley Ellis. *Balenciaga*. London: V & A Publications, 2007.

Miller, Lesley Ellis. "Perfect Harmony: Textile Manufacturers and Haute Couture 1947–1957." In *The Golden Age of Couture: Paris and London 1947–57,* edited by Claire Wilcox, 113–35. London: V & A Publishing, 2007.

Mitchell, W. J. T. *Landscape and Power*. Chicago: University of Chicago Press, 1994.

Mort, Frank. *Cultures of Consumption: Masculinities and Social Space in Late Twentieth-Century Britain*. London: Routledge, 1996.

Mottram, R. H. *Another Window Seat or Life Observed: Vol. 2 1919–1953*. London: Hutchinson, 1957.

Mountain, Moor and Loch: On The Route of the West Highland Railway. Colonsay: House of Lochar, 2002.

Murray, Norman. *The Scottish Hand Loom Weavers 1790–1850: A Social History*. Edinburgh: John Donald Publishers Ltd., 1978.

Naylor, Gillian. *The Arts and Crafts Movement*. London: Studio Vista, 1980.

North, Susan. "John Redfern and Sons, 1847–1892." *Costume* 42 (2008): 145–68.

Ormerod, Frank. *Wool*. London: Constable and Company Ltd, 1918.

Orr, W. *Deer Forests, Landlords and Crofters*. Edinburgh: John Donald Publishers Ltd, 1982.

Ostick, E. *Textiles for Tailors*. London: The Tailor and Cutter Limited, undated.

Owen, Elizabeth. *Fashion in Photographs 1920–1940*. London: B. T. Batsford in association with The National Portrait Gallery, 1993.

New Statistical Account of Scotland, Vols. III and XII. Edinburgh and London: William Blackwood and Sons, 1845.

Palmer, Alexandra. *Couture & Commerce: The Transatlantic Fashion Trade in the 1950s*. Vancouver: University of British Columbia Press, 2001.

Pattison, Jean S. "The Tweed Section of the Scottish Woollen Industry." In *Studies In Industrial Organisation,* edited by H. A. Silverman, 104–54. London: Methuen & Co. Ltd, 1946.

Pieda Consulting. *Briefing Paper on The Scottish Textile and Clothing Industry*. Edinburgh: Scottish Executive, Enterprise and Lifelong Learning Department and Scottish Textiles Network, 2000.

Platman, Lara. *Harris Tweed: From Land to Street*. London: Frances Lincoln Limited Publishers, 2011.

Ponting, Kenneth. *The Wool Trade: Past and Present*. Manchester: Columbine Press, 1961.

Ponting, Kenneth. "The Scottish Contribution to Wool Textile Design in the Nineteenth Century." In *Scottish Textile History,* edited by John Butt, 78–94. Aberdeen: Aberdeen University Press, 1987.

Price, Christopher. "Depression and Recovery." In *20th Century Britain: Economic, Cultural and Social*

Change, edited by Francesca Carnevali and Julie-Marie Strange, 145–61. Harlow: Pearson Education Limited, 2007.

Pugh, Martin. *We Danced All Night: A Social History of Britain Between the Wars.* London: Vintage, 2009.

Pugh, Martin. *State and Society: a Social and Political History of Britain Since 1870.* 4th edn. London: Bloomsbury Academic, 2012.

Rainnie, G. F. *The Woollen and Worsted Industry: An Economic Analysis.* Oxford: Clarendon Press, 1965.

Richards, Eric. *The Highland Clearances.* Edinburgh: Birlinn Limited, 2013.

Rolley Katrina and Caroline Aish. *Fashion in Photographs 1900–1920.* London: B. T. Batsford, 1992.

Ross, Geoffrey Aquilina. *The Day of the Peacock: Style for Men 1963–1973.* London: V & A Publishing, 2011.

Ross, Josephine. *Society in Vogue: The International Set Between the Wars.* London: Condé Nast Publications Ltd, 1992.

Scott, Kirsty, Maggie Marr and Ann Ritchie. *Shetland Textile Sector Review.* Weave Consult for Shetland Islands Council, 2012.

Scott, Walter. *Waverley.* London: Simpkin and Marshall, 1829 edn.

Scottish Development Agency in association with Research Associates and the Shirley Institute. *Opportunities for The Scottish Wool Textile and Knitwear Industries.* Glasgow: Scottish Development Agency, 1981.

Scottish Home Industries Association. *Scottish Home Industries.* Dingwall: Lewis Munro, 1895.

Scrope, William. *The Art of Deer-stalking; Illustrated By A Narrative Of A Few Day's Sport In The Forest Of Atholl.* London: John Murray, 1838.

Sherwood, James. *Savile Row: the Master Tailors of British Bespoke.* London: Thames & Hudson, 2010.

Silverman, Kaja. "Fragments of a Fashionable Discourse." In *Studies in Entertainment: Critical Approaches to Mass Culture* edited by Tania Modleski, 139–52. Bloomington, Indiana University Press, 1986.

Sladen, Christopher. *The Conscription of Fashion: Utility Cloth, Clothing and Footwear 1941–1952.* Aldershot: Scolar Press, 1995.

St. John, Charles. *Sportsman's and Naturalist's Tour in Sutherlandshire.* London: Simpkin, Marshall and Co., 1891.

Steele, Valerie. *Paris Fashion: A Cultural History.* New York: Oxford University Press, Inc., 1988.

Steele, Valerie. "Chanel in Context." In *Chic Thrills: A Fashion Reader,* edited by Juliet Ash and Elizabeth Wilson, 118–26. London: Harper Collins Publishers, 1992.

Stillie, T. A. "The Evolution of Pattern Design in the Scottish Woollen Textile Industry in the Nineteenth Century." *Textile History* 3 (3) (1970): 309–31.

Taylor, Lou. "Wool Cloth and Gender: The Use of Woollen Cloth in Women's Dress in Britain, 1865–85." In *Defining Dress: Dress as Object, Meaning and Identity,* edited by Amy de la Haye and Elizabeth Wilson, 30–47. Manchester: Manchester University Press, 1999.

Taylor, Lou and Fiona Anderson. "Fashion for Women and Men in the Twentieth Century." In *The Cambridge History of Western Textiles, II,* edited by David Jenkins, 1044–74. Cambridge: Cambridge University Press, 2003.

Taylor, Lou. "To attract the attention of fish as little as possible": An Object-Led Discussion of Three Garments, for Country Wear for Women, Made of Scottish Woollen Cloth Dating from 1883–1908." *Textile History* 38 (1) (2007): 92–105.

Taylor, Marjory. *Technology of Textile Properties.* London, Forbes Publications Limited, 1981.

The Major. *Clothes and the Man: Hints on the Wearing and Caring of Clothes.* London: Grant Richards, 1900.

The Scottish Woollen Industry. Edinburgh: The National Association of Scottish Woollen Manufacturers, 1970.

Tosh, John. *Manliness and Masculinities in Nineteenth-Century Britain.* Harlow: Pearson Education Ltd, 2005.

Tranter, Neil. *Sport, Economy and Society in Britain 1750–1914.* Cambridge: Cambridge University Press, 1998.

Ugolini, Laura. *Men and Menswear: Sartorial Consumption in Britain 1880–1939.* Aldershot: Ashgate, 2007.

Walker, Ann. *The Structure of the West European Wool Industry: Prospects and Strategies for a Changing Market.* London: Pearson Professional Ltd, 1995.

Watson, D. "The Early Manufactures of Hawick." *Transactions of the Hawick Archaeological Society* (1868): 9–15.

Watson, Linda. *Vogue Twentieth Century Fashion: 100 Years of Style by Decade and Designer.* London: Carlton, 1999.

Waugh, Norah. *The Cut of Men's Clothes 1600–1900.* London: Faber and Faber, 1964.

Whatley, Christopher. *The Industrial Revolution in Scotland.* Cambridge: Press Syndicate of the University of Cambridge, 1997.

Wilcox, Claire. *Vivienne Westwood.* London: V & A Publications, 2004.

Wilcox, Claire. *The Golden Age of Couture: Paris and London 1947–57.* London: V & A Publishing, 2007.

Williams, Raymond. *Keywords: A Vocabulary of Culture and Society.* London: Fontana Press, 1988.

Wilson, Elizabeth. "Fashion and the Postmodern Body." In *Chic Thrills: A Fashion Reader* edited by Juliet Ash and Elizabeth Wilson, 3–6. London: Pandora, 1992.

Wilson, Elizabeth. *Adorned in Dreams: Fashion and Modernity.* 2nd edn. London: I. B. Tauris, 2003.

Wilson, Elizabeth. *Bohemians: The Glamorous Outcasts.* London: Tauris Parke Paperbacks, 2003.

INDEX

Plate 1 J. & A. Ogilvie pattern book, 1836–7, shepherd's check and *tweel* samples. Heritage and Information Governance, Heriot-Watt University, Galashiels. G.H.1.1.4.

Plate 2 Bernat Klein, mohair and wool tweed, 1964. © National Museums Scotland, Edinburgh. K.2010.94.45.9.

Plate 3 Harris Tweed label and length of Harris Tweed, heather mixture, woven by Donald John Mackay, 2010. © National Museums Scotland, Edinburgh. K.2015.24.1&3.

Plate 4 J. & A. Ogilvie pattern book, 1836–7, green, black and orange, checked tweed sample and an overdyed, shepherd's check swatch. Heritage and Information Governance, Heriot-Watt University, Galashiels. GH 6.1.1.3

Plate 5 John Frederick Lewis (1804–76). *Highland Hospitality*, 1832. Watercolour, gouache, gum and graphite with scratching out, 22 1/8 x 28 7/8 inches (56.2 x 75.9 cm). Yale Center for British Art, Paul Mellon Collection, New Haven. 10772 – B1978.43.167.

Plate 6 R. & A. Sanderson & Co. Ltd, pattern book, 1852, black-and-white and multi-coloured samples of men's trousering cloths. Heritage and Information Governance, Heriot-Watt University, Galashiels. RAS 6.2.1.1.

Plate 7 Blenkhorn Richardson & Co. Ltd range book, winter 1907, menswear tweed samples. © National Museums Scotland, Edinburgh. A.1996.279.

Plate 8 French pattern book, titled "Plaid Patterns, 1886," woolen samples including *fantaisie* yarns, R. & A. Sanderson & Co. Ltd Archive. Heritage and Information Governance, Heriot-Watt University, Galashiels. RAS 6.1.1.1

Plate 9 Traveling coat, checked tweed, John Redfern, 1888. Photograph by Chicago History Museum/ Getty Images. 1987.471.lab.

Plate 10 Detail of woman's, checked tweed cape, c. 1870–1900. © National Museums Scotland, Edinburgh. H. TO 59.

Plate 11 Norfolk-style, jacket and skirt, c. 1908, in striped homespun tweed, Frederick Bosworth. © Victoria and Albert Museum, London. T.20 to D-1960.

Plate 12 G. & G. Kynoch Ltd, Order Book, 1933, twist suiting samples. © National Museums Scotland, Edinburgh. K.1997.1139.1.

Plate 13 R. & A. Sanderson & Co. Ltd, page from VIP Order Book, 1944. Heritage and Information Governance, Heriot-Watt University, Galashiels. RAS7.1.1.1.

Plate 14 Womenswear tweed samples from bunch, 1934, 113/1, Otterburn Mill Collection. ©National Museums Scotland, Edinburgh. K.2013.7.11.

Plate 15 Woman's brown and beige tweed suit, Chanel haute couture, c. 1927–9. © CHANEL HC.INC.1927–1929.

Plate 16 Woman's suit, Chanel haute couture, spring/summer 1963, mohair and wool tweed by Bernat Klein. © CHANEL HC.PE.1963.5.

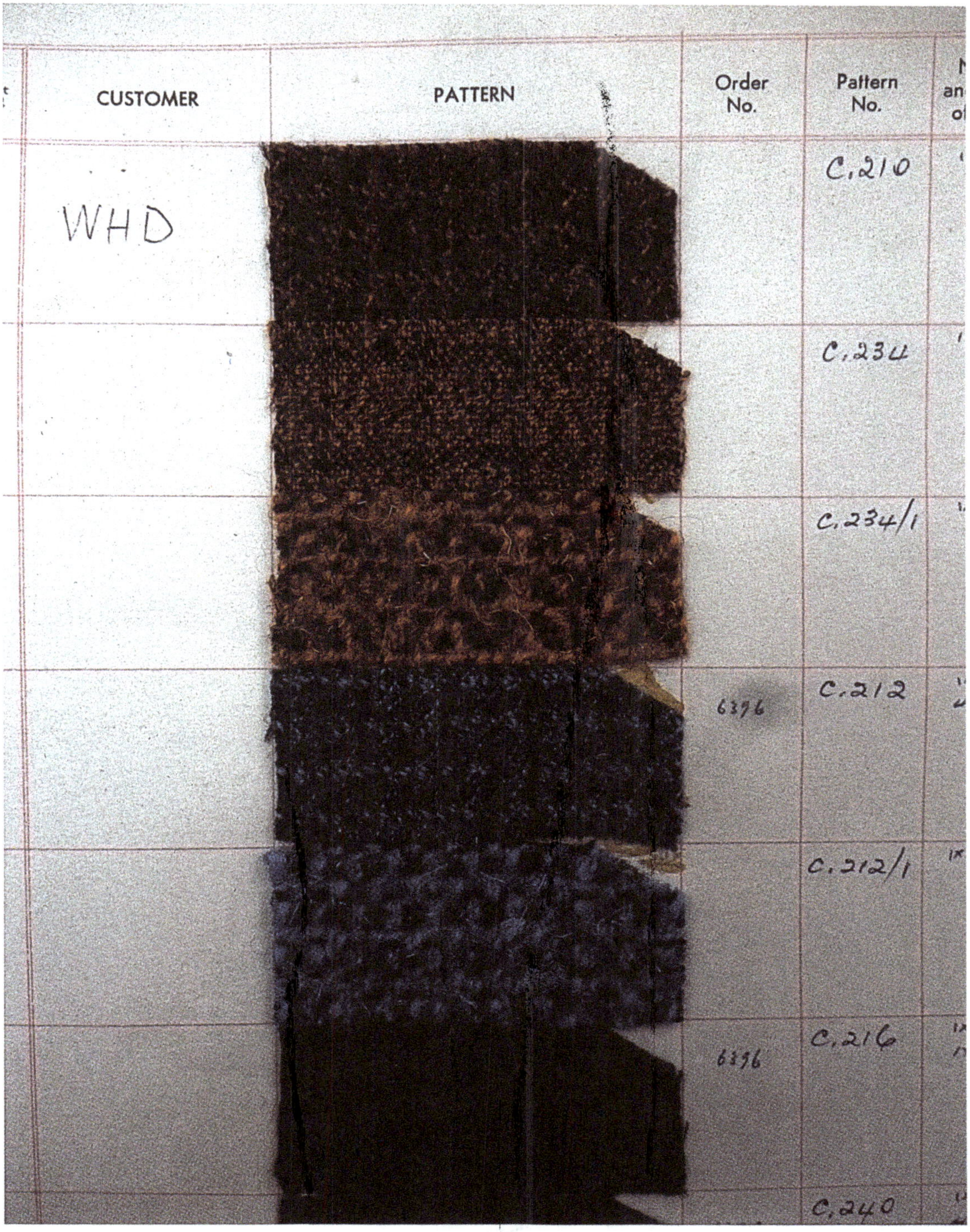

CUSTOMER	PATTERN		Order No.	Pattern No.	N and o
WHD				C.210	
				C.234	
				C.234/1	
			6396	C.212	
				C.212/1	
			6396	C.216	
				C.240	

Plate 17 Linton Tweeds, page from Order Book, 1956–7, overdyed tweed samples. Linton Tweeds archive, Carlisle. Courtesy of Fiona Anderson.

Plate 18 "Peachy" dress in red tweed, Mary Quant, 1960. © Victoria and Albert Museum, London. T.27.1997

Plate 19 Melanie Hampshire in a tweed coat by Kenneth Sweet, photograph by Norman Parkinson, *Life*, October 18, 1963. © Norman Parkinson Ltd, courtesy Norman Parkinson Archive, London.

Plate 20 Chanel, *fantaisie* tweed jacket worn with metallic dress and hat, Haute Couture collection, autumn/winter, 2013–14. Photograph by Dominique Charriau/WireImage. Getty Images.

Plate 21 Woman's outfit including brown herringbone Harris Tweed jacket, Ralph Lauren, fall 1990. Photograph by George Chinsee/WWD. © Condé Nast.

Plate 22 Red Harris Tweed jacket and mini-crini, Harris Tweed Collection, Vivienne Westwood, autumn/winter, 1987–8. © Victoria and Albert Museum, London.

www.ingramcontent.com/pod-product-compliance
Lightning Source LLC
Chambersburg PA
CBHW080417270326
41929CB00018B/3060